PRINCI
of Reinsurance

MW01181659

Information That Works

Information That Works

LOMA (Life Office Management Association, Inc.) is an international association founded in 1924. LOMA is committed to a business partnership with its worldwide members in the insurance and financial services industry to improve their management and operations through quality employee development, research, information sharing, and related products and services. Among LOMA's activities is the sponsorship of the FLMI Education Program—an educational program intended primarily for home office and branch office employees.

The *Associate, Reinsurance Administration (ARA) Program* is designed for people who work in reinsurance, reinsurance administration, and related areas of both reinsurers and ceding companies. To earn the ARA designation, a student must complete all required courses as outlined in LOMA's most current *Education and Training Catalog*. Upon successful completion of all required courses, the student receives a diploma awarded by LOMA and is entitled to use the letters *ARA* after his/her name.

Statement of Purpose:
LOMA Educational Programs Testing and Designations

Examinations described in the LOMA *Education and Training Catalog* are designed solely to measure whether students have successfully completed the relevant assigned curriculum, and the attainment of the ARA and other LOMA designations indicates only that all examinations in the given curriculum have been successfully completed. In no way shall a student's completion of a given LOMA course or attainment of the ARA or other LOMA designation be construed to mean that LOMA in any way certifies that student's competence, training, or ability to perform any given task. LOMA's examinations are to be used solely for general educational purposes, and no other use of the examinations or programs is authorized or intended by LOMA. Furthermore, it is in no way the intention of the LOMA curriculum and examinations staff to describe the standard of appropriate conduct in any field of the insurance and financial services industry, and LOMA expressly repudiates any attempt to so use the curriculum and examinations. Any such assessment of student competence or industry standards of conduct should instead be based on independent professional inquiry and the advice of competent professional counsel.

PRINCIPLES
of Reinsurance

Susan Conant, FLMI, HIA, CEBS, PAHM

Miriam A. Orsina, FLMI, PCS, ARA, PAHM

LOMA
Atlanta, Georgia
www.loma.org

Associate, Reinsurance Administration
Education Program

Information in this text may have been changed
or updated since its publication date.
For current updates, visit www.loma.org.

Information That Works

ARA 440 TEXT—PRINCIPLES OF REINSURANCE

Authors:	Susan Conant, FLMI, HIA, CEBS, PAHM
	Miriam A. Orsina, FLMI, PCS, ARA, PAHM
Manuscript Editors:	Harriett E. Jones, J.D., FLMI, AIRC, ACS
	Jo Ann S. Appleton, FLMI, ALHC, PCS, HIA, CEBS
Exam Editor:	Harriett E. Jones, J.D., FLMI, AIRC, ACS
Project Manager:	Joyce R. Abrams, J.D., FLMI, PCS, AAPA, AIRC, ARA, AIAA, FLHC, PAHM, HIA, MHP
Production Manager:	Stephen J. Bollinger, ACS
Copyeditor:	Harriett E. Jones, J.D., FLMI, AIRC, ACS
Indexer:	Amy Souwan
Typesetters:	Allison Ayers
	Amy Souwan
Production Coordinator:	Amy Souwan
Print Buyer:	Audrey H. Gregory, ACS
Permissions Coordinator:	Iris F. Hartley, FLMI, ALHC
Administrative Support:	Mamunah Carter
Cover Designer:	Stephen J. Bollinger, ACS

Library of Congress Cataloging-in-Publication Data

Conant, Susan
    Principles of reinsurance / Susan Conant, Miriam A. Orsina.
        p. cm
Includes index.
    ISBN 1-57974-278-5
     1. Reinsurance. I. Orsina, Miriam A., 1958-II. Title.

HG8083.C66 2005
368'.0122--dc22

2005044926

ISBN 1-57974-278-5
Printed in the United States

Contents

Preface x

PART 1: REINSURANCE OVERVIEW 1

CHAPTER 1: Introduction to Reinsurance 3
Roles of Insurance Companies in Reinsurance Arrangements 5
    Professional and Occasional Reinsurance Providers 6
    Captive Reinsurers 7
    Reciprocal Arrangements 7
    Reinsurance Pools 8
Assumption and Indemnity Reinsurance 9
    Assumption Reinsurance 9
    Indemnity Reinsurance 10
Exchanges of Funds in Indemnity Reinsurance 11
Benefits and Costs of Reinsurance to the Direct Writer 12
Documentation of Reinsurance Arrangements 14
The Reinsurance Industry 16

CHAPTER 2: Regulation of Reinsurance 21
United States Reinsurance Regulation 23
    The National Association of Insurance Commissioners 24
    NAIC Accreditation of State Insurance Departments 24
Licensing Requirements 25
    Licensing Requirements—Direct Writers 26
    Licensing Requirements—Reinsurers 27
    Licensing Requirements—Reinsurance Intermediaries 27
Monitoring Financial Condition 28
    Financial Reports 29
    Capital and Surplus Requirements 30
    On-Site Regulatory Examinations 31
Reserves and Reserve Credit 31
    Reserve Credit for Reinsurance 32
    Forms of Security for Reinsurance 33
Risk Transfer 36

CHAPTER 3: Forms of Reinsurance 39
Cession Arrangements in Reinsurance 41
    Automatic Reinsurance 41
    Facultative Reinsurance 43
    Facultative-Obligatory Reinsurance 43
    Comparison of Cession Arrangements 44
Nonproportional and Proportional Reinsurance Plans 45
    Nonproportional Reinsurance 45
    Proportional Reinsurance 47

The Cession Amount in Proportional Reinsurance 48
    Excess-of-Retention Arrangements 49
    Quota Share Arrangements 51
Basic Coinsurance 52
    Coinsurance Premiums 53
    Funds Withheld Coinsurance 53
Modified Coinsurance 54
Yearly Renewable Term Reinsurance 55

PART 2: THE REINSURANCE AGREEMENT 61

CHAPTER 4: Defining the Reinsurance Coverage 63
Reasons to Use Written Reinsurance Agreements 65
Life Cycle of the Reinsurance Agreement 66
Choosing a Reinsurance Partner 67
    Evaluation Criteria Used by Direct Writers 67
    Evaluation Criteria Used by Reinsurers 68
General Characteristics of a Reinsurance Agreement 69
Common Agreement Provisions 71
Scope of the Agreement 71
    Parties to the Agreement Provision 71
    Entire Agreement Provision 71
    Duration of the Agreement Provision 73
    Recapture Provision 76
Termination of the Agreement 77
Insurance Ceded and Reinsurance Provided 79
    Reinsurance Coverage Articles 79
    Schedules of Reinsurance Coverage 81

Chapter 5: Reinsurance Administration Procedures 85
Methods of Reinsurance Record Administration 87
    Individual Cession Administration 87
    Self Administration 87
    Bulk Administration 88
Procedures to Begin Reinsurance Coverage 88
    Notification for Automatic Reinsurance 88
    Notification for Facultative-Obligatory Reinsurance 91
    Notification for Facultative Reinsurance 92
    Reasons Why Reinsurance May Not Be in Effect 92
Reporting Requirements 94
Records Inspection 95
Provisions for Changes to the Reinsurance 95
    Provisions for Increases in Retention Limits and Recapture 95
    Provisions for Increasing Death Benefits 98
    Continuations Provision 100
    Conversions Provision 102
    Reinstatements Provision 103
    Provisions for Reductions and Terminations of Reinsurance 103

CHAPTER 6: Claims, Rescission, and Potential Problems 109
Claim Administration 111
    The Direct Writer's Authority to Handle Claims 111
    Claim Procedures 112
Rescission 115
Potential Problems Between a Direct Writer and a Reinsurer 116
    Errors and Omissions 116
    Arbitration 118
Insolvency 121
    Direct Writer Insolvency 124
    Reinsurer Insolvency 124

CHAPTER 7: Financial Arrangements 127
Reinsurance Premiums and Allowances 130
    Premium Rate Tables 131
    Reinsurance Premium Reporting and Payment 132
    Paying Premiums for Coinsurance, Modco, and YRT Reinsurance 135
    Nonpayment of Reinsurance Premiums 135
    Reinsurance Premium Rate Changes 136
    Reinsurance Premium Reporting 136
    Allowances 136
Miscellaneous Other Payments Under Coinsurance and Modco 136
    Policy Cash Values 137
    Policy Dividends 137
    Experience Refunds 138
    Modco Reserve Adjustments 138
Provision for Premium Taxes 139
Currency for Reinsurance 140
    Currency Fluctuations 141
    Consequences for Late Payment Due to Decreases in Currency Exchange Values 141

CHAPTER 8: Risk Management and Reinsurance 143
Approaches to Risk Management 145
Balancing Risks and Returns 146
Leverage 147
    Positive and Negative Leverage Effects 147
    Leverage Ratios 148
Surplus Strain and Surplus Relief 148
The Surplus Relief Ratio 149
Retention Limits: Mechanisms for Redistributing Risks 151
Types of Retention Limits 151
    Cession Basis and Retention Limits 152
    Retention Limit Corridors 152
Setting, Monitoring, and Changing Retention Limits 154
    Influences on Retention Limits 154
    Changing Retention Limits 154

Limitations of Reinsurance 155
   Limitations for a Direct Writer 155
   Limitations for a Reinsurer 156

PART 3: REINSURANCE ADMINISTRATION 157

CHAPTER 9: Reinsurance Activities, Staff, and Systems 159
Reinsurance Administration Activities 161
Reinsurance Administration Staff 162
   Reinsurance Analysts 162
   Other Staff Involved in Reinsurance Activities 163
Reinsurance Communications with Third Parties 171
   Reinsurance Intermediaries 171
   Consumer Reporting Agencies 171
   MIB Group, Inc. 173
Reinsurance Information Systems 173
   Telecommunications 174
   Document Management Systems 175
   Security for Information Systems 175

CHAPTER 10: Administering New Business 179
Preplacement of Reinsurance 181
   Reviewing a Request for Coverage 183
   Establishing Records and Reserving Capacity 184
   Following Up on Reserved Capacity 193
Placement of Reinsurance 193
   Facultative and Fac-Ob Cessions 196
   Automatic Cessions 196

CHAPTER 11: Administering In-Force Business and Terminations of Reinsurance 201
Administering In-Force Business 203
   Reports Used to Administer In-Force Business 203
   Processing Changes in Reinsurance Coverage 208
   Processing Billing Statements 209
   Recording Policy Reserves 213
   Administering Mergers and Acquisitions 213
Administering Terminations of Reinsurance 213
Administering Claims 214
   Establishing the Claim File 215
   Examining the Claim 218
   Approving the Claim 224
   Settling the Claim 224
   Notifying Retrocessionaires of a Claim 225

CHAPTER 12: Quality Control in Reinsurance 227
Principles of Quality Control 230
    Segregation of Duties 230
    Execution of Transactions as Authorized 230
    Recording of Transactions as Executed 230
    Safeguarding of Assets 231
    Physical Comparison of Recorded Amounts 231
Control Requirements of the Sarbanes-Oxley Act 231
Quality Control Approaches 232
Process Controls 232
    Suspense Account Reconciliation 232
    Data Integrity Checks 233
    Trend Analysis 233
    Checking Overdue Reports 234
Audits 235
    Internal Audits 236
    External Audits 237
    Desk Audits 243
    Comparison of Internal Audits, External Audits, and Desk Audits ... 244

Glossary 247

Index 285

Preface

Principles of Reinsurance introduces the reinsurance industry, the regulatory environment of reinsurance, the forms of reinsurance, the reinsurance contract, arrangements for reinsurance administration, and the financial mechanics of reinsurance.

This text has been designed for students who are preparing to take the examination for ARA 440—*Reinsurance Administration,* part of LOMA's Associate, Reinsurance Administration (ARA) education program. The examination is based exclusively on the assigned study materials, including information in the body of the text as well as the Figures in the text. The texts and study aids for LOMA courses may be revised periodically. To ensure that you are studying from the correct materials, check the current *LOMA Education and Training Catalog.*

The text includes features designed to help you organize your studies, reinforce your understanding of the materials, and prepare for the examination. As we describe each of these features, we give you suggestions for studying the material.

- **Learning Objectives.** The first page of each chapter contains a list of learning objectives to help you focus your studies. Before reading each chapter, review these learning objectives. Then, as you read the chapter, look for material that will help you meet the learning objectives.

- **Chapter Outline.** At the beginning of each chapter is an outline of the chapter. Review this outline to gain an overview of the major topics that will be covered; then scan through the chapter to familiarize yourself with the presentation of the information. Looking at the headings and figures will give you a preview of how the various subjects relate to each other.

- **Key Terms.** This text explains the key terms associated with reinsurance. Important terminology is highlighted with ***bold italic type*** when the term is defined, and a list of these key terms appears at the end of each chapter. All key terms also appear in a comprehensive glossary at the end of the book. As you read each chapter, pay special attention to the key terms.

- **Figures and Examples.** Figures and examples throughout the text illustrate and amplify the text's discussions of important topics. Note that information contained in figures and examples may be tested on the examination for this course.

- **Glossary.** A comprehensive glossary containing definitions of all key terms and other important concepts appears at the end of the book. Following each glossary entry is a number in brackets that indicates the chapter in which the key term is defined. The glossary includes references to important equivalent terms and acronyms.

Test Preparation Guide. LOMA's *Test Preparation Guide (TPG) for ARA 440* is assigned reading for students preparing for the ARA 440 examination. Used along with this textbook, the TPG will help you master the course material. The TPG includes practice exam questions, a full-scale sample examination, and answers to every question in the TPG.

LOMA recommends that you use the Test Preparation Guide for this course. **Studies indicate that students who use LOMA study aids consistently perform significantly better on LOMA examinations than students who do not use these study aids.**

Acknowledgments

Principles of Reinsurance is a joint effort of industry experts from reinsurance, insurance, and financial services companies and LOMA staff. Much of *Principles of Reinsurance* is adapted from *Reinsurance Administration* (Atlanta: LOMA, © 2000), written by Jane Lightcap Brown, FLMI, ALHC, ACS and Jennifer W. Herrod, FLMI, ACS, AIAA, PAHM. The textbook development panel members for *Reinsurance Administration* made valuable contributions that we have retained in *Principles of Reinsurance*. For those contributions, LOMA and the financial services industry owe a debt of gratitude to the following people: Margaret Barry; Suzanne L. Bathke, ACS, AIRC, CPIW; Randall M. Benton, FLMI, ALHC; Diane Brûlé, B.Sc., BAA, FLMI/M, ALHC; Diane M. Currier; Jill Dupuis, ACS; Jennifer Jones-Lapointe, FLMI/M, ALHC, HIA; Emmanuel Kintu, M.B.A., HIA, D.Mgt. (ADB); Rosita Kraml, FLMI; Vincent J. Montelione, CPA, CLU, ChFC, ACS; Marisa Cristina Mota, FLMI, HIA, ACS; Sandy Peterson; Jane Y. Tiu, FLMI, ACS; Melanie Tullett, B.Sc., FLMI, ACS; and Ava M. Zils, FLMI. Numerous other industry experts reviewed selected portions of the text.

Textbook Development Panel

During development, *Principles of Reinsurance* underwent extensive review by a panel of industry experts. The source materials, suggestions, and critical evaluations supplied by LOMA's text reviewers were essential to this book's accuracy, relevance, and completeness. For reviewing the entire text, answering numerous author questions, and providing ideas and documents for supporting materials, we wish to thank the following individuals:

- Ania Antus, Ph.D., FLMI, ARA, ACS, Reinsurance Technician, Minnesota Life Insurance Company; Adjunct Professor, University of Wisconsin—River Falls

- Diane Brûlé, FLMI/M, ALHC, Senior Vice President, Systems, Optimum Re Insurance Company

- Gary L. Corliss, FSA, MAAA, RHU, President & CEO, Avon Long Term Care Leaders

- Jill Y. Dupuis, ACS, Manager, Operations Analysis, Manulife Financial

- David Eng, FLMI, ACS, HIA, AIAA, ARA, Complex Claims Adjudicator, Industrial Alliance Insurance and Financial Services, Inc.

- Sarah Grose, FLMI, ACS, ARA, IS Project Leader, Securian Financial Group, Inc.

- Josée Malboeuf, FLMI, ALHC, Vice President, Underwriting & Claims, RGA Reinsurance

- Priscilla J. Merriweather, FLMI, ALHC, ACS, ARA, Executive Director, Retrocession Administration, RGA Reinsurance

- Julio E. Payés, FLMI, ACS, Technical Manager, Reinsurance and Statistics, Interseguros

- Nina Rhines, ACS, ARA, Financial Reporting and Reinsurance Specialist, Minnesota Life Insurance Company

- Gerald T. Stewart, ASA, MAAA, FFSI, FLMI, ARA, AIRC, AAPA, ACS, Assistant Actuary, Corporate Actuarial, West Coast Life Insurance Company

We also thank the following individuals who contributed their time and knowledge by participating in planning this project and in reviewing portions of the text:

- Peggy Barusta, FLMI, ACS, PMP, Assistant Vice President, Reinsurance Planning and Projects, Manulife Financial

- Suzanne L. Bathke, ARA, ACS, AIRC, CPIW, Vice President, Hannover Life Reassurance Company of America

- Warren A. Carter, ASA, MAAA, Teachers Insurance and Annuity Association (retired), Recipient, 1991 FLMI Insurance Education Award

- Maria Guadalupe Covarrubias, Life and Health Director, Hannover Services México

- Shaun Downey, FLMI, ARA, ACS, Assistant Vice President, Client Services, Manulife Financial

- John Haungs, FLMI, ACS, AIRC, ARA, AIAA, Manager of Professional Services, Transamerica Reinsurance (deceased)

- David Howard, FLMI, ACS, Director, Membership and Marketspace, MIB Group, Inc.

- Melanie M. Pappalardo, FLMI, ACS, ARA, Senior Medical Underwriter, StanCorp Financial

- Joseph Sebbag, FLMI, ACS, ARA, Manager, Individual Reinsurance, SCOR Life US Reinsurance Company, Inc.

- Holly Schultz, ARA, Senior Disability Benefit Analyst, National Accounts Benefits, Standard Insurance Company

- Lauren Szwiec, FLMI, ARA, Reinsurance Analyst, Guarantee Trust Life Insurance Company

- Ann Wenzl, FLMI, ALHC, FLHC, ACS, HIA, MHP, AIAA, AIRC, ARA, Vice President, Administration, Credit Protection Services, Central States Health & Life Company of Omaha

LOMA Staff

Writing a LOMA textbook is a collaborative effort not only with our industry reviewers, but also with other LOMA staff members who generously contribute their time and expertise. These individuals from Education & Training include Harriett E. Jones, J.D., FLMI, AIRC, ACS, Senior Associate, who served as manuscript editor, examinations editor, and copyeditor for the project; Joyce R. Abrams, J.D., FLMI, PCS, AAPA, AIRC, ARA, AIAA, FLHC, PAHM, HIA, MHP, Assistant Vice President; and Jo Ann S. Appleton, FLMI, ALHC, PCS, HIA, CEBS, Senior Associate. Thanks go to Mamunah Carter, Administrative Assistant III, who provided administrative support.

From LOMA's Examinations Department, Lisa Kozlowski, FLMI, CLU, ChFC, FLHC, ACS, AIAA, PAHM, AIRC, ARA, AAPA, Senior Associate, and Cynthia Mathis Henry, FLMI, ACS, ALHC, PAHM, Senior Associate, co-authored the test preparation guide and gave much helpful direction, and Robert H. Hartley, FLMI, ACS, ALHC, CLU, ChFC, RHU, PAHM, Assistant Vice President, oversaw the examinations aspects of the text development.

In LOMA's Production Department, thanks go to Stephen J. Bollinger, ACS, Production Manager, who oversaw the production of the book; Amy Souwan, who served as Production Coordinator, performed typesetting, and developed the index; and Allison Ayers, who performed typesetting for the text. Audrey H. Gregory, ACS, made all printing arrangements. In LOMA's Information Center, Olivia Blakemore, ACS, Technical Administrator, and Mallory Eldridge, Research Analyst/Writer, provided valuable research services for this textbook

Former LOMA staff members and co-authors of *Reinsurance Administration,* Jane Lightcap Brown, Ph.D., FLMI, ALHC, Senior Associate, and Jennifer W. Herrod, FLMI, ACS, AIAA, PAHM, Senior Associate, provided a strong foundation for *Principles of Reinsurance.* Jane Brown made numerous important contributions to this book, particularly in the planning stages. Iris F. Hartley, FLMI, ALHC, obtained the permissions for use of copyrighted materials.

We also thank Katherine C. Milligan, FLMI, ACS, ALHC, Vice President, Education and Training Division, for her continuing support and encouragement throughout the project.

Susan Conant, FLMI, HIA, CEBS, PAHM
Miriam Orsina, FLMI, PCS, ARA, PAHM

Atlanta, Georgia
2006

Part 1:
Reinsurance Overview

CHAPTER 1

Introduction to Reinsurance

After studying this chapter, you should be able to

- Identify the roles that insurance companies can take in a reinsurance transaction

- Describe arrangements in which reinsurers combine forces, including reciprocal arrangements and reinsurance pools

- Discuss the differences between assumption reinsurance and indemnity reinsurance

- Describe four broad benefits that direct writers can gain when they use reinsurance and four types of costs that direct writers incur when they use reinsurance

- Describe market concentration and geographic dispersion in the reinsurance industry

OUTLINE

Roles of Insurance Companies in Reinsurance Arrangements

Professional and Occasional Reinsurance Providers

Captive Reinsurers

Reciprocal Arrangements

Reinsurance Pools

Assumption and Indemnity Reinsurance

Assumption Reinsurance

Indemnity Reinsurance

Exchanges of Funds in Indemnity Reinsurance

Benefits and Costs of Reinsurance to the Direct Writer

Documentation of Reinsurance Arrangements

The Reinsurance Industry

The business of reinsurance involves vast amounts of money, many insurance companies, and countries around the globe. Major reinsurers maintain offices on multiple continents and actively seek to geographically disperse risk among their subsidiaries and business partners.

Insurance companies are in the business of sharing in the various risks that their customers transfer to them.[1] In turn, insurance companies must manage the insurance risks they assume from their customers. One tool insurers use to manage the risks they assume is **reinsurance**. Reinsurance is insurance that one insurance company obtains for its business risks from another insurance company. The business of reinsurance involves vast amounts of money, many insurance companies, and countries around the globe. To complicate matters, reinsurance terminology in the English language varies throughout the world. This textbook is about reinsurance purposes and reinsurance practices. In this chapter, we first introduce some fundamental concepts of reinsurance; then we describe the reinsurance industry.

Roles of Insurance Companies in Reinsurance Arrangements

Many insurance companies engage in reinsurance activities. These companies fall into several categories. All companies that enter into reinsurance arrangements are insurance companies. An insurer can act as a buyer of reinsurance in one transaction and a seller of reinsurance in another transaction. With respect to any given reinsurance arrangement, though, each company takes on a specific role, as follows:

- A **direct writer**, also called a *ceding company*, is an insurer that sells insurance coverage to the public. A direct writer can transfer—or *cede*—its insurance risks by obtaining reinsurance on those insurance risks. A **cession** is the unit of insurance risk that a direct writer transfers to a reinsurer. *Cession* also refers to the document used to record the transfer of risk from a direct writer to a reinsurer. In this textbook, whenever we refer to a direct writer in a reinsurance transaction, we mean the company that cedes the risk.

- A **reinsurer**, also called a *reinsurance company* or an *assuming company*, is an insurer that provides reinsurance coverage by accepting, or *assuming*, insurance risk from a direct writer or another reinsurance company. In this textbook, whenever we refer to a reinsurer in a reinsurance transaction, we mean the company that assumes insurance risk from another insurer.

- A reinsurer can transfer some of the risks it has assumed under a reinsurance arrangement by obtaining reinsurance from a third insurance company. In such a situation, the third insurer is a *retrocessionaire*. A **retrocessionaire** is an insurance company that accepts risks from—and provides reinsurance to—a reinsurer. A **retrocession** is the unit of reinsurance that a reinsurer cedes to a retrocessionaire. *Retrocession* also refers to the document used to record the transfer of risk from a reinsurer to a retrocessionaire.

Example: The Fox Insurance Company reinsures 75 percent of $200 million of directly written insurance business with Wolf Reinsurance. Thus, the amount of risk that Fox transfers to Wolf Re is $150 million. Wolf Re does not wish to keep this entire $150 million of risk for itself, and thus retrocedes $50 million to another company, Bear Reinsurance. Because Bear Re is accepting a retrocession, Bear Re is acting as a retrocessionaire in this transaction.

Fox Insurance	Wolf Re	Bear Re
On a block of business worth $200 million, cedes $150 million of risk to Wolf Re and retains $50 million of risk	Reinsures Fox's cession for $150 million Retrocedes one-third of Fox's risk to Bear Re in a retrocession of $50 million of risk, retaining $100 million of risk	Reinsures Wolf Re's cession of $50 million

Professional and Occasional Reinsurance Providers

In the United States, virtually any licensed insurance company can write reinsurance. Although some insurance companies act as both direct writers and reinsurers, other insurance companies deal only in reinsurance, as follows:

	Professional	Occasional
Reinsurer	**Professional reinsurer** An insurance company whose sole or primary line of business is selling reinsurance to direct writers	**Occasional reinsurer** An insurer that accepts some reinsurance business but is not a professional reinsurer
Retrocessionaire	**Professional retrocessionaire** A reinsurer whose primary business is providing reinsurance to reinsurers	**Occasional retrocessionaire** A reinsurer whose primary business is not retrocessions but who accepts retrocessions

Generally, a professional reinsurer or professional retrocessionaire is licensed to do business in multiple jurisdictions, often on an international basis. We describe the licensing of reinsurers in Chapter 2.

Captive Reinsurers

An insurance company that acts both as a direct writer and a reinsurer may create a subsidiary company that is dedicated to reinsurance business. A **captive reinsurer** is a reinsurer that was formed by an insurer for the purpose of providing reinsurance and that is controlled by the insurance company that formed it. A captive reinsurer's activities may be limited by its corporate charter. For example, a captive reinsurer could be limited to offering reinsurance only to the organization that formed it. Not all captive reinsurers, however, have such a limitation.

Example: The Mammoth Global Insurance Company has three subsidiaries, including a captive reinsurer, as shown:

Reciprocal Arrangements

A **reciprocal arrangement**, also called *reciprocity*, is a two-way reinsurance arrangement wherein two insurance companies cede business to each other and assume risk from each other. In a reciprocal arrangement, both insurance companies variously take on the roles of a direct writer and a reinsurer.

Example: Ahab Insurance Company and Ishmael Insurance Company have entered into a reciprocal arrangement in which each company has agreed to provide reinsurance on $40 million of the other company's directly written business.

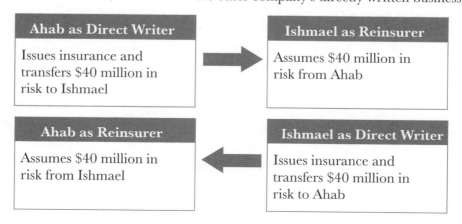

Several types of insurers may participate in a reciprocal arrangement. For example, a direct writer and a reinsurer may reciprocate; a reinsurer and a retrocessionaire may reciprocate; two reinsurers may reciprocate; and so on. Two direct writers can reciprocate only if they both are *authorized reinsurers*; in a given transaction, though, one insurer acts as a direct writer and the other acts as a reinsurer. We discuss authorized reinsurers in Chapter 2.

The insurance companies that exchange business through reciprocal arrangements usually issue the same type of business, but they typically do not compete against each other in the same geographic areas.

Insurance companies that enter into a reciprocal arrangement try to exchange approximately equal amounts of business or otherwise to maintain equality in their relationship. Insurers often measure the equality in their reciprocal arrangements on the basis of either premiums or results.

- *Premium-based reciprocity* involves the exchange of blocks of reinsurance business representing approximately the same amount of gross premium on the reinsured risks

- *Results-based reciprocity* involves the exchange of blocks of reinsurance business representing approximately the same projected monetary amount of claims experience on the reinsured risks

Reinsurance Pools

A *reinsurance pool*, also known as a *reinsurance syndicate*, is a group of two or more insurance companies or individuals who jointly reinsure risks accepted on their behalf by an appointed representative who represents them in a marketplace. A reinsurance pool may operate in a subscription market or an open market.[2] A *subscription market* is an exchange market where appointed agents for insurance companies accept shares of coverage on given risks; the shares accepted vary from company to company. Lloyd's of London is a subscription market for reinsurance pools. An *open market* is usually more formal in that each member of the pool has a set amount or percentage that it will accept.

A pool might handle new or unusual risks that represent less well known risks, large amounts at risk, or hazardous risks. Each participant in a pool has an individual liability and is not responsible for the liabilities of other pool members. The reinsured risk usually is spread between or among the pool members according to specified portions, known as quota shares. Generally, a *quota share* is an insurance company's percentage share of a reinsurance transaction. In a pool, a *quota share*, also known as a *subscription*, is the amount each pool member accepts as its liability under a specific reinsurance arrangement.

Example: As illustrated in the following table, a quota share (subscription) is the portion of risk assumed by each member of a reinsurance pool. These shares need not be equally divided among the pool members.

100% of Reinsured Risk		Quota Share	Reinsurance Pool Members
Divided		30%	Reinsurer A
among		20%	Reinsurer B
pool		40%	Reinsurer C
members		10%	Reinsurer D

Figure 1.1 displays types of reinsurance providers and arrangements.

FIGURE 1.1

Reinsurance Providers and Arrangements Involving Multiple Reinsurers

REINSURANCE PROVIDERS	REINSURANCE ARRANGEMENTS
Professional reinsurer	Reciprocal arrangements
Occasional reinsurer	Reinsurance pools (syndicates)
Professional retrocessionaire	
Occasional retrocessionaire	
Captive reinsurer	

Source: Adapted from Jane Lightcap Brown and Jennifer W. Herrod, *Reinsurance Administration* (Atlanta: LOMA, © 2000), 8. Used with permission; all rights reserved.

Assumption and Indemnity Reinsurance

Reinsurance can be divided into two broad classifications—assumption reinsurance and indemnity reinsurance. Although this book primarily focuses on indemnity reinsurance arrangements, assumption reinsurance also has important roles in the insurance industry.

Assumption Reinsurance

Assumption reinsurance, also known as *portfolio reinsurance*, is reinsurance designed to permanently and entirely transfer blocks of existing insurance business from one company to another. In assumption reinsurance, the reinsurer assumes the entire legal obligation formerly borne by the insurer that issued the business. The assuming company (reinsurer) issues new insurance certificates, known as ***assumption certificates***, to all affected policyowners. These assumption certificates show policyowners that the assuming insurer has taken responsibility for all risk under their insurance policies. Under an assumption reinsurance arrangement, the direct writer, the reinsurer, and the policyowners are parties to the reinsurance transaction.

Assumption reinsurance is the most common method of buying and selling blocks of insurance business. Insurance regulators must approve assumption reinsurance transactions, just as they must approve insurance company mergers and acquisitions. Assumption reinsurance has the following applications:

- An insurer can exit a line of business by ceding the business to a reinsurer

- An insurer can enter a new line of business or expand its participation in an existing line of business by assuming a line of business from another insurer

- A guaranty association or an insurance regulator can use assumption reinsurance to transfer the business of a failed insurer to other insurers, so as to provide continuation coverage to the failed company's policyowners

- An assumption reinsurance transaction can be used to complete the purchase and sale of an entire insurance company

Indemnity Reinsurance

In indemnity reinsurance, a direct writer transfers a stated portion of its accepted risk to a reinsurer. Under indemnity reinsurance, a reinsurer is obligated to reimburse a direct writer only after the direct writer pays benefits under reinsured policies. Indemnity reinsurance, the type of reinsurance most commonly used to transfer risk, includes traditional indemnity reinsurance and finite reinsurance. In practice, *indemnity reinsurance* can refer to both traditional indemnity reinsurance and finite reinsurance. Here, to minimize any confusion between the two types of indemnity insurance, we use the term *traditional indemnity insurance* to distinguish it from finite reinsurance.

Traditional Indemnity Reinsurance

Traditional indemnity reinsurance is a reinsurance arrangement that is used to transfer a portion of a direct writer's accepted risk on an ongoing basis and that is intended to be a permanent transfer. This form of risk transfer is the original purpose of reinsurance transactions. The parties to a traditional indemnity reinsurance arrangement directly negotiate the terms of the arrangement, which vary from one arrangement to another, to meet the specific needs of both parties.

Traditional indemnity reinsurance typically transfers risk on a direct writer's new business rather than its in-force business. Traditional indemnity reinsurance arrangements create an ongoing contractual relationship between the parties to the arrangement.

Although the parties to a traditional indemnity reinsurance arrangement intend for the risk transfer to be permanent, such arrangements typically include a means for the direct writer and the reinsurer to end or otherwise modify the reinsurance arrangement. For example, reinsurance arrangements usually allow the direct writer to take back—or *recapture*—specified reinsured risks or for the reinsurer to return—or *commute*—specified reinsured risks. Indemnity reinsurance arrangements also allow for termination of the entire arrangement either through mutual agreement or automatically due to the insolvency of one of the parties to the arrangement.

Unlike assumption reinsurance transactions, a traditional indemnity reinsurance arrangement is not disclosed to the direct writer's customers, who are not parties to the agreement. Under traditional indemnity reinsurance, the direct writer retains the entire legal liability to its customers whose policies are reinsured.

Finite Reinsurance

Finite reinsurance, also known as *financial reinsurance*, is a form of indemnity reinsurance that allows the direct writer to improve its financial position by the timing of and method by which it transfers risk to a reinsurer. Usually, finite reinsurance is intended to be a temporary arrangement, and its primary purpose is to enable the direct writer to transfer expenses and profits to the reinsurer. Finite reinsurance typically sets a maximum limit on the reinsurer's obligation and specifies an assumed investment earnings rate. Unlike traditional indemnity reinsurance, which involves a direct writer's new business, finite reinsurance typically involves the direct writer's in-force business. In many other respects, finite reinsurance arrangements resemble traditional indemnity reinsurance arrangements. Finite reinsurance arrangements have some controversial aspects, and we will not discuss these arrangements further in this textbook.

The remainder of this textbook is devoted to traditional indemnity reinsurance, and we will only occasionally mention assumption reinsurance. Unless we specify otherwise, we use the term indemnity reinsurance to mean traditional indemnity reinsurance. Figure 1.2 summarizes the features of the types of reinsurance arrangements we have described.

FIGURE 1.2

Types of Reinsurance and Their Characteristics

	Assumption Reinsurance	Indemnity Reinsurance	
		Traditional Indemnity Reinsurance	Finite Reinsurance
Is the arrangement intended to be temporary or permanent?	Permanent	Permanent	Temporary
Is recapture permitted?	No	Yes	Yes
Does the reinsurer become a party to the reinsured policies?	Yes	No	No
Is the arrangement used to reinsure new business or in-force business?	In-force	New	In-force, usually
What are the primary purposes of the reinsurance arrangement?	Total risk transfer	Share risks	Transfer expenses and profits
Who administers the reinsured insurance policies?	Reinsurer	Reinsurer or direct writer	Direct writer

Source: Adapted from Susan Conant, *Capital Management for Insurance Companies* (Atlanta: LOMA, © 2001), 149. Used with permission; all rights reserved.

Exchanges of Funds in Indemnity Reinsurance

In indemnity reinsurance, the direct writer makes periodic payments, known as **reinsurance premiums**, to the reinsurer. In return, the reinsurer agrees to reimburse the direct writer for a stated portion of benefits the direct writer has paid to customers under the reinsured business.

The reinsurer typically agrees to establish, for the reinsured portion of the risk, policy reserves that are similar to the policy reserves that the direct writer establishes for its portion of the business. We describe policy reserves in Chapter 2.

In some arrangements, the reinsurer grants the direct writer an **allowance**, also known as an *expense allowance*, a *reinsurance allowance*, a *ceding commission*, or a *reinsurance commission*. An allowance is an amount granted by the reinsurer to the direct writer and designed to recognize the direct writer's acquisition, maintenance, and other costs.

- **Acquisition expenses** are the costs a direct writer incurs in developing, marketing, and issuing new business. Examples of acquisition expenses covered in the reinsurance allowance are first-year commissions, underwriting costs, new business processing costs, and policy issue costs.

- **Maintenance expenses**, also known *renewal expenses* or *administration expenses*, are the direct writer's ongoing expenses for administering and servicing a policy or a book of business after it has been placed in force.

Some allowances additionally include a factor for the direct writer's profits. The amount of the allowance usually differs by policy duration, being larger in the early policy durations and lower in the later policy durations. The reinsurer deducts the allowance from the reinsurance premium that the direct writer must pay to the reinsurer. The allowance may be expressed as a percentage of the gross reinsurance premium, a flat amount per unit of coverage, or a flat amount per transaction. We present additional discussion of reinsurance premiums and allowances in Chapter 3.

A reinsurance gross premium is the reinsurance premium before the allowance. A reinsurance net premium is the cost that the direct writer pays for reinsurance coverage, after allowances. The following formula illustrates these relationships:

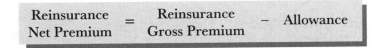

$$\text{Reinsurance Net Premium} = \text{Reinsurance Gross Premium} - \text{Allowance}$$

Figure 1.3 summarizes the costs that are incurred by the direct writer and the reinsurer.

Benefits and Costs of Reinsurance to the Direct Writer

The use of reinsurance has benefits and costs for the direct writer, which should use reinsurance only when the benefits outweigh the costs. Generally, direct writers can obtain the following broad benefits from reinsuring a portion of their risks:

- **Managing the direct writer's financial capacity.** From a practical viewpoint, every insurance company has a finite limit on (1) the amount of coverage it can approve or afford to pay on a single risk and (2) the total amount of risk it can accept. **Underwriting** is the process of selecting and classifying the risks that an insurer will accept. *Selecting* is the process of making a decision to accept or decline the risk. After a risk is accepted, *classifying* is the process of assigning the appropriate premium rate to charge for the insurance policy. Generally,

FIGURE 1.3

Assignment of Financial Responsibility Between Direct Writer and Reinsurer

DIRECT WRITER'S FINANCIAL RESPONSIBILITIES

- Pay reinsurance premiums to the reinsurer
- Pay operating expenses for the retained and reinsured business
- Pay acquisition expenses for the retained and reinsured business
- Establish reserves for the retained and reinsured business
- Pay claims to customers on all retained and reinsured business
- Pay the expenses of administering the reinsurance arrangement

REINSURER'S FINANCIAL RESPONSIBILITIES

- Grant the direct writer an allowance on reinsured business
- Establish reserves for the reinsured business
- Pay a portion of claims on reinsured business

an insurance company's ***underwriting capacity*** or risk-taking capability is the highest monetary amount of risk that the company should accept so that unusual claim volatility will not damage the ongoing solvency of the company. An insurer's ***financial capacity*** is the total monetary amount of risk an insurance company can accept based on the investable funds it has available to write new business. Reinsurance can help a direct writer to manage the timing of its product revenues and expenses and, thus, to smooth the impact of short-term and intermediate-term fluctuations in its cash flows and financial position. The timing and amount of insurance claims an insurer receives can fluctuate greatly. The direct writer can smooth the burden of these extreme fluctuations when a reinsurer participates in paying a proportion of the claim costs. Also, a direct writer's marketing efforts might enable the company to sell more insurance coverage than its financial position can support. In such cases, the direct writing company can transfer the excess risk and expense to a reinsurer.

- **Obtaining consultation from reinsurers.** Through exposure to the experience of many direct writers, reinsurers are aware of challenges that many direct writers face and of successful responses to those challenges. Reinsurers consult with their clients and apply their expertise in many areas—notably underwriting, reinsurance administration, and claim administration.

- **Managing the company's product portfolio.** A company can use reinsurance to enter or exit a particular insurance market or market niche. To enter a new product line, a direct writer can entirely reinsure another direct writer's business in the chosen product line. To exit a product line, a direct writer can transfer a book of business to a reinsurer.

- **Facilitating mergers.** Reinsurance can be used to transfer all of one company's product assets and product liabilities to another company. Mutual insurance companies, which do not have common stock, particularly tend to use reinsurance as a means for accomplishing a company merger.

Costs for activities that the reinsurer must undertake are passed along to the direct writer in the reinsurance premium.[3] The benefits of reinsurance to direct writers are offset by the costs of reinsurance, as follows:

- **Transaction costs.** The costs involved in entering into a reinsurance arrangement and setting up the processes needed to administer the contract

- **Monitoring costs.** The costs for evaluating the reinsurer's performance

- **Maintenance and administrative costs.** The ongoing cost of administering the contractual requirements and business processes of both parties

- **Termination costs.** The expenses, such as termination penalties, that the direct writer incurs to exit a reinsurance arrangement

Figure 1.4 gives examples of these costs.

Documentation of Reinsurance Arrangements

In a legal context, a reinsurance agreement is a contract, which is an agreement that is legally binding on the parties to the agreement. The documents that establish reinsurance arrangements can take a variety of forms.[4] The document that a direct writer and reinsurer create when they enter into an indemnity reinsurance arrangement has historically been referred to as a reinsurance treaty or a facultative certificate. We present several common types of reinsurance agreements in the following bullets, but, in practice, many sorts of hybrid arrangements blur the neat classifications of reinsurance agreements:

- A **reinsurance treaty** is usually a long and detailed document that provides evidence of reinsurance for a book of business covering a variety of insureds in various locations. A treaty specifies with precision the nature of the transferred risk, the responsibilities of the direct writer and the reinsurer, and the reporting requirements of both parties, among other things. Reinsurance treaties typically document a type of reinsurance cession known as *automatic reinsurance*, in which the reinsurer agrees to assume specified risks without having the opportunity to approve those risks in advance. We describe automatic reinsurance fully in Chapter 3.

- A **facultative certificate** typically is a short reinsurance contract issued by a reinsurance company to cover a specific risk—usually a casualty type of risk—under a specific insurance policy. These certificates typically document a type of reinsurance known as *facultative reinsurance*, in which the reinsurer independently evaluates each risk before assuming that

---

FIGURE 1.4

Costs of Reinsurance to the Direct Writer

Transaction Costs	Selecting a reinsurer Negotiating the new reinsurance arrangement Compensating brokers, if used Training employees to administer the new arrangement Writing the reinsurance contract Developing information technology support for reinsurance administration
Monitoring Costs	Monitoring the reinsurer's stability Resolving disputes between the parties to the reinsurance transaction
Administrative Processing Costs	Paying reinsurance premiums Incurring administrative costs Processing fund transfers Filing claims with the reinsurer Accounting for funds Resolving claim problems
Termination Costs	Incurring penalties for termination, recapture, or commutation Replacing the terminated reinsurance with new reinsurance

Source: Adapted from Stephen Forbes, *The Changing Reinsurance Industry* (Atlanta: LOMA, © 2004), 70. Used with permission; all rights reserved.

---

risk. We describe facultative reinsurance fully in Chapter 3. Facultative certificates are rarely found in life and health types of reinsurance in North America. Facultative certificates typically have a declarations section that describes how the reinsurer will participate in the underlying insurance contract. Recently, facultative certificates have expanded to include detailed clauses appended to the certificate, but these clauses generally are less inclusive than are the provisions of a treaty.

■ A **reinsurance slip** is a short document issued to a direct writer by a reinsurance salesperson to describe the essential terms of a reinsurance arrangement while the reinsurance treaty is being drafted. Until the reinsurance treaty is formally executed, the slip governs the reinsurance relationship. A reinsurance slip must be signed by the reinsurer and accepted by the direct writer to be valid and binding on the parties.

Despite the distinctions among these reinsurance documents, through the remainder of this book, we refer to reinsurance documents of all types as *reinsurance agreements*.

The Reinsurance Industry

Reinsurance is available for virtually every line of insurance. To appreciate the breadth of reinsurance activities, consider some of the many the lines of (1) life and health insurance and (2) property and casualty insurance that are reinsured, as shown in Figure 1.5. We define various lines of commercial property and casualty insurance in a glossary in Figure 1.6.

The traditional classification of coverages differs between North America and Europe, as follows:

- In North America, the types of business reinsured typically are divided between the classifications of (1) life insurance coverages and (2) property/casualty insurance coverages. In this discussion, life insurance coverages include annuities, health insurance, accident insurance, long-term care insurance, disability income insurance, and life insurance. In this book, property/casualty coverages encompass property, casualty, indemnity, liability, inland marine, and professional liability coverages.

FIGURE 1.5

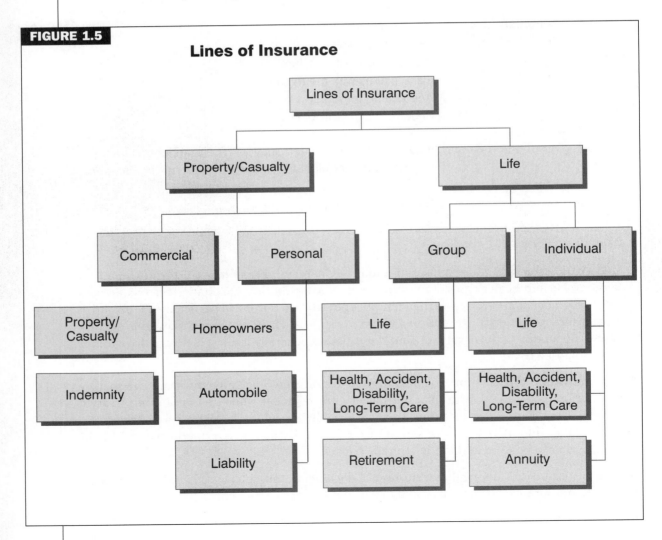

Lines of Insurance

FIGURE 1.6

Commercial Property and Commercial Liability Insurance

COMMERCIAL PROPERTY COVERAGES

- **Commercial property insurance** covers buildings, personal property in the business, and personal property of others in the care of the business.
- **Commercial automobile insurance** comes in three forms: *business automobile coverage*, which is similar to personal automobile coverage; *garage coverage*, which covers businesses that sell, service, park, or store automobiles; and *motor carrier coverage*, which covers businesses that provide transportation of people, goods, or both, as specified in the policy.
- **Business income insurance** covers losses resulting from the suspension of business operations, including loss of net income, expenses that continue during suspension of business operations, and extra expenses incurred to avoid or minimize business interruption.
- **Crime insurance** covers losses of money, securities, and tangible property resulting from the commission of certain specified crimes, such as burglary, robbery, theft, employee dishonesty, and forgery.
- **Boiler and machinery insurance** covers losses incurred to boilers and machinery as a result of boiler explosions, electrical malfunctions, and machinery breakdowns.
- **Inland marine insurance** covers property in transit over land and instruments of communication or transportation, such as tunnels and bridges.
- **Farm insurance** covers farm property and can also cover the owner's home and personal property.

COMMERCIAL LIABILITY COVERAGES

- **Commercial liability insurance** covers bodily injury and property damage liability, personal and advertising injury liability (such as defamation), and medical payments.
- **Workers' compensation and employers liability insurance** covers liability resulting from employee injury or death on the job.
- **Directors and officers (D&O) liability insurance** covers directors and officers of a corporation for their own liability resulting from failing to exercise the appropriate standard of care when discharging their corporate duties.
- **Excess and umbrella liability insurance** provides additional liability limits for underlying coverages.

Source: Adapted from Mary C. Bickley, *Principles of Financial Services and Products* (Atlanta: LOMA, © 2004), 232. Used with permission; all rights reserved.

■ In Europe, insurance usually is classified as either life or non-life, in which non-life encompasses health and accident coverages.

In this textbook, we take the North American point of view in classifying insurance coverages.

Reinsurance is an international business activity. In general, any direct writer can enter into arrangements and do business with any properly licensed or authorized reinsurer, regardless of where each company is located. (We discuss licenses and authorization in Chapter 2.) About 75 percent of the reinsurance in the United States is underwritten by non-U.S. reinsurers.[5] Major reinsurers maintain offices on multiple continents and actively seek to geographically disperse risk among their subsidiaries and business partners. Standard & Poor's lists approximately 200 major professional reinsurers domiciled throughout the world.[6] However, the majority of the global reinsurance market is concentrated among a small number of reinsurers. The dominant reinsurers play an important role in the reinsurance market because they set the contract terms and conditions for major reinsurance arrangements. Through their dominant size, they also lead the industry in innovative approaches to sharing risk, using technology, and employing large databases of statistics to better understand various risk exposures.[7] Figure 1.7 illustrates the distribution of reinsurance written by region.

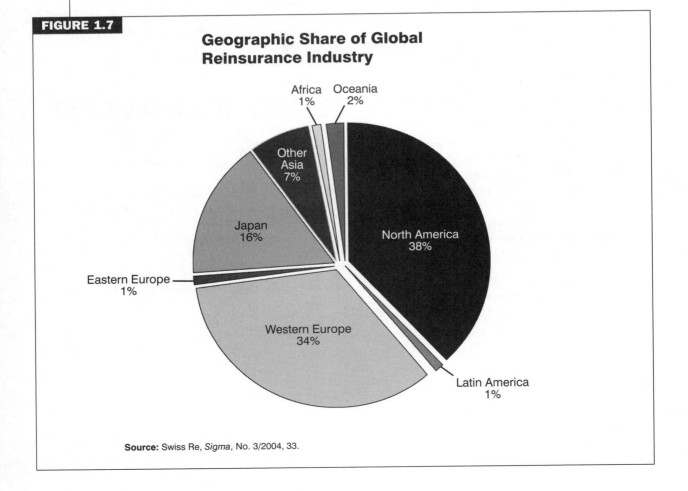

FIGURE 1.7

Geographic Share of Global Reinsurance Industry

Africa 1%
Oceania 2%
Other Asia 7%
Japan 16%
Eastern Europe 1%
North America 38%
Western Europe 34%
Latin America 1%

Source: Swiss Re, *Sigma*, No. 3/2004, 33.

Key Terms

reinsurance	quota share
direct writer	assumption reinsurance
cession	assumption certificate
reinsurer	traditional indemnity reinsurance
retrocessionaire	finite reinsurance
retrocession	reinsurance premium
professional reinsurer	allowance
occasional reinsurer	acquisition expenses
professional retrocessionaire	maintenance expenses
occasional retrocessionaire	underwriting
captive reinsurer	underwriting capacity
reciprocal arrangement	financial capacity
premium-based reciprocity	reinsurance treaty
results-based reciprocity	facultative certificate
reinsurance pool	reinsurance slip
subscription market	

Endnotes

1. This chapter represents a revision of material from Jane Lightcap Brown and Jennifer W. Herrod, *Reinsurance Administration* (Atlanta: LOMA, © 2000), 1–17. Used with permission; all rights reserved.

2   Reinsurance Evaluations, "The ABCs of Reinsurance," http://www.re-eval.co.uk/glossarys.htm (8 March 2005); and Arab Reinsurance Company, "Insurance Terms Glossary," http://www.arabre.com.lb/ins.asp (8 March 2005).

3. Stephen Forbes, *The Changing Reinsurance Industry* (Atlanta: LOMA, 2004), 18.

4. Larry P. Schiffer, "Sorting Out the Reinsurance Contract Morass," International Risk Management Institute (March 2002), http://www.irmi.com/expert/articles/2002/schiffer03.aspx. (1 August 2005).

5. Forbes, 25.

6. Ibid.

7. Ibid., 25–26.

CHAPTER

2

Regulation of Reinsurance

After studying this chapter, you should be able to

- Describe the purposes of insurance and reinsurance regulation

- Identify the parties that regulate reinsurance in the United States

- Describe the role of the National Association of Insurance Commissioners (NAIC)

- List and describe the model laws and regulations affecting reinsurance in the United States

- Describe and differentiate among licensed, authorized, accredited, and unauthorized reinsurers in the United States

- Describe how regulators monitor the financial condition of insurers through required financial reporting and regulatory examinations

- Explain the purposes of required policy reserves

- Explain the relationships among issuing new business, experiencing surplus strain, and obtaining surplus relief through reserve credit

- Describe the regulatory requirements related to reserve credit and risk transfer in reinsurance transactions

21

OUTLINE

United States Reinsurance Regulation
The National Association of Insurance Commissioners

NAIC Accreditation of State Insurance Departments

Licensing Requirements
Licensing Requirements—Direct Writers

Licensing Requirements—Reinsurers

Licensing Requirements—Reinsurance Intermediaries

Monitoring Financial Condition
Financial Reports

Capital and Surplus Requirements

On-Site Regulatory Examinations

Reserves and Reserve Credit
Reserve Credit for Reinsurance

Forms of Security for Reinsurance

Risk Transfer

A major concern of insurance regulators is risk transfer in reinsurance. To protect the solvency of insurers, regulators seek to ensure that each reinsurance transaction for which an insurer takes reserve credit involves a genuine and substantial transfer of risk to the reinsurer.

Whether in the role of direct writers or reinsurers, insurance companies with reinsurance activities are regulated by the laws that govern all other insurance companies, and their reinsurance activities are additionally subject to specific reinsurance regulation. To preserve the financial stability of licensed insurers, insurance companies with reinsurance activities must meet requirements for licensing, financial reporting, reserves, reserve credit for reinsurance, and risk transfer in reinsurance. Direct writers and reinsurers also must comply with the laws that govern all businesses—for example, taxation laws, laws against unfair competition, laws against deceptive business practices, and laws affecting securities transactions.

In this chapter, we discuss the entities that regulate insurance companies and their reinsurance activities, and we describe the general framework for insurance and reinsurance regulation in the United States. We discuss licensing of direct writers, reinsurers, and the reinsurance intermediaries that work with them. We also discuss how regulators monitor and oversee the financial condition of direct writers and risk transfer in reinsurance arrangements.

United States Reinsurance Regulation

In the United States, regulation of the insurance industry is primarily the responsibility of the individual states and territories for so long as the Congress, the national legislative body, considers state regulation to be adequate. Thus, insurance companies must comply with the laws of every state and territory in which they conduct business. As a general rule, however, each state insurance department has primary responsibility for overseeing the operations of those insurers domiciled in the state. An insurer's **domicile**, or *domiciliary state*, is the state in which the insurer incorporated.

State insurance laws are designed to protect the public interest and can be classified into two broad categories:

1. **Solvency laws** are designed to ensure that insurance companies are financially able to meet their debts and to pay policy benefits when they come due. In general terms, **solvency** is a business organization's ability to meet its financial obligations on time. **Insolvency** is a condition in which a business is consistently unable to meet its financial obligations on time.

2. **Market conduct laws** are designed to make sure that insurance companies conduct their businesses fairly and ethically. Market conduct laws regulate virtually all of the nonfinancial operations of insurers.

Both solvency laws and market conduct laws apply to direct writers. Regulation of reinsurance, however, focuses on solvency issues, and it focuses specifically on the reinsurance arrangements that direct writers enter into and how those arrangements affect the direct writers' financial condition. Differences among states' laws can make complying with state laws difficult for reinsurers that offer reinsurance products in more than one state. Typically, a reinsurer accommodates a direct writer by offering reinsurance that complies with the laws of each of their domiciliary states.

In many other countries, the insurance business is regulated by the national government through specialized entities, such as an Insurance Superintendent. For an overview of how insurance regulation and reinsurance regulation are structured in Canada, refer to Figure 2.1.

The National Association of Insurance Commissioners

In an effort to promote uniformity among state laws and regulations in the United States, the *National Association of Insurance Commissioners (NAIC)*, a nongovernmental association of state insurance commissioners, develops model laws and regulations. A *model law*, also referred to as a *model act* or *model bill*, is a sample law designed for use as a basis for the enactment of statutes by legislatures of each state or territory. State enactment of a model law is voluntary, and each state can alter the wording of the model law to reflect the state's particular concerns. Thus, the enacted laws can vary significantly from state to state and also from the original model law. A *model regulation* is a sample regulation designed for use as a basis for the adoption of regulations by the states' administrative agencies. The administrative branch of each state government is headed by the governor and includes a number of administrative agencies such as the state insurance department. Regulations adopted by state administrative agencies have the same force and effect as statutes. Figure 2.2 describes a number of NAIC model laws and regulations focused on reinsurance. We discuss most of these model laws and regulations later in this chapter and again throughout this book. Most states have enacted versions of these model laws and regulations and, thus, regulation of reinsurance is fairly uniform throughout the country.

NAIC Accreditation of State Insurance Departments

As mentioned earlier, insurers are primarily subject to regulatory oversight in their domiciliary states. Nevertheless, all states monitor the financial condition of all insurers operating within their jurisdictions and will increase their oversight activities if they believe an insurer's domiciliary state is not adequately overseeing the insurer's financial condition.

The NAIC's *Financial Regulation Standards and Accreditation Program* provides a method by which states can demonstrate that their solvency regulation systems meet specified minimum standards. To qualify for accreditation, a state must adopt in substance certain model laws and regulations and the state insurance department must have adequate resources to oversee the solvency of insurers domiciled in the state. To maintain its accreditation, a state must undergo an annual evaluation and a full recertification review every five years. The accreditation program helps the various state insurance departments ensure that a domiciliary state's regulation is effective so that they can concentrate their own resources on monitoring the condition of insurers domiciled in their states.

Licensing Requirements

Licensing is one regulatory tool that enables regulators to monitor the solvency of insurance companies. In the United States, licensing requirements apply to insurance companies, reinsurers, and reinsurance intermediaries. In addition, the individuals and entities that market insurance products to the public must be licensed as insurance producers in each state in which they conduct business.

FIGURE 2.1

Regulation in Canada

In Canada, insurers can be federally incorporated or provincially incorporated. Whether the federal or a provincial government has primary authority to regulate an insurer depends on how the insurer is incorporated. Thus, both the federal government and the provinces regulate insurance.

Office of the Superintendent of Financial Institutions

The *Office of the Superintendent of Financial Institutions (OSFI)* is the federal office responsible for overseeing the financial aspects of federally licensed financial institutions in Canada. The OSFI thus oversees federally incorporated insurance companies. The OSFI also publishes guidelines that specifically address reinsurance, such as the *Guideline on Unregistered Reinsurance and Reinsurance in the Ordinary Course of Business*. Each province has its own Financial Services Commission that monitors the financial operations of insurers in that province.

Insurance Companies Act

The *Insurance Companies Act* exercises the federal government's constitutional authority to incorporate insurance companies that conduct business extending outside a single province and to legislate with regard to foreign insurance companies incorporated in a country other than Canada. Sections of the Act related to reinsurance include the

- Reinsurance (Canadian Companies) Regulations
- Reinsurance (Foreign Companies) Regulations

Each province—except Newfoundland, which has a number of separate insurance acts—also has a provincial Insurance Act that governs how companies conduct an insurance business within the province.

Canadian Reinsurance Conference and Canadian Reinsurance Guidelines

Each year, Canadian direct writers and reinsurers hold an annual reinsurance meeting known as the *Canadian Reinsurance Conference (CRC)*. The CRC provides a forum for current life and health insurance and reinsurance issues and attracts significant international participation. The *Canadian Reinsurance Guidelines*, created and revised by the CRC, are a set of common reinsurance principles that companies can voluntarily use as a basis for writing and interpreting new reinsurance arrangements. These guidelines, last reviewed in 2003, are regarded as official standards of practice for the industry.

Source: Jane Lightcap Brown and Jennifer W. Herrod, *Reinsurance Administration* (Atlanta: LOMA, 2000), 38.

FIGURE 2.2

NAIC Model Laws Focused on Reinsurance

CREDIT FOR REINSURANCE MODEL LAW

Specifies requirements for taking reserve credits for the risk transfer in reinsurance. The Model Law is designed to protect the interests of the public and ensure payment of valid reinsurer obligations.

CREDIT FOR REINSURANCE MODEL REGULATION

Provides guidance for using trusts and escrow accounts, letters of credit, and funds withheld to provide financial backing for reserve credits in reinsurance transactions. Specifies how to implement requirements of the *Credit for Reinsurance Model Law.* Provides language for a certificate, Form AR-1, for an assuming insurer (reinsurer) to provide to the proper insurance commissioner.

REINSURANCE INTERMEDIARY MODEL ACT

Regulates the activities of reinsurance intermediaries and of direct writers and reinsurers that use the services of reinsurance intermediaries. Requires each intermediary to be licensed in each state in which it has an office. The Model Act is designed to (1) ensure that reinsurance intermediaries are qualified to perform their services and (2) enable regulators to account for any funds the intermediary may have handled in the event of the insolvency of a reinsurer.

LIFE AND HEALTH REINSURANCE AGREEMENTS MODEL REGULATION

Provides guidelines to help determine whether enough risk is transferred in a reinsurance agreement to permit the direct writer to claim reserve credit. Requires that all reinsurance agreements and amendments be in writing and be signed by the insurer and the reinsurer. The Model Regulation does not apply to all forms of nonproportional reinsurance.

ASSUMPTION REINSURANCE MODEL ACT

Provides for the regulation of the transfer and novation of insurance contracts by way of assumption reinsurance. Defines assumption reinsurance. Establishes notice and disclosure requirements. Defines the rights and responsibilities of policyholders, regulators, and the parties to assumption reinsurance agreements.

Source: National Association of Insurance Commissioners.

Licensing Requirements—Direct Writers

To conduct business within a state, an insurance company must obtain a license from that state's insurance department. Each state establishes its own licensing standards, which are designed to (1) make sure that companies can meet their financial obligations when they become due and (2) establish a mechanism for regulatory oversight of insurer operations. Typical requirements for licensing in a state require an insurance company to

■ Hold a minimum dollar amount of capital and surplus

- Deposit in trust a minimum dollar amount of securities or other liquid assets

- Name the state's insurance commissioner as the insurer's attorney-in-fact for service of process in any legal action filed against the insurer in that state

Licensing Requirements—Reinsurers

Reinsurers that market and sell insurance to the public must be licensed according to the regulatory requirements that apply to all direct writers. In addition, the states have established systems to license reinsurers.

Authorized or Admitted Reinsurers

An **authorized reinsurer**, also called an *admitted reinsurer*, is a company that is licensed or otherwise recognized by the insurance department in a given state. Just as the licensing process for a direct writer subjects the company to the jurisdiction's regulation, when a reinsurer is authorized or admitted, the reinsurer becomes subject to regulation by the authorizing jurisdiction's insurance laws and is subject to that jurisdiction's courts. The reinsurer is required to submit financial statements and other documents to the state insurance department. These documents enable the insurance department to monitor the reinsurer's financial condition.

From a direct writer's perspective, an authorized reinsurer is a reinsurer that is authorized by the direct writer's domiciliary state. Most professional reinsurers in the United States are authorized or accredited in all 50 states.

Accreditation for Reinsurers

Most states in the United States offer a status of accreditation for reinsurers. An **accredited reinsurer** is a reinsurer that is not licensed in a given state but that meets specified financial and reporting requirements of that state and is licensed to transact insurance or reinsurance in at least one other state. Because solvency regulation is relatively uniform across the United States, requiring a reinsurer to be licensed in another state provides assurance to regulators in other states that the reinsurer is subject to solvency requirements that are similar to those imposed by such other states.

Unauthorized Reinsurers

Unauthorized reinsurers, also known as *nonadmitted reinsurers*, are reinsurers that are not authorized or accredited in a given state. Regulators may not be able to adequately monitor an unauthorized reinsurer's solvency. An unauthorized reinsurer could become insolvent and harm the financial condition of a direct writer. For this reason, many states prohibit direct writers domiciled in the state from taking a reserve credit for reinsurance with a reinsurer that is not authorized by the state without at the same time obtaining security for the ceded risk. We describe reserve credits later in the chapter.

Licensing Requirements—Reinsurance Intermediaries

Marketing representatives are employees of a reinsurer, and they are not required to meet normal agent or broker licensing requirements in order to market reinsurance. These employees might have job titles such as reinsurance marketing officer or reinsurance account executive. In some cases, however, reinsurance intermediaries who are not employees of a licensed company are required to be licensed as reinsurance intermediaries in the United States. A *reinsurance intermediary* is a third party who is not employed by a licensed insurer or reinsurer, but who acts on behalf of a direct writer or reinsurer to place reinsurance.

As shown in Figure 2.2, the ***Reinsurance Intermediary Model Act*** regulates the activities of reinsurance intermediaries and of the companies that use the services of reinsurance intermediaries. The Model Act identifies two types of reinsurance intermediaries:

- A *reinsurance intermediary—broker* is any person, firm, or corporation that solicits, negotiates, or places reinsurance cessions or retrocessions on behalf of a direct writer but that is not authorized to enter into a binding reinsurance contract on behalf of the direct writer.

- A *reinsurance intermediary—manager* is any third party that acts as an agent of a reinsurer and either has authority to bind the reinsurer to a reinsurance contract or manages all or part of the reinsurer's assumed business.

The Model Act, which has been enacted by almost all of the states, is designed to (1) ensure that reinsurance intermediaries are qualified to perform their services and (2) enable regulators to—in the event of the insolvency of a reinsurer—account for any funds the intermediary may have handled. The Model Act requires each reinsurance intermediary to be licensed in each state in which the intermediary has an office. Further, for a reinsurance intermediary in one state to take cessions from an insurer incorporated in another state, the reinsurance intermediary must be licensed in that other state or in yet another state that has a law similar to the Model Act.

The Model Act also imposes certain requirements on the agreements that insurers and reinsurers enter into with reinsurance intermediaries, as follows:

- Such agreements must be evidenced by a written contract that contains specified provisions

- The company that hires a reinsurance intermediary must be able to terminate the reinsurance intermediary's authority at any time

- The company that hires a reinsurance intermediary must have access to the intermediary's records and annual financial statements

- The reinsurance intermediary must adhere carefully to stated rules of recordkeeping and reporting

Monitoring Financial Condition

Regulators monitor the solvency of various types of insurers and reinsurers operating in their jurisdictions by (1) examining required financial reports from each company, (2) setting capital and surplus requirements and monitoring compliance with those requirements, and (3) conducting on-site financial condition examinations. Each jurisdiction specifies the exact accounting and financial reporting systems to be used in the monitoring process.

Regulators generally use accounting and financial reporting systems to evaluate two specific areas of an insurer's or a reinsurer's financial condition, as follows:

- **Adequate capital**. Does the insurer have enough long-term financial resources to conduct business into the future? In finance, **capital** is the money that a company's owners either originally invested in the company and/or that the company has accrued from retained earnings.

- **Adequate liquidity**. Does the insurer have available enough cash or assets that can readily be turned into cash to pay bills and meet other obligations as they become due? In finance, **liquidity** is defined as the ease with which an asset can be converted into cash without incurring any significant loss.

Financial Reports

The primary financial report that U.S. insurance regulators use to monitor a life insurer's financial strength is the Annual Statement. The **Annual Statement** is a financial statement format that reports information about an insurer's operations and financial performance. Each year, every life insurer operating in the United States must file an Annual Statement with the NAIC and with the insurance department of every state in which the company conducts business. Companies operating as authorized or accredited reinsurers within a given state are subject to the same reporting requirements as licensed insurers operating in the state.

One report included in the Annual Statement and in other sets of financial reports is a balance sheet. A **balance sheet** is a financial document that lists the values of a company's assets, liabilities, and capital as of a specific date.

- **Assets** are all the things of value owned by a company. For insurers, assets include such items as stocks, bonds, mortgages, cash, buildings, furniture, and land.

- **Liabilities** are a company's debts and future obligations. The liabilities of insurance companies typically consist of a relatively small share of traditional debt obligations and a vast share of reserves for future contractual obligations on insurance policies in force. For insurers, the major liability item on the balance sheet is **policy reserves**—a liability account that identifies the amount that, together with future premiums and investment income, an insurer estimates it will need to pay policy benefits as claims occur.

- **Capital and surplus** are the amounts remaining after liabilities are subtracted from assets. Capital and surplus reflect a company's value. Capital and surplus are also known as *owners' equity* because they represent the owners' financial interest in the company. For mutual insurers, owners' equity may be called *policyholders' and shareholders' equity*. **Surplus** is the worth that an insurer has accumulated since its inception. By convention, though, *surplus* alone or *capital* alone can refer to both capital and surplus.

A balance sheet takes its form from an equation known as the **basic accounting equation**, which states that a company's assets equal the sum of the company's liabilities and capital and surplus. Figure 2.3 shows a simple form of balance sheet and the basic accounting equation, which defines the balance sheet relationships among assets, liabilities, and capital and surplus.

FIGURE 2.3

A Simplified Balance Sheet

Mammoth Insurance Company
Simplified Balance Sheet
December 31

Assets = Liabilities + Capital + Surplus

Assets	**Liabilities**
Investments	Policy reserves
Cash	Other liabilities
Other assets	
	Capital and Surplus (or Owners' Equity)
	Capital
	Surplus

The relationship of assets, liabilities, capital, and surplus in the basic accounting equation can be expressed in the following alternative forms:

Assets = Liabilities + Capital + Surplus

Surplus = Assets – (Liabilities + Capital)

Assets – Liabilities = Capital + Surplus

Source: Susan Conant, *Capital Management for Insurance Companies* (Atlanta: LOMA, 2001), 7–8.

Capital and Surplus Requirements

The insurance authorities of most jurisdictions are not equipped to extensively examine the accounts of every insurer operating there. Instead of examining every document in detail, regulators use financial ratios to determine whether each insurer has enough capital and surplus to remain solvent and to identify potentially impaired insurers. In the United States, all insurers must meet the following two types of capital and surplus requirements:

■ *Minimum capital and surplus requirements*, also known as *statutory minimum capitalization requirements*, set a required minimum flat dollar amount of capital and surplus for a company as a whole and for each of the company's product lines. Each jurisdiction sets its own minimum capital and surplus requirements. For insurers, **statutory solvency** refers to the legal minimum standard of capital and surplus that every insurance company must maintain. Insurers must monitor both their overall solvency positions and their statutory solvency, because one of these conditions can exist without the other.

■ The **risk-based capital (RBC) ratio** developed by the NAIC is required for companies operating in the United States. These requirements enable state regulators to evaluate the adequacy of an insurer's capital relative to the riskiness of the insurer's operations. In its most basic form, a **capital ratio** is a ratio that expresses the relationship between an insurer's capital and surplus and its liabilities. Each insurer uses the NAIC's complex formula to calculate the company's capital ratio value, using information reported in required financial statements. An insurer must meet or exceed the minimum ratio value to be considered solvent. Generally, the greater the value of the capital ratio, the better an insurer's solvency. Ratio values below an acceptable level alert regulators to more closely examine a company's financial condition.

Regulators additionally use early warning financial ratio tests to monitor insurance company solvency. **Early warning financial ratio tests** are a set of standards and financial ratios that regulatory examiners use to analyze an insurer's financial statements and to create a customized examination plan that focuses on the risks identified from the insurer's financial information. For example, in the United States, the Financial Analysis and Solvency Tracking (FAST) System is one such early warning system.

On-Site Regulatory Examinations

In most states in the United States, each insurer domiciled in a particular state must undergo a regulatory examination every three to five years. **Examiners**, representing the regulators of one or more states, visit the offices of insurers and review their business records, operating procedures, business plans, and management. Regulators in the United States conduct the following two types of on-site regulatory examinations:

- A **financial condition examination** is a routine on-site regulatory examination of an insurer for the purpose of identifying and monitoring any threats to the insurer's solvency

- A **market conduct examination** is a routine on-site regulatory examination of an insurer for the purpose of verifying that, in dealings with customers, the insurer is complying with all applicable statutes and regulations regarding marketing, sales, advertising, underwriting, and claims

Working through the NAIC, the states have developed a zone system of financial examinations to oversee the operations of multistate insurers. Each insurer is domiciled within one of four geographic zones in the United States. Examiners representing various states in the zones in which an insurer is licensed participate in examining the insurer. Such an on-site regulatory examination is known as an **association examination**. By participating in and relying on association examinations, the state insurance departments are able to work together to monitor the financial condition of multistate insurers.

Reserves and Reserve Credit

Direct writers must meet regulatory requirements for their policy reserves. Regulators use information from required financial statements to monitor insurers' policy reserve levels. **Required reserves**, also called *statutory reserves*, are the reserves calculated according to regulatory requirements. The required method of calculating the appropriate amount of policy reserves an insurer must hold varies among jurisdictions. Each state in the United States requires policy reserves that meet NAIC standards. For various other purposes, insurers in the United States use the following other reserve standards:

- Generally accepted accounting principles (GAAP) reserves, calculated using methods set by the Financial Accounting Standards Board (FASB)

- Tax reserves, calculated using methods and assumptions set by federal tax laws

- Internal management-basis reserves, also known as modified reserves, calculated using methods and assumptions set by each insurer

Insurers have some latitude in determining the size of their reserves. Each insurer adopts appropriate reserves based on the combination of legal requirements, its own circumstances, and its business objectives. In addition, some reserve calculations incorporate the insurer's claim projections. In the United States, statutory requirements set a minimum reserve amount, but no maximum amount.

Reserve Credit for Reinsurance

Surplus strain, also called *new business strain*, refers to a decrease in an insurer's surplus caused by the high initial costs and policy reserve requirements associated with issuing new insurance policies. Insurers can ease surplus strain by using reinsurance to decrease the amount of their required policy reserves on new business. A direct writer in some situations may obtain **surplus relief**—a decrease in potential surplus strain—through the use of some types of reinsurance. Reserve credits, if available, are one important mechanism for accomplishing surplus relief through reinsurance.

In some reinsurance arrangements, when the reinsurance company assumes a portion of the insurer's risk, the reinsurer establishes reserves for the reinsured portion of the risk. A **reserve credit** is the accounting entry a direct writer uses to record an offset of its required reserves due to the use of reinsurance. Taking reserve credit can improve an insurer's financial condition. Thus, direct writers seek to cede risks to reinsurers that meet the specified requirements for reserve credit.

As we saw in Figure 2.2, some of the requirements for taking reserve credits in the United States are outlined in the two closely related model laws. The **Credit for Reinsurance Model Law** specifies requirements for taking reserve credits, and the **Credit for Reinsurance Model Regulation** specifies how to implement the requirements of the Model Law.

The Credit for Reinsurance Model Law permits reserve credit for reinsurance if the reinsurer meets any one of the following requirements:

- The reinsurer is licensed to transact reinsurance in the direct writer's domiciliary state.

- The reinsurer is accredited in the direct writer's domiciliary state.

- The reinsurer is domiciled or licensed in a state in which the standards regarding credit for reinsurance are similar to those in the Model Law. In addition, the reinsurer must

  - Maintain a surplus of at least $20 million.

  - Submit its books and records to be examined by the insurance department of the direct writer's domiciliary state.

■ The reinsurer maintains a trust fund in a qualified U.S. financial institution for the payment of valid claims. The reinsurer must annually submit specified information to the insurance department of the direct writer's domiciliary state for a determination of the adequacy of the fund. The form of the trust must be approved by the insurance department and must consist of a trusteed account representing the reinsurer's liabilities in the United States. The reinsurer also must maintain a trusteed surplus of $20 million.

In one exception, the Model Law permits a direct writer to take reserve credit for reinsurance ceded to a reinsurer that does not meet any of the above requirements if the reinsured risk is located in a jurisdiction that requires reinsurance by law.

Otherwise, if the reinsurer fails to meet any of the above requirements, including the exception just noted, the reserve credit will not be allowed unless the reinsurer agrees to submit to the jurisdiction of any appropriate court in the United States and to abide by the court's final decisions. The reinsurer also must designate the insurance commissioner or a designated attorney as its attorney upon whom a legal action can be served on behalf of the direct writer.

Forms of Security for Reinsurance

As we noted earlier, insurers can take reserve credit for reinsurance ceded to an unauthorized reinsurer if the reinsurer establishes a trust or another binding arrangement for security in the amount of the reserve credit. The Credit for Reinsurance Model Regulation provides guidance for using trusts, escrow accounts, letters of credit, and funds withheld to provide financial backing for reinsurance transactions, as specified in the Credit for Reinsurance Model Law.

Trusts and Escrow Accounts

Two arrangements used for security in reinsurance transactions involve escrow accounts and trusts:

■ An *escrow account* is an amount of money that one party to a transaction puts aside in a restricted account for the benefit of the other party to the transaction until specified requirements of an agreement have been met.

■ A *trust* is a legal arrangement whereby one or more persons—called the trustees—hold legal title to property on behalf of another person—called the trust beneficiary—and are responsible for administering the property for the benefit of the trust beneficiary.

A trust fund used for security in a reinsurance transaction holds funds intended to pay claims in the event that a reinsurer becomes insolvent. The Credit for Reinsurance Model Law allows trusts to be established with cash, certificates of deposit (CDs), or other investments specified by the state insurance code. The value of the assets in a trust must be determined using fair market value. For reinsurance purposes, a trust fund may take any of the following forms:

■ Cash or securities qualified by the NAIC as admitted assets and held in a qualifying trust account. *Admitted assets* for an insurer are assets whose full value is acceptable for reporting on the assets page of the Annual Statement.

■ Clean, irrevocable, unconditional letters of credit issued by a qualified U.S. financial institution on an approved form.

■ Funds withheld by and under the control of the direct writer.

■ Any other form of security acceptable to the state insurance department.

The Credit for Reinsurance Model Regulation states that the trust must allow the trust beneficiary to remove assets from the trust at any time. The trust document must name the direct writer as beneficiary of the trust. The reinsurer may limit the use of withdrawn assets to the following purposes:

■ To reimburse the direct writer for the reinsurer's share of the premiums that the direct writer must return to policyowners who cancel reinsured policies

■ To reimburse the direct writer for the reinsurer's share of the surrender benefits or losses paid under the reinsured policies

■ To fund an account with the direct writer in the amount of the policy reserves, claims and losses incurred, unearned premium reserves, and any other amounts for which the direct writer takes a deduction for reinsurance

■ To pay any other amounts the direct writer asserts are due under the reinsurance arrangement

Letters of Credit

The most common form of security offered by unauthorized reinsurers is the letter of credit. In reinsurance transactions, a *letter of credit* issued by a bank is a document that permits the letter's addressee—in this case, usually the direct writer—to use the letter as security and to draw funds from the bank in the event of a valid, unpaid claim against the letter's issuer—in this case, the reinsurer. The letter of credit guarantees payment of funds up to a specified maximum amount. A letter of credit protects the direct writer from financial harm caused by the insolvency or other financial difficulty of the reinsurer. Under the Credit for Reinsurance Model Regulation, letters of credit must be clean, unconditional, irrevocable, and evergreen, defined as follows:

■ *Clean* means that the direct writer must be able to receive the funds merely by requesting them from the bank

■ *Unconditional* means that the letter of credit must establish all qualifications for payment

■ *Irrevocable* means that the letter of credit can be modified only with the consent of all parties specified in the letter of credit

■ *Evergreen* means that the letter of credit will be renewed automatically each year unless the bank gives ample notice to the parties to the letter of credit

Figures 2.4 shows a letter of credit.

Withheld Funds

Withheld funds in reinsurance are amounts of money that the direct writer would otherwise pay to the reinsurer, but by agreement, the direct writer continues to hold as security for the reinsurance transaction. Reinsurers can provide security for reinsurance transactions by depositing money with the direct writer or by allowing the direct writer to withhold funds that the direct writer would otherwise pay to the reinsurer under the reinsurance arrangement. The amount of the withheld funds must at least equal the direct writer's reserve credit. The direct writer pays the reinsurer interest on these withheld funds.

FIGURE 2.4

A Letter of Credit

 **Horizon Bank**

December 29, 2005
Letter of Credit No. 443566
Effective December 31, 2005
Applicant: Overlook Reinsurance Company

Mr. George Roberts
Chief Financial Officer
Atlantica Insurance Company
One Atlantica Way
Anytown, NY 55555

Dear Mr. Roberts:

We have established this clean, irrevocable, and unconditional letter of credit in your favor as beneficiary for drawing up to U.S. $9,000,000.00 (NINE MILLION AND 00/100 U.S. DOLLARS), effective December 31, 2005. This letter of credit is issued, presentable, and payable at Horizon Bank, 100 Main Street, Anytown, NY 55555. Except when the amount of this letter of credit is increased, this credit cannot be modified or revoked without your consent.

The term beneficiary includes any successor by operation of law of the named beneficiary including without limitation any liquidator, rehabilitator, receiver, or conservator. Drawing by any liquidator, rehabilitator, receiver, or conservator shall be for the benefit of all of the beneficiary's policyholders.

We hereby undertake to promptly honor your sight draft(s) drawn on us, indicating our credit number 443566, for all or any part of this credit upon presentation of your draft drawn on us at our office specified in paragraph one on or before the expiration date hereof or any automatically extended expiry date.

Except as expressly stated herein, this undertaking is not subject to any agreement, requirement, or qualification. The obligation of Horizon Bank under this credit is the individual obligation of Horizon Bank and is in no way contingent upon reimbursement with respect thereto, or upon our ability to perfect any lien, security interest, or any other reimbursement.

This letter of credit is deemed to be automatically extended without amendment for one year from the expiration date or any future expiration date unless at least 30 days prior to such expiration date we notify you by registered mail that this letter of credit will not be renewed for any such additional period.

This letter of credit is subject to and governed by the laws of the State of New York.

Yours very truly,

Hannah M. Blakemore

Hannah M. Blakemore
Authorized Signature

Risk Transfer

A major concern of insurance regulators is risk transfer in reinsurance. To protect the solvency of insurers, regulators seek to ensure that each reinsurance transaction for which an insurer takes reserve credit involves a genuine and substantial transfer of risk to the reinsurer. If a direct writer reports a reinsurance reserve credit on risk that is not actually transferred to a reinsurer, the direct writer's financial statements do not reflect the company's actual risk exposure. Such financial reporting would be misleading.

To protect against potential inaccuracy, the NAIC developed the ***Life and Health Reinsurance Agreements Model Regulation***, which provides guidelines to help determine whether enough risk is transferred in a reinsurance arrangement to permit the direct writer to take reserve credit. The Model Regulation—which does not apply to all forms of reinsurance—requires that reinsurance arrangements be in writing and be signed by the insurer and the reinsurer. Figure 2.5 discusses circumstances in which a direct writer would be denied reserve credit for inadequate transfer of risk.

The Model Regulation contains a table of risk categories and product types to identify significant risk categories, which enable regulators to determine if risk has been adequately transferred. If a risk type is significant for a particular product, the risk must be transferred to the reinsurer for reserve credit to be allowed.

FIGURE 2.5

Basis for Denial of Reserve Credit

The *Life and Health Reinsurance Agreements Model Regulation* denies reserve credit to a direct writer in the following circumstances:

- The renewal expense allowances owed by the reinsurer are not adequate to cover the direct writer's actual renewal expenses for the reinsured portion of each policy.

- The reinsurance arrangement requires the direct writer to repay the reinsurer for losses, to recapture or terminate all or part of the reinsurance, and/or to pay amounts not realized from the reinsured policies

- The reinsurance arrangement fails to provide for the transfer of all significant risk of the reinsured coverage

- The direct writer is required to make guarantees of the future performance of the reinsured business

Source: Adapted from Jane Lightcap Brown and Jennifer W. Herrod, *Reinsurance Administration* (Atlanta: LOMA, © 2000), 50. Used with permission; all rights reserved.

Key Terms

domicile
solvency laws
solvency
insolvency
market conduct laws
Office of the Superintendent of
  Financial Institutions (OSFI)
Insurance Companies Act
Canadian Reinsurance Conference (CRC)
Canadian Reinsurance Guidelines
National Association of Insurance
  Commissioners (NAIC)
model law
model regulation
Financial Regulation Standards and
  Accreditation Program
authorized reinsurer
accredited reinsurer
unauthorized reinsurer
reinsurance intermediary
Reinsurance Intermediary Model Act
reinsurance intermediary—broker
reinsurance intermediary—manager
capital
liquidity
Annual Statement
balance sheet
assets

liabilities
policy reserve
capital and surplus
surplus
basic accounting equation
minimum capital and surplus requirements
statutory solvency
risk-based capital (RBC) ratio
capital ratio
early warning financial ratio tests
examiner
financial condition examination
market conduct examination
association examination
required reserves
surplus strain
surplus relief
reserve credit
Credit for Reinsurance Model Law
Credit for Reinsurance Model Regulation
escrow account
trust
admitted assets
letter of credit
withheld funds
Life and Health Reinsurance Agreements
  Model Regulation

CHAPTER 3

Forms of Reinsurance

After studying this chapter, you should be able to

- Compare and contrast the automatic, facultative, and facultative-obligatory methods of transferring reinsurance risk

- Explain how nonproportional reinsurance differs from proportional reinsurance

- Describe and differentiate among the approaches used in nonproportional reinsurance: excess-of-loss reinsurance, stop-loss reinsurance, catastrophe coverage, spread-loss coverage, and extended-time reinsurance

- Describe basic coinsurance and modified coinsurance (modco)

- Discuss the excess-of-retention and first-dollar quota share methods that direct writers and reinsurers use for sharing a risk

- Describe yearly renewable term (YRT) reinsurance

OUTLINE

Cession Arrangements in Reinsurance
Automatic Reinsurance
Facultative Reinsurance
Facultative-Obligatory Reinsurance
Comparison of Cession Arrangements

Nonproportional and Proportional Reinsurance Plans
Nonproportional Reinsurance
Proportional Reinsurance

The Cession Amount in Proportional Reinsurance
Excess-of-Retention Arrangements
Quota Share Arrangements

Basic Coinsurance
Coinsurance Premium
Funds Withheld Coinsurance

Modified Coinsurance

Yearly Renewable Term Reinsurance

Proportional reinsurance typically is used for life insurance products, because the liability for a life insurance policy generally is known at the outset. Most life reinsurance and long-term care reinsurance conducted in North America is proportional reinsurance.

Indemnity reinsurance arrangements are quite complex and can take a variety of forms. In this chapter, we discuss some important distinctions among the forms of reinsurance. Each of these forms assigns a different set of rights and obligations to the direct writer and the reinsurer, who are the parties to the reinsurance arrangement.[1]

Cession Arrangements in Reinsurance

A direct writer can cede reinsurance risk on an automatic, a facultative, or a facultative-obligatory (fac-ob) basis, as illustrated in Figure 3.1.

Automatic Reinsurance

In **automatic reinsurance,** the direct writer agrees in advance to cede and the reinsurer agrees in advance to assume all cases that meet the specifications in the reinsurance agreement. For a case that meets all agreement specifications, automatic reinsurance allows a direct writer to *automatically* bind a reinsurer to a risk without first providing the reinsurer with underwriting evidence for the case and without asking the reinsurer's approval in advance.

The automatic reinsurance agreement states the premium rates for automatic reinsurance. Thus, for a given case under an automatic arrangement, the direct writer and the reinsurer can independently calculate the amount of the reinsurance premium payable.

The automatic cession is the only cession basis in which the direct writer must cede and the reinsurer must assume a qualifying case based on only the direct writer's underwriting evaluation. If a case under automatic reinsurance meets the requirements for automatic cession, then the direct writer generally *must* reinsure the case and the reinsurer *must* accept the case, without question. However, many automatic reinsurance agreements include a facultative provision that

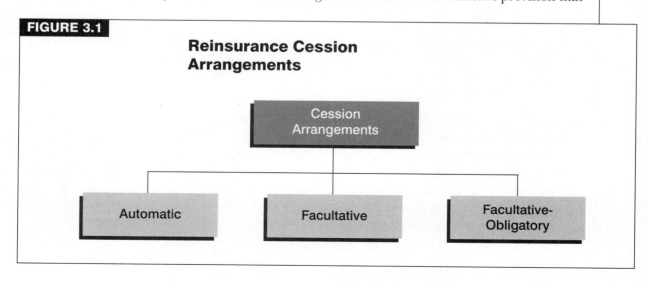

FIGURE 3.1

Reinsurance Cession Arrangements

Cession Arrangements

Automatic

Facultative

Facultative-Obligatory

allows a direct writer to submit certain applications facultatively to its reinsurance partner and to other reinsurers. We discuss facultative reinsurance arrangements in the next section of this chapter.

Automatic reinsurance arrangements may limit cessions based on factors such as the plan of insurance; age of the insured; policy issue date; standard or substandard underwriting class; direct writer's retention limit; and amount of risk. A **retention limit** is a specified maximum monetary amount of insurance that an insurer is willing to carry at its own risk without transferring some of the risk to a reinsurer. Direct writers and reinsurers have retention limits. Automatic reinsurance cessions often specify the following monetary limits on the amount of risk a reinsurer will accept:

■ A reinsurer's **automatic binding limit** represents the maximum monetary amount of risk the reinsurer will obligate itself to accept automatically on a given policy or case without making an independent underwriting assessment. The reinsurer must accept the entire ceded risk on all policies when that risk does not exceed the automatic binding limit.

■ A reinsurer's **minimum cession** is the smallest monetary amount of risk the reinsurer will accept in an automatic cession. The high expense of a small cession affects both direct writers and reinsurers. Having a minimum cession allows a reinsurer to avoid the obligation to accept amounts of risk that are relatively small in comparison to the administrative costs associated with the risk amounts. For a direct writer, a minimum cession is the smallest monetary amount of risk that the direct writer will cede in an automatic cession.

■ A **jumbo limit** for an automatic cession is the maximum allowable monetary amount of total insurance—in force plus yet-to-be-placed—with all companies on any one life that a reinsurer will accept for automatic cession. If a case exceeds the reinsurer's jumbo limit, the direct writer may submit the case on a facultative basis to the reinsurer and the reinsurer may accept the case. Jumbo limits for automatic cessions control the reinsurer's exposure to risk on any one life. A jumbo limit on life reinsurance protects a reinsurer from excessive risk resulting from the accumulation of several policies on the same life. Only automatic reinsurance arrangements for life insurance or critical illness coverage are subject to jumbo limits. For life insurance coverage, reinsurers cumulate the total life insurance amounts. For critical illness coverage, reinsurers cumulate the total critical illness coverage. Reinsurers, however, never cumulate both life and critical illness coverages.

Example: A reinsurer with a jumbo limit of $20 million receives an automatic cession of $10 million in life insurance for an insured who already has $15 million of insurance on her life. This cession of $10 million would exceed the reinsurer's jumbo limit of $20 million.

■ A reinsurer's **participation limit** specifies the reinsurer's maximum limit on coverage currently in force plus yet-to-be-placed on any given person.[2] If the total amount of insurance—currently in force plus yet-to-be-placed—with all companies on a given person exceeds a reinsurer's participation limit, the reinsurer will automatically refuse to provide reinsurance on a policy covering that person, regardles of the cession basis. Participation limits are used with all types of reinsurance cession bases. Participation limits are most common for disability income and accidental death coverages, and they may be used with life coverages.

An automatic cession arrangement may be subject to a number of these foregoing limits. For example, an automatic arrangement could be subject to a minimum cession, an automatic binding limit, a jumbo limit, and a participation limit.

Facultative Reinsurance

Under *facultative reinsurance,* a direct writer chooses whether to cede a risk and the reinsurer chooses whether to accept that risk. For a facultative case, a reinsurer underwrites the case, assigns the case a risk classification, and can quote a price based on its own underwriting guidelines and terms. A reinsurer has no obligation to submit a quote for a case submitted on a facultative basis. Facultative reinsurance is the only cession basis wherein the reinsurer must perform an independent underwriting evaluation and has the option to reject cases on the basis of the underwriting.

Many direct writers choose facultative reinsurance because facultative reinsurance allows them to obtain the benefit of the reinsurer's underwriting judgment before accepting a case. All other factors held constant, the cost of facultative reinsurance to direct writers is generally higher than the cost of automatic reinsurance. One reason for the higher cost is that direct writers often submit facultative cases to several reinsurers simultaneously to obtain several price quotes. Also, direct writers often use facultative reinsurance for hard-to-place, complex cases involving multiple risk factors. Thus, a reinsurer's premium rates include the costs to underwrite, evaluate, and provide coverage for facultative cases.

Many automatic reinsurance agreements include a facultative provision that allows a direct writer to facultatively submit cases that do not qualify for automatic cession. The facultative provision usually specifies that the direct writer may facultatively submit the case to multiple reinsurers but the direct writer must submit the case to the reinsurer under the automatic agreement. In general, a facultative provision also indicates that the case must be awarded to the reinsurer under the automatic agreement if that reinsurer and another reinsurer respond with similar offers that both would otherwise represent winning bids.

Facultative-Obligatory Reinsurance

Facultative-obligatory (fac-ob) reinsurance arrangements specify that (1) the direct writer may choose to submit cases to the reinsurer and (2) the reinsurer must accept the submitted cases based on the direct writer's underwriting, up to a stated maximum monetary amount, if the reinsurer has available capacity. Under a fac-ob arrangement, the reinsurer determines whether the requested coverage exceeds the reinsurer's capacity. If the reinsurer lacks capacity and therefore cannot accept the risk, it immediately notifies the direct writer. If the reinsurer fails to decline a fac-ob case within a specified maximum period, the reinsurer is automatically bound to the risk within the agreed-upon acceptance limits. If the reinsurer in such a situation lacks capacity to cover the case, the reinsurer will have to retrocede the excess risk with its own reinsurers.

With one exception, the reinsurer in a fac-ob arrangement has the same rights and obligations as in an automatic reinsurance arrangement. The exception is that the reinsurer can refuse a fac-ob case if the reinsurer lacks capacity, whereas under a fac-ob cession basis, the reinsurer cannot refuse a qualifying case if the reinsurer has the capacity to accept it.

Comparison of Cession Arrangements

The strength of a direct writer's financial incentive to perform a thorough underwriting evaluation on a case depends on the amount of risk the direct writer intends to retain. A direct writer must retain a portion of the risk under an automatic or a facultative-obligatory arrangement; for these arrangements, the direct writer thus will have a financial incentive to perform a detailed underwriting evaluation. However, a direct writer may cede the entire risk under facultative cases. Thus, a direct writer may not have a strong financial incentive to perform a detailed underwriting evaluation for a case under a facultative arrangement, particularly if the direct writer plans to cede the entire risk.

The three cession arrangements just described have the following similarities and differences:

- In all three arrangements, the direct writer ideally should perform an underwriting evaluation of every application for insurance

- For only the automatic cession basis, the direct writer must cede and the reinsurer must assume a qualifying case based on only the direct writer's underwriting evaluation

- Only the automatic cession basis includes both an automatic binding limit and a jumbo limit

- In only the facultative arrangement, the reinsurer both performs an independent underwriting evaluation and, on the basis of that risk evaluation, has the option to reject qualifying cases

- All other factors held constant, the direct writer's cost of administering facultative reinsurance is generally higher than the cost of administering automatic reinsurance

- In a fac-ob arrangement, the reinsurer has the same rights and obligations as in an automatic arrangement and the reinsurer has the additional right to reject a case if the reinsurer lacks financial capacity

The following table summarizes the typical options or requirements for the direct writer and the reinsurer under the various cession arrangements we have discussed:

	Direct Writer	Reinsurer
Automatic	Must cede all qualifying cases	Must assume all qualifying cases Does not perform any underwriting evaluation before its assumption of risk
Facultative	Has the option to cede or retain qualifying cases	Has the option to reject cases Performs an underwriting evaluation before accepting a risk
Fac-Ob	Has the option to cede or retain qualifying cases	Must assume all qualifying cases if capacity is available May reject qualifying cases if financial capacity is not available

Nonproportional and Proportional Reinsurance Plans

Typically, reinsurance arrangements structure the sharing of monetary risk between the direct writer and the reinsurer in either a nonproportional or proportional manner.

Nonproportional Reinsurance

Nonproportional reinsurance limits the direct writer's total loss on a specified segment of the direct writer's insurance business. Under nonproportional reinsurance, after a direct writer's monetary losses exceed a specified maximum limit, the reinsurer begins to share in expenses for future claims.

Direct writers most frequently use nonproportional reinsurance for non-life coverages. They also use some forms of nonproportional reinsurance for life insurance business, although the use of nonproportional reinsurance for life insurance cases may be limited in Europe and North America.

Under nonproportional reinsurance, the reinsurer's liability is determined by actual claims the direct writer receives, so the amount of the reinsurer's liability is not precisely known in advance. The reinsurer begins to reimburse a direct writer for claims when the direct writer's losses on a business segment exceed a specified monetary limit within a specified period, such as one year. The specified monetary limit at which the direct writer's obligation transfers to the reinsurer is known as the reinsurer's ***attachment point***.

Nonproportional reinsurance arrangements do not describe the reinsurer's specific percentage share of the total monetary risk. Nonproportional reinsurance generally defines the risk level for each party in terms of (1) the monetary amount of reinsured claims or (2) the number of the reinsured claims.

> **Example:** For a specified block of the direct writer's business within a specified calendar year, a reinsurer agrees to cover the direct writer's total claim benefits greater than $50 million.

The most common plans of nonproportional reinsurance include excess-of-loss reinsurance, stop-loss reinsurance, and catastrophe coverage. Less commonly used plans of nonproportional reinsurance are spread-loss coverage and extended-time reinsurance. Figure 3.2 compares essential characteristics of the most common plans of nonproportional reinsurance.

Excess-of-Loss Reinsurance

Excess-of-loss reinsurance is a type of nonproportional reinsurance in which a reinsurer is responsible for paying a specified amount of a direct writer's claim benefits paid on a single loss, within a specified range of monetary amounts. In this context, a *single loss* could refer to the monetary loss per policy, per person, or per occurrence. An excess-of-loss reinsurance plan generally specifies both a lower and an upper limit on the reinsurer's monetary obligation for a single loss. The reinsurance coverage extends to each loss that falls within the specified range or *layer* of monetary amounts. Excess-of-loss reinsurance typically covers the entire monetary amount of the loss within the coverage range.

FIGURE 3.2

Comparison of Common Nonproportional Reinsurance Plans

Plan	Amount of a reinsurer's liability for covered business	Upper limit on reinsurer's liability?
Excess-of-Loss Reinsurance	Within a specified range of monetary amounts, a specified amount of a direct writer's claim expenses on a single loss	Yes
Stop-Loss Reinsurance	Within a specified range of monetary amounts, a portion of the direct writer's total claims for a specified operating period	Yes
Catastrophe Coverage	The direct writer's total claims above a stated amount, subject to a minimum number of qualified claims and a maximum total reinsurance payout	Yes

Example: In the event of an insured's total disability, a disability income policy promises a benefit of $3,000 per month for as long as the disability continues. The direct writer retains its normal retention limit of $2,500 per month and maintains reinsurance for the remainder—$500 per month. If a claim for total disability arises, the reinsurer is responsible for paying $500 per month. The risk assumed by the reinsurer is not proportional and the cumulative amount of the reinsurer's liability is not known before a claim occurs.

Stop-Loss Reinsurance

Stop-loss reinsurance, also known as *stop-loss ratio reinsurance* or *excess-of-loss ratio reinsurance*, is a type of nonproportional reinsurance in which the reinsurer agrees to pay for a portion of total claims on a block of business in an amount between stated lower and upper limits for a specified operating period. In stop-loss reinsurance coverage, the stated lower limit could be either (1) an agreed monetary amount or (2) an agreed percentage of some other monetary measure of business volume, such as (a) aggregate net premiums over the same period or (b) average insurance in force for the same period.

Example: On reinsurance for all coverage issued under a health insurance plan, the direct writer may retain the first $250,000 of benefits paid in a year. The reinsurer will be liable for the remainder of benefits, up to a maximum of $1,000,000. Thus, if the direct writer received a total of $400,000 in claims under the plan, the reinsurer would be liable for $150,000 of the loss. The risk assumed by the reinsurer is not proportional, and the amount of the reinsurer's liability is unknown before the claims occur.

Both stop-loss and excess-of-loss reinsurance cover situations in which unexpectedly large claims would cause a financial strain for the direct writer. Note that the main difference between excess-of-loss and stop-loss reinsurance is that excess-of-loss reinsurance applies to a single loss, whereas stop-loss reinsurance typically applies to a block of business within a stated period of operations.

Catastrophe Coverage

Catastrophe coverage, commonly known as *cat cover*, is a type of nonproportional reinsurance designed to partially protect direct writers from (1) a single catastrophic event resulting in multiple claims or (2) an annual total of claims in a catastrophic amount. Cat cover usually is a backup for accident or casualty coverages. In rare instances, cat cover can be applied to life insurance, health insurance, disability income insurance, or long-term care insurance coverages. Cat cover usually requires the reinsurer to pay claims on the direct writer's total claims above a stated amount, subject to (1) a minimum number of qualified claims or minimum amount of claim benefits and (2) a maximum total reinsurance payout. Examples of such single catastrophic events involving multiple claims are building fires, earthquakes, volcanic eruptions, commercial airplane crashes, environmental accidents, epidemics, and tsunamis. Typically, a cat cover arrangement for a single catastrophic event requires a minimum of three claims from the same event.

Spread-Loss Coverage

Spread-loss coverage is a nonproportional reinsurance arrangement—similar to a loan—between a direct writer and a reinsurer. In spread-loss coverage, the reinsurer agrees to pay the direct writer if the direct writer's total claims for a specified block of business in a stated period exceed a specified monetary amount. In return, the direct writer is required to repay the reinsurer's funds over time with interest payable according to specified terms.

Extended-Time Reinsurance

Extended-time reinsurance, also called *excess-of-time reinsurance*, is a type of nonproportional reinsurance in which the reinsurer takes over paying benefits for reinsured policies after the direct writer has paid benefits for a specified amount of time. An extended-time reinsurance plan may or may not set an upper limit on the reinsurer's obligation. Extended-time reinsurance is commonly used with disability income and long-term care insurance. In contrast to spread-loss coverage, the direct writer is not required to repay the reinsurance liability.

> **Example:** A long-term care insurance policy provides a maximum benefit period of 5 years. Under that plan of insurance, the direct writer retains the liability for the first 2 years of each claim. If any claim extends longer than the first 2 years, then the reinsurer pays the benefits incurred after the first 2 years, up to the policy maximum of 5 years.

Proportional Reinsurance

Proportional reinsurance is an arrangement under which the reinsurer agrees to assume specified risks in exchange for a specified reinsurance premium. The direct writer and the reinsurer agree to share the direct writer's premiums and the direct writer's expenses in a specified amount or percentage. A key characteristic of proportional reinsurance is that the reinsurer's percentage of the liability is known in advance of any claims. In proportional business, the direct writer and reinsurer share the policy reserve proportionately. Proportional reinsurance typically is used for life insurance products, because the liability for a life insurance policy generally is known at the outset. Most life reinsurance and long-term care reinsurance conducted in North America is proportional reinsurance.

A proportional reinsurance arrangement specifies the share of the direct writer's premium that the reinsurer will collect and the claim liabilities that the reinsurer is obligated to pay. The proportional arrangement may express the reinsurer's share as a percentage or ratio of the face amount of life insurance issued. The proportional arrangement may express the risks reinsured in terms of criteria such as type of plan, age limits, underwriting rating, or benefit amounts.

Example: A proportional reinsurance arrangement states that the reinsurer will accept 60 percent of the face amount of each of the direct writer's whole life claims. For a $1 million policy, we can calculate the direct writer's and reinsurer's proportionate responsibilities, as follows:

	Proportionate Share	×	Face Amount	=	Liability
Direct Writer	0.40	×	$1,000,000	=	$400,000
Reinsurer	0.60	×	$1,000,000	=	$600,000

Proportional reinsurance can take the forms of coinsurance, modified coinsurance (modco), funds withheld coinsurance, funds withheld modco, and partially modified coinsurance (partco), and other variations. For reasons that go beyond the scope of this textbook, industry usage varies as to whether YRT reinsurance is proportional. Our discussion uses the definition of proportional reinsurance that excludes YRT reinsurance. However, many practitioners consider YRT reinsurance to be proportional.

Figure 3.3 illustrates the types of nonproportional and proportional reinsurance discussed in this chapter. Figure 3.4 presents a comparison of the characteristics of nonproportional and proportional reinsurance.

The Cession Amount in Proportional Reinsurance

A proportional reinsurance arrangement generally specifies a method for determining the amount of risk the direct writer will cede. Although companies may use any reasonable method for dividing risks, the two most common methods are excess-of-retention and first-dollar quota share.

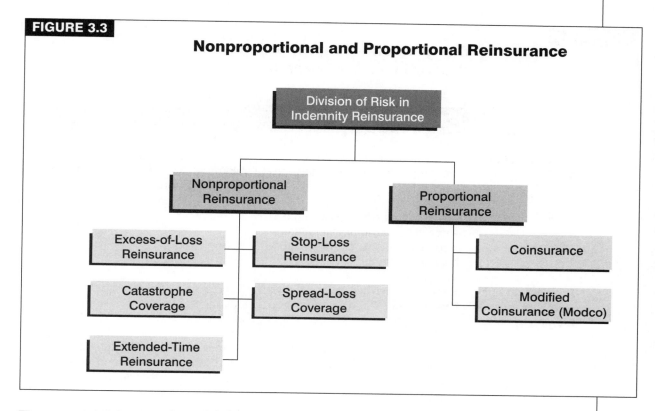

FIGURE 3.3

Nonproportional and Proportional Reinsurance

Excess-of-Retention Arrangements

The **excess of retention** generally is the monetary amount of risk remaining after the direct writer's retention limit is subtracted from the net amount at risk on a case. The **net amount at risk (NAAR)** is the difference between the face amount of a life insurance policy—other than a universal life policy—and the policy reserve the direct writer has established at the end of any given policy year. Thus, the excess of retention for a case generally is the amount of risk the direct writer cedes and the reinsurer assumes, as shown:

$$
\begin{array}{ccccc}
\text{Direct Writer's} & & \text{Direct Writer's} & & \text{Direct Writer's} \\
\text{Excess of} & = & \text{Net Amount} & - & \text{Retention} \\
\text{Retention} & & \text{at Risk} & & \text{Limit}
\end{array}
$$

In the next section of this chapter we discuss coinsurance, an important form of proportional reinsurance. The excess of retention for coinsurance is calculated in a different manner. For coinsurance, the excess of retention is calculated as follows:

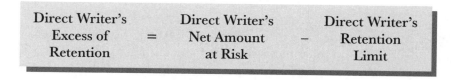

$$
\begin{array}{ccccc}
\text{Excess of} & & \text{Direct Writer's} & & \text{Initial Reinsurance} \\
\text{Retention for} & = & \text{Net Amount at} & \times & \dfrac{\text{Amount}}{\text{Policy Face Amount}} \\
\text{Coinsurance} & & \text{at Risk} & &
\end{array}
$$

FIGURE 3.4

Comparison—Nonproportional and Proportional Reinsurance

	Nonproportional	Proportional
Arrangements for Assumption of Risk	The reinsurance arrangement does not describe the reinsurer's specific percentage share of the total monetary risk. After a direct writer's losses exceed a specified maximum limit, the reinsurer begins to share in future benefit payments.	The direct writer and the reinsurer agree to share the direct writer's premiums and benefit payments in a specified amount or percentage.
Predictabilty of Reinsurer's Liability	Reinsurer's liability depends upon level of claims and is not known precisely in advance.	Reinsurer's liability is defined in advance in terms of a monetary amount or percentage.
Treatment of Reserves	Shared non-proportionally, with the reinsurer holding the larger share.	Shared proportionally, with reserves held by the direct writer and reinsurer in proportional shares. Direct writer takes reserve credit for the proportion of the risk ceded to the reinsurer.
Types of Business Reinsured	Mostly non-life business Health insurance Disability income insurance Some long-term care coverage Some life business	Life insurance Annuities Health insurance Disability income insurance Long-term care coverage

Example: Suppose a case has a face amount of $100,000; the direct writer's retention is $25,000; and the direct writer's net amount at risk (NAAR) is $90,000. The general approach and the coinsurance approach result in different values for the excess of retention on a given case, as follows:

General Approach	Coinsurance Approach
The reinsurer will assume the risk for $65,000, calculated as $$\$90,000 - \$25,000$$	The reinsurer will assume the risk for $67,500, calculated as $$\$90,000 \times \frac{\$75,000}{\$100,000}$$ or $\$90,000 \times 0.75$

In an ***excess-of-retention arrangement*** for assigning risk in proportional reinsurance cessions, the direct writer establishes a retention limit and the reinsurer agrees to assume monetary amounts greater than the direct writer's specified retention limit, up to the reinsurer's automatic binding limit. The excess-of- retention arrangement is used with automatic reinsurance arrangements. In an excess-of-retention arrangement, the direct writer automatically obtains reinsurance for specified amounts of coverage that exceed its retention limit. The applicable retention limit may be from the direct writer's standard retention schedule or from a special retention schedule designed for the specific reinsurance arrangement. In an excess-of-retention arrangement, because the retention limit is a fixed monetary amount, the percentages retained and ceded vary from one case to the next according to the monetary amount of coverage under each case.

Quota Share Arrangements

As we have already discussed, a quota share is the portion of a direct writer's risk that is ceded to one or more reinsurers. Quota share arrangements can be applied to an entire block of a direct writer's business rather than being applied to individual cases. Under a ***quota share arrangement*** for assigning risk in reinsurance, the direct writer retains a specified amount or percentage of the risk and cedes the remaining risk to a reinsurer. Quota share arrangements usually are used with automatic cessions, but they can be used with facultative cessions. Sometimes the direct writer is subject to a maximum monetary amount of retention.

Two forms of quota share arrangements are excess quota share and the more popular first-dollar quota share. An ***excess quota share arrangement*** is a method of ceding proportional reinsurance in which the direct writer keeps its full retention limit and cedes the remaining risk to two or more reinsurers on a percentage basis. Excess quota share arrangements are found mostly in old business, as the popularity of excess quota share has declined in recent decades. Most present-day quota share arrangements are first-dollar quota share arrangements, which are suitable for most common insurance coverages. A ***first-dollar quota share (FDQS) arrangement*** is a proportional reinsurance arrangement in which the direct writer retains a stated percentage of the entire risk on a given book of business and cedes the remaining risk to one or more reinsurers, despite the presence of a retention limit. In FDQS arrangements, the direct writer cedes coverage from the "first dollar." The FDQS arrangement usually states a maximum monetary amount of risk that the reinsurer is willing to accept.

Compared to excess quota share arrangements, FDQS arrangements give the reinsurer greater participation in the direct writer's risks. Under FDQS the direct writer cedes a fixed percentage of the risk on each policy; thus, in FDQS the reinsurer shares the risk on *every* policy, not on only the policies that have an excess of retention. Because under FDQS the reinsurer has greater participation and the direct writer cedes more risk in the first year, the direct writer receives a greater overall first-year allowance and reserve credit than it would under an excess quota share arrangement.

Excess-of-retention arrangements typically provide less relief from surplus strain than do quota share arrangements, because under excess-of-retention arrangements the direct writer receives smaller allowances. These allowances usually are smaller under excess-of-retention arrangements because, compared with quota share arrangements, the direct writer often has a higher retention under excess-of-retention arrangements and, thus, less risk is transferred to the reinsurer.[3]

Basic Coinsurance

Basic coinsurance is a standard approach used in proportional reinsurance arrangements. In a basic **coinsurance** arrangement, the direct writer and reinsurer proportionately share monetary responsibility for almost every aspect of each policy covered under the arrangement. Before entering into a coinsurance arrangement, the reinsurer must evaluate the values incorporated into the direct writer's product design.

Every retail insurance product has a financial design or model that includes critical elements for the product's financial success. This financial design process often is called *product pricing*. When an insurance company designs a product, the actual values of the critical design elements are unknown. Thus, the financial values incorporated in product pricing are based on estimates, so that the actual values will differ from the estimated values in the product model. The financial success of the product depends on the difference between the actual experience with these elements and the values incorporated into the product model. Product pricing is intended to have the best financial results when the product's experience is at least as favorable for the direct writer as the statistics, known as *assumptions*, used in the product design. Insurance product design can include the risks described in Figure 3.5.

FIGURE 3.5

Risks Estimated in Product Modeling

Mortality risk for an insurance product is the risk that (1) a life insured will die earlier than the levels built into the product design or (2) a life annuitant or long-term care insured will live longer than the levels built into the product design.

Morbidity risk for an insurance product is the risk that a health insured will experience sickness, accidents, or impaired condition more frequently or for a longer period than the levels built into the product design.

Lapse risk for an insurance product is the risk that (1) an insurance policy will terminate prior to the recovery of the insurer's initial expenses for the product or (2) the insured will retain a health or disability income insurance policy long enough to make a claim.

Expense risk for an insurance product is the risk that an insurance company's first-year or renewal expenses to support the product will exceed the expense level built into the product's design and pricing.

Asset risk for an insurance product is the risk that the assets supporting the product will lose value or will fail to earn at least the rate of return used in the product model.

Reinvestment risk for an insurance product is the risk that funds reinvested will earn a lower rate of return than was built into the policy design.

Disintermediation risk for an insurance product is the risk that interest rates will change and (1) policy loans and surrenders will increase or (2) maturing contracts will renew less frequently than was built into the product design.

A coinsurance arrangement specifies each party's proportionate share of the shared risk in terms of either (1) a percentage of risk—say, 45 percent of a risk—or (2) a flat monetary amount of risk—say, the first $50,000 of a risk. The direct writer and reinsurer share the premiums and various obligations of the primary coverage—any death benefit, other policy benefits, nonforfeiture values, and policy reserves. The reinsurer, however, very rarely shares in the direct writer's responsibility for the amounts of outstanding policy loans.[4] In addition, the reinsurer proportionately shares in the direct writer's expenses—for commissions, administration, and sometimes premium taxes—in the form of a ***coinsurance allowance***. As we have seen, the direct writer withholds the allowance from the coinsurance premium paid to the reinsurer. This coinsurance allowance can be a proportionate share of the coinsurance gross premium, as shown:

$$\begin{array}{ccc} \text{Coinsurance} \\ \text{Allowance} \end{array} = \begin{array}{c} \text{Coinsurance} \\ \text{Gross} \\ \text{Premium} \end{array} \times \begin{array}{c} \text{Reinsurer's Proportionate} \\ \text{Share of Expenses for} \\ \text{Administration, Commissions,} \\ \text{and Premium Taxes} \end{array}$$

Alternatively, the coinsurance allowance can be applied as a charge per unit, such as a monetary amount per policy issued or per policy in force.

Coinsurance is suitable for life insurance, health insurance, disability income insurance, long-term care insurance, and annuity coverages.

Coinsurance Premiums

In coinsurance, the ***coinsurance net premium*** is the amount that the direct writer must pay to the reinsurer after subtracting the coinsurance allowance from the coinsurance gross premium, as shown:

$$\begin{array}{c} \text{Coinsurance} \\ \text{Net Premium} \end{array} = \begin{array}{c} \text{Coinsurance} \\ \text{Gross Premium} \end{array} - \begin{array}{c} \text{Coinsurance} \\ \text{Allowance} \end{array}$$

Thus, the ***coinsurance gross premium*** is equal to the coinsurance net premium plus coinsurance allowance.

Funds Withheld Coinsurance

Funds withheld coinsurance is a variation on basic coinsurance and, thus, is similar to basic coinsurance in many ways.[5] Funds withheld coinsurance requires the direct writer and the reinsurer to proportionately share responsibility for some aspects of a reinsured policy. This plan allows the direct writer and reinsurer to limit cash flows between them over the life of the reinsurance arrangement. The main differences between the initial handling of the allowance under basic coinsurance versus funds withheld coinsurance are as follows:

- Under basic coinsurance, the direct writer usually initially pays the reinsurer a reinsurance premium and the reinsurer pays an allowance to the direct writer. Each party maintains its own share of the required policy reserves.

- Under funds withheld coinsurance, the reinsurer retains the initial reinsurance allowance and the direct writer retains the initial gross reinsurance premium. The parties record any difference between these amounts in an account payable or account receivable, as appropriate, for *net funds withheld*. Both parties maintain accounting records and, thus, track changes in the net balance of the withheld funds. Because both parties must track the net values over the life of the arrangement, funds withheld coinsurance requires exceptionally careful and accurate recordkeeping and administration.

- For all coinsurance, the direct writer and the reinsurer have responsibility for their portion of the policy reserves. Funds withheld coinsurance is distinctive in that the direct writer holds the reserves, invests the corresponding assets, and credits the reinsurer's reserve fund with the reinsurer's portion of the investment earnings.

Modified Coinsurance

Modified coinsurance (modco) is a type of proportional reinsurance in which the direct writer and reinsurer share proportionately in the policy reserve obligation, the reinsurance premium, and the risks of loss from expenses for death, surrender, other benefits, or lapse. Modco typically is used for cash value life insurance and annuity products, and it is particularly appropriate for interest-sensitive products.

Although the parties to a modco arrangement share responsibility for policy reserves, the direct writer holds the entire reserve and interest earnings on the reserve for each reinsured policy. The reinsurer deposits its proportionate share of the required reserve, known as a reserve credit, with the direct writer. Both the direct writer's share of the policy reserve and the reinsurer's reserve credit amount are adjusted periodically, usually quarterly.

Modco premiums and allowances are calculated in a manner similar to coinsurance. Modco requires a *modified coinsurance (modco) reserve adjustment*, as shown:[6]

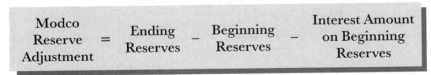

$$\text{Modco Reserve Adjustment} = \text{Ending Reserves} - \text{Beginning Reserves} - \text{Interest Amount on Beginning Reserves}$$

The interest on beginning policy reserves is calculated using a *modco interest rate*. The value of the modco interest rate is specified in the modco arrangement. In the United States, the modco interest rate typically must meet requirements of the *Credit for Reinsurance Model Regulation*.

For any given period, the value of a modco reserve adjustment may be positive or negative:

- A positive modco reserve adjustment value indicates that the reinsurer owes funds to the direct writer.

- A negative modco reserve adjustment value indicates that the direct writer owes funds to the reinsurer.

Variations on modco reinsurance include *funds withheld modco* and *partially modified coinsurance (partco)*. These modco variations are beyond the scope of this text. Figure 3.6 compares features of coinsurance and modco arrangements.

FIGURE 3.6

Comparison of Coinsurance and Modco

Type(s) of Coverage Reinsured	
Coinsurance	Suitable for life, health, disability income, and long-term care insurance and annuities
Modco	• Usually annuities and cash value life products • Particularly appropriate for interest-sensitive products

Reinsurance Obligations	
Coinsurance	Proportionate share in the policy reserve obligation, the reinsurance gross premium, and expenses for death, surrender, lapse, or other benefits
Modco	Proportionate share in the policy reserve obligation, the reinsurance gross premium, and expenses for death, surrender, lapse, or other benefits

Treatment of Policy Reserve Obligation	
Coinsurance	The direct writer and reinsurer proportionately share responsibility for the policy reserve obligation and maintain the reserves within each company
Modco	The direct writer and reinsurer proportionately share responsibility for the policy reserve obligation, but the direct writer holds the entire policy reserve and interest earnings on the reserve

---

Yearly Renewable Term Reinsurance

Yearly renewable term (YRT) reinsurance is a type of reinsurance typically used for life insurance policies. YRT reinsurance reinsures only the mortality portion of a life insurance risk. For YRT reinsurance, the direct writer pays a one-year term insurance premium to the reinsurer on the anniversary date of each reinsured policy. The direct writer remains responsible for paying policy dividends and cash values, and for holding most reserves on the reinsured business. Thus, YRT reinsurance does not significantly reduce the direct writer's surplus strain.

Under YRT reinsurance, the reinsurance liability amount equals the net amount at risk on the reinsured portion of a policy. For a term life insurance policy, the NAAR is equal to the death benefit. The NAAR for a cash value life insurance policy is the policy's death benefit minus the policy's cash value, as shown:

$$\begin{array}{c} \text{Cash Value Life} \\ \text{Policy's Net Amount} \\ \text{at Risk (NAAR)} \end{array} = \begin{array}{c} \text{Policy's} \\ \text{Death} \\ \text{Benefit} \end{array} - \begin{array}{c} \text{Policy's} \\ \text{Cash} \\ \text{Value} \end{array}$$

For cash value life insurance, reinsurers often use the amount of policy reserves as a convenient estimate for the policy cash value. Thus, companies can obtain a reasonable estimate for NAAR by using the following formula:

$$\text{Cash Value Life Policy's Estimated Net Amount at Risk (NAAR)} = \text{Policy's Death Benefit} - \text{Policy Reserves}$$

The amount of the YRT reinsurance coverage a direct writer needs decreases each policy year. When a life policy reaches maturity, the direct writer's accumulated reserves equal the entire mortality risk, leaving no NAAR, and the YRT reinsurance terminates. Figure 3.7 illustrates the decreasing NAAR phenomenon.

In effect, under YRT reinsurance, the direct writer cedes only the life insurance policy's mortality risk. The YRT mortality cost for a cash value life insurance policy increases every year, because the mortality risk increases every year.

A reinsurer develops the YRT reinsurance premium rates independently of the direct writer's gross premiums. The YRT reinsurance premium rate reflects mostly the mortality risk reinsured. The YRT reinsurance premium rate increases each year as the insured ages and mortality risk increases. Figure 3.8 shows how to calculate the mortality cost of a yearly renewable term life insurance policy.

FIGURE 3.7

Decreasing Net Amount at Risk on Life Insurance Policies

Policy Year	Anniversary Date	NAAR (Net Amount at Risk)
1	11/26/07	$2,900,000
2	11/26/08	$2,700,000
3	11/26/09	$2,500,000
4	11/26/10	$2,300,000
5	11/26/11	$2,100,000
6	11/26/12	$1,900,000
...Maturity	11/26/XX	$0

Source: Adapted from Jane Lightcap Brown and Jennifer W. Herrod, *Reinsurance Administration* (Atlanta: LOMA, © 2000), 23. Used with permission; all rights reserved.

FIGURE 3.8

Calculation of Mortality Cost
for Term Life Insurance

For a yearly renewable term life insurance policy with a $100,000 face amount, the amount of a potential claim is $100,000. We can approximate the probability of a claim for a given year by using the probability that the insured will die during that year, which is the mortality rate. Thus, the estimated mortality cost for a yearly renewable term policy is the mortality risk for the insured's age at issue, multiplied by the $100,000 face amount. For a male aged 35, let's assume that the tabular life insurance mortality rate is 0.00251. Now, we can use this information to derive the mortality cost of $100,000 of YRT coverage on a male aged 35, as follows:

Product: $100,000 yearly renewable term life insurance, male aged 35				
Mortality Cost	=	**Number of Claims**	×	**Amount of Claims**
	=	Mortality Rate	×	Face Amount
	=	0.00251	×	$100,000
	=	$251		

This procedure shows that the mortality cost is $251 for such a $100,000 yearly renewable term life insurance policy.

Source: Adapted from Susan Conant, *Product Design for Life Insurance and Annuities* (Atlanta: LOMA, © 2001) 71–72. Used with permission; all rights reserved.

For a given cash value life insurance policy, as the policy reserve and cash value accumulate, the NAAR declines, reducing the total amount of reinsurance liability. So, the reinsurance liability decreases with the passage of time. Eventually, the reinsurer's liability terminates when the NAAR has grown to equal the policy reserve. However, as the insured ages, the YRT reinsurance premium rate increases. Thus, the YRT premium rate increases with the passage of time even as the reinsurance liability decreases. For YRT reinsurance arrangements, these important elements change in the following directions as time passes:

With the passage of time,	
As the following amounts increase...	**The following amounts decrease...**
Policy reserve	Net amount at risk
Policy cash value	Reinsurer's liability
Age of insured	
YRT reinsurance premium rate	
Mortality risk	
Mortality cost	

Figure 3.9 summarizes important characteristics of YRT reinsurance.

FIGURE 3.9

Characteristics of YRT Reinsurance

Type of Business Covered
Life insurance

Reinsurance Obligations
The entire net amount at risk (NAAR) on the reinsured portion of a life insurance policy.

Policy Reserve Obligation
The direct writer and the reinsurer share responsibility for the policy reserve obligation.

The direct writer is entitled to reduce its reserve holdings in the amount of a reserve credit from the reinsurer.

Key Terms

automatic reinsurance
retention limit
automatic binding limit
minimum cession
jumbo limit
participation limit
facultative reinsurance
facultative-obligatory (fac-ob)
   reinsurance
nonproportional reinsurance
attachment point
excess-of-loss reinsurance
stop-loss reinsurance
catastrophe coverage
spread-loss coverage
extended-time reinsurance
proportional reinsurance
excess of retention
net amount at risk (NAAR)

excess-of-retention arrangement
quota share arrangement
excess quota share arrangement
first-dollar quota share (FDQS)
   arrangement
coinsurance
mortality risk
morbidity risk
lapse risk
expense risk
asset risk
reinvestment risk
disintermediation risk
coinsurance allowance
coinsurance net premium
coinsurance gross premium
funds withheld coinsurance
modified coinsurance (modco)
yearly renewable term (YRT)
   reinsurance

Endnotes

1. This chapter represents a revision of material from Jane Lightcap Brown and Jennifer W. Herrod, *Reinsurance Administration* (Atlanta: LOMA, © 2000), 19–33. Used with permission; all rights reserved.

2. John E. Tiller and Denise Fagerberg Tiller, *Life, Health, and Annuity Reinsurance*, 2nd ed. (Winsted, CT: ACTEX Publications, 1995), 31–32.

3. Insurance Accounting and Systems Association, *Financial Accounting for Life Insurance* (Charlotte, NC: IASA, 2004), 2.9.

4. Tiller and Tiller, 87.

5. Ibid., 139.

6. Ibid., 97.

Part 2:
The Reinsurance Agreement

CHAPTER 4

Defining the Reinsurance Coverage

After studying this chapter, you should be able to

- Explain why written reinsurance agreements are used

- List the criteria that direct writers and reinsurers use to evaluate potential reinsurance partners

- Describe the general characteristics of a reinsurance agreement

- Explain the reinsurance agreement provisions that define the scope of the agreement, including the parties to the agreement provision, the entire agreement provision, the duration of the agreement provision, and the recapture provision

- Describe the reinsurance agreement provisions that concern the termination of the agreement

- Describe the reinsurance agreement provisions that relate to (1) the plans of insurance to be retained and ceded and (2) the reinsurance coverage to be provided

OUTLINE

Reasons to Use Written Reinsurance Agreements

Life Cycle of the Reinsurance Agreement

Choosing a Reinsurance Partner

Evaluation Criteria Used by Direct Writers

Evaluation Criteria Used by Reinsurers

General Characteristics of a Reinsurance Agreement

Common Agreement Provisions

Scope of the Agreement

Parties to the Agreement Provision

Entire Agreement Provision

Duration of the Agreement Provision

Recapture Provision

Termination of the Agreement

Insurance Ceded and Reinsurance Provided

Reinsurance Coverage Articles

Schedules of Reinsurance Coverage

Reinsurance is not a one-size-fits-all product. Each reinsurance agreement is tailored to meet the requirements of the direct writer and the reinsurer.

A written indemnity reinsurance agreement attempts to outline every foreseeable aspect of the business conducted between the reinsurance parties at the inception of the agreement, during the effective period of the agreement, and even after the termination of the agreement.[1] To help you understand the general types of provisions in a reinsurance agreement, consider the following example.

Example: Suppose you are about to enter into an important contract with another person. Before the contract becomes effective, you need to know certain facts:

- Exactly what you are agreeing to do

- When the agreement begins and how long it will last

- How to end the agreement if you or the other person want to do so

- The amount of money involved (if any), who has to pay it, and when and how it is to be paid

- Your responsibilities under the contract and the responsibilities of the other person

- How to resolve any problems that arise under the contract

Reinsurance agreements address these same kinds of concerns. The provisions in indemnity reinsurance agreements typically fall into four categories:

- Defining the coverage to be ceded and assumed and any applicable limitations on this coverage

- Establishing procedures for administering the reinsurance, such as the method of administering records and reports and instructions for handling changes in coverage

- Handling claims, rescission, potential problems, and insolvency

- Specifying the financial terms of the agreement, such as the currency to be used and the payment of reinsurance premiums

In this chapter, we discuss the ways that reinsurance agreements define the coverage to be ceded and the reinsurance to be provided. We address additional aspects of reinsurance agreements in Chapters 5, 6, and 7.

Reasons to Use Written Reinsurance Agreements

A reinsurance agreement is a contract that, like most contracts, can be valid and binding on the parties even if it is an oral agreement. To protect themselves, however, the parties to a reinsurance agreement typically create a written document that spells out the terms of the arrangement. The principal reason for having a written reinsurance agreement is to document the terms of the agreement, including the details of the risk transfer, administration procedures, information exchanges, and rights and duties of the parties to the agreement. A written agreement also protects the financial security of the parties. Because the parties' risk transfers and information exchanges could potentially damage the financial strength of the parties, the details of the arrangement must be disclosed in the written agreement's provisions.

Reinsurance is not a one-size-fits-all product. Each reinsurance agreement is tailored to meet the requirements of the direct writer and the reinsurer. By specifically describing the terms of the reinsurance arrangement, a written agreement can help (1) prevent misunderstandings that may result from vague or overlooked details and (2) identify and resolve mistakes.

Although agreements differ substantially in the details—such as plans covered, reinsurance premium rates, and quota shares—the provisions that are included in agreements have become increasingly standardized, in part due to guidelines created by groups such as the NAIC, the Society of Actuaries, and the American Council of Life Insurers (ACLI).

Further, a written agreement documents the terms of the agreement for the future. Some reinsurance agreements remain in effect for many years, and the written agreement allows the next generation of administrators to understand how to handle a reinsured policy. Figure 4.1 presents the reasons to use written reinsurance agreements.

Life Cycle of the Reinsurance Agreement

Although the details of each reinsurance agreement vary, the life cycle of an indemnity reinsurance agreement generally includes the following stages:

- Selection of a reinsurance partner and negotiation of the terms of the agreement

- Cessions of specific risks

FIGURE 4.1

Reasons to Use Reinsurance Agreements

☑ Document the basis for conducting reinsurance transactions

☑ Describe the terms of the reinsurance arrangement

☑ Document the rights and duties of each party to the agreement

☑ Protect the financial security of the parties relative to the agreement

☑ Protect the parties from misunderstandings

☑ Help identify and resolve mistakes

Source: Jane Lightcap Brown and Jennifer W. Herrod, *Reinsurance Administration* (Atlanta: LOMA, 2000), 81.

- Ongoing administration of in-force reinsurance, which may continue after the agreement ends

- Termination of the agreement

Ideally, the reinsurance partners establish a written reinsurance agreement before any reinsurance cessions occur under the reinsurance arrangement. In practice, however, the formal agreement can take effect before, during, or after the direct writer transfers business to the reinsurer. A reinsurance agreement may cover one policy, a group of policies, a line of business, or any combination of policies, policy groups, or lines of business.

Choosing a Reinsurance Partner

Before entering a reinsurance agreement, direct writers and reinsurers generally conduct a careful investigation into potential reinsurance partners' financial circumstances, abilities, and integrity. To enter into a reinsurance arrangement in good faith, the direct writer and the reinsurer must undertake a required investigation process, known as *due diligence*. The due diligence investigation usually includes evaluating whether the other party's (1) policy reserves are adequate, (2) current pricing techniques are sound, and (3) products are likely to be profitable.

Evaluation Criteria Used by Direct Writers

Because reinsurance agreements often last many years, a direct writer is particularly concerned with the financial stability of its potential reinsurance partners.[2] The direct writer analyzes a reinsurer's recent financial statements and reports from independent auditors to determine whether the reinsurer has the ability to (1) accept the size and type of cases the direct writer needs to reinsure and (2) pay claims appropriately and promptly. To evaluate a reinsurer's financial position, a direct writer also can consider the following quantitative factors:

- **Quality ratings.** A *quality rating* is an alphabetical grade or rating assigned to an insurance company by an insurance rating agency to indicate the level of the insurance company's financial strength, its ability to pay its obligations to customers, or its ability to pay its obligations to creditors.

- **Profitability measures.** *Profitability* refers to a company's overall degree of success in generating returns for its owners, including its abilities to generate profit and to increase the company's wealth. Profitability measures include financial ratios such as the gross profit ratio and investment yield ratio. The *gross profit ratio* measures the growth in an insurance company's capital. The *investment yield ratio* shows how efficiently a company has used its investment portfolio to earn a return. Figure 4.2 shows the calculation of these ratios.

- **Liquidity measures.** As you learned in Chapter 2, liquidity is the ease with which an asset can be converted into cash without any significant loss. One measure of liquidity is the *insurance liquidity ratio*, which compares the market value of an insurer's *liquid assets*—which include cash and readily marketable assets—to some measure of its total reserves.

- **Leverage.** *Leverage* can be defined as a financial effect in which the presence of fixed costs—either operating or financing costs—automatically magnifies risks and potential returns to a company's owners. Evaluating a company's leverage includes an evaluation of the adequacy of the company's capital.

FIGURE 4.2

Ratio Calculations

$$\text{Gross Profit Ratio} = \frac{\text{Gross Contributions to Capital and Surplus}}{\text{Beginning Capital and Surplus}}$$

$$\text{Investment Yield Ratio} = \frac{\text{Investment Portfolio Income}}{\text{Average Invested Assets}}$$

$$\text{Insurance Liquidity Ratio} = \frac{\text{Liquid Assets at Market Value}}{\text{Total Reserves}}$$

In addition, the direct writer gathers information about a reinsurer from the reinsurer and the reinsurer's current and past clients. The direct writer seeks to gather the following types of information about a reinsurer:

■ The cost of reinsurance coverage from the reinsurer relative to the cost of similar coverage from other reinsurers

■ The reinsurer's ability and willingness to tailor reinsurance coverage and services to the direct writer's requirements

■ The extent of the reinsurer's expertise, particularly in the areas of underwriting and claim administration

■ The quality of client services provided by the reinsurer, including its ability to provide expert advice and help the direct writer solve reinsurance-related problems

■ The reinsurer's reputation in the industry, especially for appropriately protecting its reinsurance partners' proprietary procedures and information

Evaluation Criteria Used by Reinsurers

Before a reinsurer submits a proposal offering coverage to a direct writer, the reinsurer investigates the direct writer's financial circumstances, abilities, and integrity. The reinsurer analyzes the direct writer's recent financial statements and other financial information, including information about the direct writer's pricing, the anticipated profitability rates of its products, and the integrity of its accounting procedures.

The reinsurer also closely examines the direct writer's underwriting policies and procedures to ensure that the quality of the direct writer's underwriting is acceptable. The direct writer's underwriting practices are of particular importance for automatic reinsurance agreements, under which the reinsurer accepts the risk on a case based on the direct writer's underwriting without performing its own assessment of the risk. The reinsurer's decision on whether to enter into a reinsurance agreement with a direct writer also may be influenced by the following factors:

- Actuarial studies of the business to be reinsured

- Anticipated policy lapse rates

- The extent of the reinsurer's ability to monitor the direct writer's actual financial results and to investigate any deviations from projected results

- The reinsurer's business experience with the direct writer, if any

- The reinsurer's experience with similar types of business and reinsurance agreements

- The frequency and content of reports that the direct writer agrees to provide to the reinsurer

- Information about the direct writer's marketing procedures and results, claim administration procedures, and actuarial policies

After a direct writer and a reinsurer have agreed to do reinsurance business together, they negotiate the terms of one or more reinsurance agreements.

General Characteristics of a Reinsurance Agreement

Some reinsurance agreements—particularly those between reinsurance parties that have had a long-term, ongoing relationship—describe the reinsurance arrangement in broad terms that give both parties considerable discretion in implementing and administering the agreement. Other reinsurance agreements are quite specific concerning the accountabilities of each party and the procedures the parties agree to follow. Regardless of the amount of detail expressed in an agreement, every reinsurance agreement contains certain provisions that protect the interests of the parties.

The body of the reinsurance agreement is made up of *articles*, which are relatively standard contract provisions. The parties tailor the reinsurance agreement by adding schedules to cover the more variable elements of the agreement. *Schedules*, which also may be called *exhibits* or *conditions*, typically address details of the agreement such as the plans covered, retention limits, binding limits, reinsurance premium rates, and allowances. Because each reinsurance agreement is unique, details about the types of reinsurance covered by an agreement may be in an article in one agreement, and they may be in a schedule in another agreement.

When negotiating the terms of a reinsurance agreement, the direct writer and the reinsurer may start with a template that contains the articles typically used by one of the parties for the particular type of reinsurance involved. The direct writer and the reinsurer make changes to the standard provisions to meet the needs of both parties. The parties then add various other articles and schedules to describe the specific details of their particular arrangement. Figure 4.3 describes the process for establishing a reinsurance agreement.

FIGURE 4.3

Establishing a Reinsurance Agreement

The establishment of a reinsurance agreement typically involves six steps: (1) research, (2) request for proposal, (3) reply to the request for proposal, (4) evaluation of the proposal, (5) negotiation of terms, and (6) documentation. In many cases, reinsurance intermediaries provide assistance to the direct writer or the reinsurer with one or more of the steps.

1 Research
First, the direct writer identifies a need for reinsurance coverage and assembles information about its reinsurance needs and goals. The direct writer also identifies potential providers of the desired reinsurance coverage. Marketing communications from and previous experience with individual reinsurers and reinsurance pools can help direct writers identify the reinsurers that can provide the needed reinsurance.

2 Request for Proposal
The direct writer then notifies a reinsurer—or, if the business is to be submitted for bids, several reinsurers— of the need for reinsurance and provides the reinsurer with information about the business to be reinsured. The direct writer often sends the reinsurer a *request for proposal (RFP)*, which is a detailed bidding document that states the direct writer's needs and provides the product, pricing, and service details that the reinsurer must address in its proposal. In the RFP, the direct writer requests a quote for reinsuring the business and sometimes indicates the reinsurance premium rates it proposes to pay for the reinsurance. The direct writer also may ask the reinsurer for advice about details of a new product, such as policy provisions, pricing, and intended market. If the product to be covered is an existing product, the direct writer includes marketing and claims experience statistics concerning the business covered by the product.

3 Reply to the RFP
The reinsurer evaluates the direct writer's request. If the reinsurer wishes to accept the risk, then the reinsurer quotes its rates—or reinsurance premiums—in a proposal to the direct writer. The reinsurer's proposal to accept a risk is sometimes called an *offer*, a *quote offer*, or an *authorization*. If the reinsurer cannot offer the requested level of reinsurance at the rate suggested by the direct writer, the reinsurer may propose a higher rate or a lower level of coverage for the same or even a lower rate.

Example: Suppose a direct writer has asked a reinsurer to accept 80 percent of the risk on a new product at a specified schedule of rates. The reinsurer may reply to the request by stating that it will accept only 50 percent of the risk, but will do so according to a rate schedule that is lower than that quoted by the direct writer.

The reinsurer also may give advice to the direct writer. For instance, the reinsurer may note that the direct writer's intended insurance premium rates for a certain class of proposed insureds are too high or too low.

4 Proposal Evaluation
The direct writer examines the terms of each proposal submitted and invites the preferred candidates to discuss the proposed reinsurance coverage further. The direct writer might choose to negotiate with only one or two top candidates among the reinsurers that responded to the RFP.

5 Negotiations
The direct writer and a reinsurer may negotiate the terms of the reinsurance agreement for a considerable time to reach an agreement on reinsurance premium rates and coverage. Pricing actuaries at each company usually manage these negotiations.

After concluding negotiations, the direct writer makes a final decision on reinsuring the risk. The direct writer may decide to not reinsure the risk at all or to allocate the business among multiple reinsurers in various ways—for instance, to award 70 percent of the business to one reinsurer and 10 percent to each of three other reinsurers. The direct writer then notifies each reinsurer of its risk-allocation decision.

6 Documentation
Either the direct writer or the reinsurer may develop the written reinsurance agreement. The party that does not draft the agreement must review and approve the document.

If a direct writer plans to split its coverage among several reinsurers, the direct writer attempts to use the same reinsurance agreement for all reinsurers. Ideally, the direct writer is able to establish the same procedures for multiple reinsurers—for instance, setting up the same claim handling procedures and retention limits for large-amount cases. However, the specific rates may vary from one reinsurer to another.

Some jurisdictions require the reinsurance parties to file indemnity reinsurance agreements with insurance regulators before implementing the agreements. Most jurisdictions do not require approval of indemnity reinsurance agreements by insurance regulators.

Source: Adapted from Jane Lightcap Brown, *Insurance Administration* (Atlanta: LOMA, © 1997), 309–312 and Susan Conant, *Introduction to Institutional Investing* (Atlanta: LOMA, © 2005), 232–235. Used with permission; all rights reserved.

Common Agreement Provisions

Because a direct writer and a reinsurer negotiate each agreement to meet their specific needs, no two reinsurance agreements are exactly alike. Most indemnity reinsurance agreements, however, have similar versions of the basic provisions described in Figure 4.4. We describe each of these provisions in this and later chapters.

As we mentioned, reinsurance agreements contain schedules that provide key information such as retention limits, reinsurance premium rates, allowances, and sample forms. Figure 4.5 lists information typically presented in schedules in a reinsurance agreement.

In the remainder of this chapter, we describe the reinsurance agreement provisions that define the reinsurance coverage, including the provisions that describe the (1) scope of the agreement, (2) termination of the agreement, and (3) specific insurance to be ceded and the reinsurance coverage to be provided.

Scope of the Agreement

The provisions that describe the scope of the reinsurance agreement include the parties to the agreement provision, the entire agreement provision, the duration of the agreement provision, and the recapture provision.

Parties to the Agreement Provision

In an indemnity reinsurance agreement, the ***parties to the agreement provision*** typically states that the reinsurance agreement exists solely between the direct writer and the reinsurer. The reinsurance agreement does not create any legal relationship between the reinsurer and the insured, the policyowner, any beneficiary, any assignee, or any party other than the direct writer. Further, the agreement limits the business relationship between the reinsurer and the direct writer to *only* the coverage to be reinsured.

Entire Agreement Provision

The ***entire agreement provision*** states that the written agreement and any amendments represent the whole agreement between the parties, which have no further agreement than that stated in the written document. The intent of the entire agreement provision is to protect both parties from any liability implied, but not expressed, by the written agreement. Thus, only the reinsurance arrangements that are specifically stated in the written document and its amendments—and not arrangements not stated in the written document, even though they may be typical in the industry—are binding on the parties.

If a reinsurer cedes to a retrocessionaire part of the risk it has assumed from a direct writer, such a retrocession does not affect the agreement between the direct writer and the reinsurer in any way.

FIGURE 4.4

Basic Provisions in a Reinsurance Agreement

Scope of the Agreement

Names the direct writer and the reinsurer as the sole parties to the reinsurance agreement. States the effective date of the reinsurance agreement. Specifies that the agreement articles, schedules, and amendments constitute the entire agreement between the parties. Includes
- Parties to the agreement
- Entire agreement
- Duration of the agreement
- Recapture

Termination of the Reinsurance Agreement

Identifies the terms and conditions under which the reinsurance agreement may end. Describes the procedures for notification of termination. Describes the handling of the reinsurance in force under the agreement.

Reinsurance Coverages

Identifies the basis of reinsurance, such as facultative or automatic; the type of reinsurance coverage, such as YRT or coinsurance; the method of reinsurance coverage, such as first dollar quota share or excess of retention; and the plan of insurance coverage, such as whole life products or disability income products, allowed under the reinsurance agreement. Also describes any policy riders covered and any limits on the reinsurance. Includes
- Plans of reinsurance
- Amounts of reinsurance and related limits

Reinsurance Rates and Payment

Describes the calculation of reinsurance premiums, allowances, and other payments and specifies when the payments are due. Also explains the ways in which the reinsurance coverage will change if the face amount of a reinsured policy changes. Describes
- Reinsurance premium payments
- Allowances
- Reinsurance premium changes
- Modco reserve adjustment
- Reinsurance premium reporting
- Policy dividends and cash values
- Experience refunds

Premium Taxes

Describes the manner in which the reinsurer will reimburse the direct writer for premium taxes the direct writer pays, if the reinsurance agreement calls for such reimbursements.

Procedures to Begin Coverage

Describes the notification process for automatic, facultative, and facultative-obligatory reinsurance.

Reporting

Describes the procedures for reporting reinsurance transactions and the types of reports required.

Records Inspection

States that either party to the agreement can inspect the other party's records relating to the agreement.

Changes to the Reinsurance

States the procedures required for notification and handling of changes to reinsurance coverage as a result of increases, continuations, conversions, reinstatements, replacements, reductions, and terminations of reinsured policies.

continued on next page

Basic Provisions in a Reinsurance Agreement

Claims

States the circumstances under which a reinsurer will pay claims and outlines the procedures required for notification, settlement, and denial of claims. Also describes how the reinsurance parties will handle claim expenses in various situations. Discusses contests of claim denials.

Rescission

Describes the notification and handling procedures required when the direct writer rescinds a reinsured policy.

Errors and Omissions

States that, under certain circumstances, if an unintentional error occurs because of misunderstanding or oversight, both parties normally are restored to the positions they would have occupied if the error had not occurred.

Arbitration

Describes the arbitration process to be used if a dispute arises that the parties to the agreement cannot resolve to their mutual satisfaction.

Insolvency

Describes the procedures that will be followed if either party to the reinsurance agreement becomes unable to meet its financial obligations on time.

Source: Adapted from Jane Lightcap Brown and Jennifer W. Herrod, *Reinsurance Administration* (Atlanta: LOMA, © 2000), 84–85. Used with permission; all rights reserved.

The entire agreement provision further specifies that any future changes or modifications to the agreement will be void unless the reinsurance parties make the changes by amendment or in writing signed by appropriate representatives of both the direct writer and the reinsurer.

In addition, some reinsurance agreements state that neither party can sell, assign, or transfer the agreement or the reinsurance covered by the agreement without prior written permission from the other party. This provision protects the direct writer from having the reinsurance coverage changed to another reinsurance provider without the direct writer's knowledge and consent. The provision also protects the reinsurer from having the reinsured business sold to a direct writer with less stringent underwriting guidelines and claim practices than the original direct writer.

Duration of the Agreement Provision

The duration of the agreement provision addresses when the reinsurance agreement becomes effective and when it ends.

Commencement of the Agreement

Most reinsurance agreements provide that the agreement takes effect on an agreed-upon date, known as the ***agreement effective date***. The agreement effective date may be either (1) the date on which the written agreement is signed by authorized representatives of the direct writer and the reinsurer and a copy of the agreement is delivered to each party or (2) any date when the

FIGURE 4.5

Typical Reinsurance Agreement Schedules

- Description of the percentage or dollar amount of risk retained and ceded per type of benefit
- Description of the business covered (policy forms or product names)
- Direct writer's retention schedule
- Automatic binding limits and jumbo limits
- Exclusions to automatic reinsurance coverage
- Reporting requirements, including
  - Type of report
  - In-force policy reports
  - Policy exhibits
  - New business reports
  - Policy change reports
  - Billing statements
  - Policy reserve listings
  - File layout
  - File security
  - Data elements
  - Data definitions
- Premium taxes
- Rates and allowances, including
  - Rates for reinsurance premiums and allowances
  - Substandard risk table ratings
  - Rates for flat extra premiums
  - Rates for additional benefits—such as waiver of premium or accidental death benefit—if reinsured

Source: Adapted from Jane Lightcap Brown and Jennifer W. Herrod, *Reinsurance Administration* (Atlanta: LOMA, © 2000), 86. Used with permission; all rights reserved.

direct writer submits cessions to the reinsurer for automatic reinsurance or the reinsurer approves cessions for facultative reinsurance. In many cases, the effective date of reinsurance coverage occurs before the date on which the written reinsurance agreement is actually signed; however, the parties to the agreement will have agreed to the terms of the agreement before any risk is ceded. Figure 4.6 shows a typical provision that establishes the date when a reinsurance agreement becomes effective.

Each reinsurance agreement also specifies how the reinsurance effective date will be determined. The ***reinsurance effective date*** is the date on which the reinsurance coverage for a specific risk takes effect. Some agreements specify that reinsurance coverage for a given policy begins on the

FIGURE 4.6

Effective Date of Agreement Provision

This agreement has been signed by an officer of the company or an authorized representative and delivered in duplicate on the dates indicated below. This agreement and all its terms shall be effective as of _____.

Direct Writer

By _____   Attested By _____

_____   _____

_____   _____

Reinsurer

By _____   Attested By _____

_____   _____

_____   _____

Source: Adapted from Jane Lightcap Brown and Jennifer W. Herrod, *Reinsurance Administration* (Atlanta: LOMA, © 2000), 88. Used with permission; all rights reserved.

date the application for the policy is submitted to the direct writer; other agreements state that reinsurance coverage begins on the policy issue date. Typically, reinsurance on a given risk is not in force until all three of the following conditions are met:

1. The underlying insurance is in force for an automatic case or a fac-ob case, the direct writer specifically accepts an offer of reinsurance on a facultative case, or temporary insurance under a premium receipt is in force. Figure 4.7 describes temporary coverage under premium receipts.

2. The marketing, issue, and delivery of the underlying insurance policy are in compliance with the laws of applicable jurisdictions.

3. The direct writer is in compliance with all applicable terms, provisions, and conditions of the reinsurance agreement.

A facultative reinsurance agreement provides that the liability of the reinsurer for a given risk will begin at the same time as that of the direct writer, provided that both of the following conditions are met:

1. The reinsurer has given the direct writer an unconditional offer to reinsure.

2. The direct writer has notified the reinsurer in writing of its acceptance of the reinsurer's offer. In lieu of written notification, the direct writer may be permitted to send the reinsurer an individual cession form or pay a reinsurance premium when the policy is added to the direct writer's self-administered billing report, which is then sent to the reinsurer.

FIGURE 4.7

Temporary Coverage under Premium Receipts

The reinsurer may accept risk for facultative, fac-ob, or automatic cases under a premium receipt. In exchange for the initial premium payment, an insurance producer often gives an applicant for individual life insurance a premium receipt to provide the proposed insured with some type of temporary insurance coverage while the application is being underwritten. A premium receipt can be a binding premium receipt or a conditional premium receipt.

- A *binding premium receipt*, also known as a *temporary insurance agreement (TIA)*, provides temporary insurance coverage from the time the applicant receives the receipt. If the proposed insured dies before the insurer completes its evaluation of the application, the receipt generally provides a death benefit.

- A *conditional premium receipt* specifies certain conditions that must be met—for example, the insurer must find the proposed insured to be insurable—before the temporary insurance coverage provided by the receipt becomes effective.

When a direct writer issues a premium receipt to an applicant for insurance, the insurer agrees to provide specified temporary insurance coverage, and a reinsurer also may agree to provide reinsurance coverage under the premium receipt. If the proposed insured dies and the direct writer is obligated to pay a death claim under a premium receipt, the reinsurer is responsible for paying its portion of the claim. If no death claim is filed, the coverage provided by the direct writer and reinsurer under the premium receipt ends when the direct writer declines the application or accepts the application and issues a policy.

Conclusion of the Agreement

Although some reinsurance agreements state when the agreement will end, most agreements specify that, when the agreement has taken effect, it continues to be effective for an unlimited period of time. The intent of an unlimited period of effectiveness is to allow the parties to avoid spending time and money to renew an agreement that is fulfilling its intended purposes. However, agreements also typically specify allowable circumstances for termination of the agreement. We discuss the termination of reinsurance agreements in detail later in this chapter.

Recapture Provision

Recapture is the process by which a direct writer takes back some or all ceded business from a reinsurer. A direct writer may increase its retention limit and then choose to recapture amounts of risk from its reinsurers. The direct writer must notify the reinsurer of its intent to apply the new retention limit to its existing business. When a recapture results from an increase in the direct writer's retention limit, the recapture of a reinsured policy usually takes effect on the next policy anniversary date.

To protect the financial stability of the reinsurer, reinsurance agreements typically do not allow the direct writer to recapture coverage before the end of a specified policy year—usually the tenth year of the cession. A reinsurer wants to avoid the expenses of assuming and administering cessions for a short time because the reinsurer would not be able to recover these costs if the direct writer recaptures those cessions after only a few years.

Most reinsurance agreements do not allow a direct writer to recapture coverage if it did not retain its maximum retention limit when it first ceded the coverage. If the direct writer recaptures risk on any single policy, then the direct writer also must recapture risk in a similar manner on all ceded risks that are eligible for recapture. By preventing the direct writer from selectively recapturing only the lowest risks and leaving the highest risks covered by the reinsurer, this provision protects the reinsurer from adverse selection by the direct writer. Depending on the circumstances of the recapture, the reinsurance agreement may require the direct writer to pay the reinsurer a recapture fee.

Termination of the Agreement

Most reinsurance agreements—particularly those that cover life insurance—stay in effect indefinitely until the agreement is canceled by one or both parties to the contract. The complete cancellation of a reinsurance agreement for both new business and in-force business is called a ***termination***. Under a ***termination for new business***, the parties to a reinsurance agreement no longer cede or assume new business, but reinsurance coverage continues on business already in place.

Either party to a reinsurance agreement has the right to cancel the agreement with regard to new business, assuming that the canceling party provides proper notification—usually 30 to 90 days in advance of the intended termination—to the other party. The reinsurance parties typically consider the day that the termination notice is mailed to be the first day of the advance notice period. Reinsurance agreements generally require the reinsurer to continue accepting—or for facultative coverage, considering—new business during this advance notice period.

However, unless the parties mutually agree to completely end the entire agreement established under a written reinsurance agreement, existing reinsurance typically remains in force until the natural termination or expiration of the reinsured policies. That is, an in-force policy remains reinsured until the policy terminates due to lapse, surrender, or payment of a life insurance claim, or for term insurance, until the term of coverage has ended. Thus, under a termination for new business, reinsurance coverage issued earlier than the termination date is still in force, unless other arrangements are made to discontinue that coverage. The agreement requires the reinsurer to remain liable for losses that have occurred prior to the termination, but that have not yet been settled.

Each jurisdiction determines the circumstances under which the parties may terminate a reinsurance agreement. Insurance regulators may limit policy reserve credit for direct writers whose reinsurance agreements allow the reinsurer to terminate in-force coverage for reasons not deemed acceptable. Figure 4.8 describes the most common circumstances for termination of reinsurance agreements for new business and, in some cases, for existing business.

FIGURE 4.8

Common Circumstances for Termination of Reinsurance Agreements

- **Mutual agreement.** The parties to a reinsurance agreement can mutually agree to terminate the agreement at any time. For example, termination through mutual agreement can occur because the direct writer has increased its retention limit and recaptured all risks ceded under the agreement. Typically, the parties avoid terminating a reinsurance agreement for reasons other than mutual agreement.

- **A notice of cancellation offered by either party.** One party can notify the other party of termination for new business by sending a written statement, known as a *notice of cancellation*. For example, a direct writer might send the reinsurer a notice of cancellation for new business if the direct writer decides to stop selling the product covered by the reinsurance agreement. The parties can tender a notice of cancellation at any time, as long as the canceling party provides the other party with the advance notice required by the agreement.

- **Nonpayment of reinsurance premiums.** Most reinsurance agreements allow the reinsurer to unilaterally cancel the agreement for new business and in-force business if the direct writer fails to pay reinsurance premiums owed to the reinsurer. In this situation, the agreement typically calls for a reinsurer to provide the direct writer with adequate notice of the nonpayment so that the direct writer has the opportunity to pay any overdue reinsurance premiums and keep the reinsurance in force.

- **Extraordinary business circumstances.** If a reinsurer experiences a specified business event—such as the loss of its insurance license or the loss of a significant proportion of its capital and surplus—the reinsurance agreement may allow the direct writer to completely withdraw from the agreement by invoking its right to a *special termination*.

- **Termination of every policy reinsured under the agreement.** If no policy remains in force under the agreement, the reinsurance agreement automatically ends.

- **Rescission of the reinsurance agreement by either party.** Rescission of a reinsurance agreement is rare, and it typically occurs as a result of fraud or failure to disclose material information by one of the parties. We define rescission in Chapter 6.

- **The expiration of a reinsurance agreement that contains a limitation on its term.** The agreement may specify whether the termination can be for new business only, for new business and in-force business, or for either type of termination.

Source: Adapted from Jane Lightcap Brown and Jennifer W. Herrod, *Reinsurance Administration* (Atlanta: LOMA, © 2000), 90–91. Used with permission; all rights reserved.

The requirements of the termination provision may vary according to whether the reinsurance is proportional or nonproportional. For proportionally reinsured policies, the provision for termination of the reinsurance agreement may call for the reinsurer to

- Keep the reinsurance in force on policies reinsured during the term of the agreement until those policies expire or mature

- Retain liability for any claims arising from losses that have occurred but have not been settled prior to the termination of the reinsurance agreement

For nonproportional reinsurance, the provision for termination of the reinsurance agreement generally requires the reinsurer to

- Retain liability for all losses incurred or partially incurred during the term of the agreement until the reinsurance agreement has terminated

- Retain responsibility for losses on policies written during the term of the reinsurance agreement until the next renewal date of the policies following termination of the reinsurance agreement

Insurance Ceded and Reinsurance Provided

A reinsurance agreement describes in detail the plans of insurance to be retained and ceded and the reinsurance coverage to be provided. Otherwise, the reinsurance parties could run the risk of misunderstanding each other. Consider the following example of the need to be specific:

> **Example:** Suppose that a reinsurance agreement provides coverage for universal life insurance products. After the agreement has been in effect for a number of years, the direct writer introduces a variable universal life product. In this situation, neither the direct writer nor the reinsurer could be certain that the agreement, as written, covers the variable universal life product. The two companies would likely negotiate a change to their agreement to specifically include the new product.

Reinsurance Coverage Articles

The articles included in a reinsurance agreement define in general terms the

- Plans of insurance to be covered by the reinsurance—for example, whole life, term life, or universal life

- Reinsurance cession basis—for example, automatic or facultative

- Type of reinsurance—for example, YRT, modified coinsurance, or coinsurance

- Method of reinsurance coverage—for example, a first-dollar quota share or an excess-of-retention arrangement

The articles generally refer to schedules for the specific retention limits and acceptance limits on the reinsurance coverage. A typical reinsurance coverage article might be worded as follows:

> Amounts of individual life insurance that have been issued by the direct writer or its subsidiaries to standard and substandard lives on any of the plans of insurance listed in Schedule I shall be automatically coinsured under this agreement with the participating reinsurers, as defined in Schedule III, on a 50 percent first-dollar quota share basis up to the maximum retention limit specified in Schedule I.

Automatic and Facultative Reinsurance

As a general rule, an automatic reinsurance agreement contains more specific and restrictive parameters than does a facultative agreement. Because the reinsurer *must* accept risks that are automatically reinsured, an automatic reinsurance agreement specifies the parameters under which the direct writer can submit a risk to the reinsurer. For example, the agreement may specify that only "individual life insurance policies issued to standard or preferred risks" may be submitted for automatic reinsurance. In contrast, a facultative reinsurance agreement can contain more general parameters because the reinsurer has the opportunity to underwrite each policy individually and then to accept or decline each risk.

In describing the reinsurance to be provided, an automatic reinsurance agreement may exclude certain risks from coverage. Most automatic agreements state that if (1) the direct writer intends to retain less than its available retention for the insured's age and mortality rate under an excess-of-retention agreement or (2) the direct writer has submitted a case for facultative consideration, then that case cannot be submitted for automatic reinsurance. Further, most automatic reinsurance agreements state that if the reinsurer has declined to issue facultative coverage on a case, the direct writer may not resubmit that case to the reinsurer as an automatic cession. Figure 4.9 lists situations in which most agreements exclude automatic cession.

The reinsurance agreement typically states that the direct writer may facultatively submit to the reinsurer any cases that do not qualify for automatic reinsurance—perhaps because the insured's age, amount of reinsurance requested, risk classification, financial justification for the insurance coverage, or some other aspects do not match the specified requirements for automatic cession. In addition, the direct writer may submit a policy facultatively because it prefers to have the reinsurer's underwriters review the case and the direct writer's underwriting decision.

Further, the reinsurance agreement usually states that all facultative offers made by the reinsurer with underwritten acceptance will automatically terminate within a certain number of days from the date on which the offer was made. The number of days allowed for the direct writer to consider a facultative offer from the reinsurer is usually between 90 and 120 calendar or business days, with the reinsurer retaining the right to extend or shorten the time period by stating so in writing when it makes the offer.

Reinsurance Pools

If a direct writer plans to cede risk to a reinsurance pool, the reinsurance agreement describes the quota shares that will be apportioned to each reinsurer in the pool. An automatic reinsurance agreement may include a provision specifying that the pool members will automatically accept their prescribed share of the risk whenever coverage is available in the reinsurance pool and when no exclusions apply. Such a provision ensures that the direct writer will have the expected and agreed-upon reinsurance coverage when needed and that each reinsurer must accept no more risk than its anticipated share.

Schedules of Reinsurance Coverage

A reinsurance agreement typically includes schedules that describe the plans of insurance to be covered, the amounts to be reinsured and the limits on those amounts, and the reinsurance

---

FIGURE 4.9

Typical Exclusions from Automatic Cession

Most reinsurance agreements exclude a specific risk from automatic cession if

- The direct writer intends to retain less than its available retention for the insured's age and mortality rate under an excess-of-retention agreement

- The direct writer has already submitted the case for facultative consideration

- The reinsurer has already declined to issue facultative coverage on a case

- The total amount of life insurance in force on a life in all companies plus the amount currently being applied for with all companies exceeds the jumbo limit

- The total amount of life insurance previously reinsured and currently applied for and to be reinsured under the agreement exceeds the specified automatic binding limit

- The substandard underwriting rating assigned by the direct writer to the risk exceeds a specified level

- The plan of reinsurance requested by the direct writer is not included in the agreement

- The direct writer is issuing the insurance in a manner not specified in the agreement— for example, as a conversion of group insurance or as a policy exchange

- The underwriting guidelines used by the direct writer differ from the agreed-upon selection criteria specified in the agreement

- The policy's suicide exclusion clause and/or incontestability clause are not fully applicable

- The policy is a continuation of coverage of a previously issued policy that has been reinsured under another agreement or that was fully retained by the direct writer

- The direct writer has not paid full first-year commissions on the policy

- The insured does not meet criteria set by both parties—for example, the insured is not a resident of a specified jurisdiction or the insured exceeds the maximum age allowed

Source: Adapted from Jane Lightcap Brown and Jennifer W. Herrod, *Reinsurance Administration* (Atlanta: LOMA, © 2000), 94. Used with permission; all rights reserved.

---

premium rates. We discuss the plans of insurance and amounts to be covered in the next section. Chapter 7 examines the agreement articles and schedules that describe reinsurance premiums.

Plans of Insurance

A reinsurance agreement typically includes a schedule that lists all of the insurance plans to be covered by the agreement. The schedule also describes any riders—such as waiver of premium (WP) for disability benefits and accidental death benefit (ADB) riders—that provide coverage that may be reinsured. Figure 4.10 shows an example of a schedule for the plans of insurance that will be covered by a reinsurance agreement.

Amounts of Reinsurance and Related Limits

A schedule—or in some cases, an article—in the reinsurance agreement specifies the method to be used to calculate the direct writer's net amount at risk (NAAR) and retention limits. The schedule may specify a retention limit for each risk level and a retention limit for additional benefits offered by the reinsured policies, such as waiver of premium or accidental death benefits. For automatic reinsurance, the direct writer usually reinsures only amounts that exceed the company's stated retention limit for a certain insurance product up to a specified maximum amount. Most automatic reinsurance agreements also state a minimum cession, which, as you learned in Chapter 3, is the smallest amount of risk that the direct writer may cede. For facultative reinsurance, the reinsurer may or may not require the direct writer to keep its stated retention on a given policy. Figure 4.11 shows a retention limits schedule in a reinsurance agreement.

For nonproportional reinsurance, the reinsurance agreement generally includes a schedule that specifies the amount the reinsurer will pay based on the number or amount of claims submitted under the coverage.

Another schedule in the reinsurance agreement specifies the lower and upper issue ages and the acceptable risk level for each type of coverage. For instance, a reinsurance agreement for term life insurance may state that no one under the age of 6 or above the age of 70, and no one with a mortality rate greater than a specified level, can be reinsured under the agreement.

FIGURE 4.10

Plans of Insurance Covered

This agreement covers single, joint-first-to-die, and joint-last-to-die individual life insurance, and supplementary benefits and riders issued directly by the direct writer on insureds who are residents of the United States of America or its territories or Canada at the time of issue of the policy.

Source: Adapted from Jane Lightcap Brown and Jennifer W. Herrod, *Reinsurance Administration* (Atlanta: LOMA, © 2000), 95. Used with permission; all rights reserved.

FGURE 4.11

Schedule of Retention Limits

Limits of Retention: RightWay Life Insurance Company
Whole Life Insurance

Issue Ages	Standard–Table 4	Table 5–Table 8	Table 9–Table 16
0–60	$100,000	$50,000	$25,000
61–70	$50,000	$25,000	$25,000
71–80	$25,000	$25,000	$25,000

Waiver of Premium
Same as Whole Life Insurance

Source: Adapted from Jane Lightcap Brown and Jennifer W. Herrod, *Reinsurance Administration* (Atlanta: LOMA, © 2000), 96. Used with permission; all rights reserved.

The reinsurer's binding limits are listed in a schedule, which also typically specifies the jumbo limit. Figure 4.12 shows an example of a binding limits schedule.

FIGURE 4.12

Schedule of Binding Limits

Automatic Acceptance Limits of Exceptional Re

Life Insurance: Retroceded

Exceptional Re will automatically accept 50% of the excess on assumed business, subject to the following maximums:

Issue Ages	Standard	Substandard 101%–300%	Substandard 301%–500%	Substandard 501%+
0–80	$1,000,000	$1,000,000	$500,000	$500,000

Waiver of Premium for Disability Benefits

Provided that the underwriting classification of the life risk does not exceed 200% of total mortality, the reinsurer will automatically accept 50% of the excess over the direct writer's retention for an amount up to, but not exceeding, the lesser of (a) the amount corresponding to the life insurance being automatically reinsured and (b) the amount corresponding to $50,000 of the annual premium waived. Under no circumstances will the reinsurer automatically accept any waiver of premium for disability benefits risk when the total face amount of the life insurance associated with the waiver of premium for disability benefits in all companies exceeds $10,000,000.

Source: Adapted from Jane Lightcap Brown and Jennifer W. Herrod, *Reinsurance Administration* (Atlanta: LOMA, © 2000), 96. Used with permission; all rights reserved.

Key Terms

quality rating
profitability
gross profit ratio
investment yield ratio
insurance liquidity ratio
liquid assets
leverage
article
schedule
request for proposal (RFP)
parties to the agreement provision

entire agreement provision
agreement effective date
reinsurance effective date
binding premium receipt
conditional premium receipt
recapture
termination
termination for new business
notice of cancellation
special termination

Endnotes

1.   This chapter represents a revision of material from Jane Lightcap Brown and Jennifer W. Herrod, *Reinsurance Administration* (Atlanta: LOMA, © 2000), 77–97. Used with permission; all rights reserved.

2.   Adapted from Jane Lightcap Brown, *Insurance Administration* (Atlanta: LOMA, © 1997), 290–293. Used with permission; all rights reserved.

CHAPTER

5

Reinsurance Administration Procedures

After studying this chapter, you should be able to

- Describe the following methods of reinsurance record administration: individual cession administration, self administration, and bulk administration

- Explain how a direct writer notifies a reinsurer of an automatic or a fac-ob reinsurance liability

- Explain how a direct writer requests facultative coverage for a specific risk

- Describe the reinsurance agreement provisions that

address submission of reports and records inspection

- Explain the administration of the following changes that can affect reinsurance coverage:

  - Recapture of ceded risk
  - Increasing death benefits
  - Continuations of reinsured policies
  - Conversions of reinsured policies
  - Reinstatements of reinsured policies
  - Reductions and terminations of reinsurance

OUTLINE

Methods of Reinsurance Record Administration
Individual Cession Administration
Self Administration
Bulk Administration

Procedures to Begin Reinsurance Coverage
Notification for Automatic Reinsurance
Notification for Facultative-Obligatory Reinsurance
Notification for Facultative Reinsurance
Reasons Why Reinsurance May Not Be in Effect

Reporting Requirements

Records Inspection

Provisions for Changes to the Reinsurance
Provisions for Increases in Retention Limits and Recapture
Provisions for Increasing Death Benefits
Continuations Provision
Conversions Provision
Reinstatements Provision
Provisions for Reductions and Terminations of Reinsurance

Because reinsurance arrangements may remain in force for years, the reinsurance agreement provides specific instructions for handling changes in coverage on reinsured policies.

In Chapter 5, we address the administrative provisions generally included in reinsurance agreements.[1] Clarity in the agreement sections that deal with administration is critical because the agreement will be ineffective unless both parties understand how to carry out reinsurance administration. This chapter describes the provisions that typically are included in indemnity reinsurance agreements regarding methods of reinsurance record administration, procedures for beginning reinsurance coverage, reporting requirements, inspections of reinsurance records, and administering changes in reinsurance coverage.

Methods of Reinsurance Record Administration

The reinsurance parties typically use one of three methods to administer their reinsurance records: individual cession administration, self administration, or bulk administration.

Individual Cession Administration

Individual cession administration is a method of reinsurance record administration under which the reinsurer prepares its own cession records based on detailed information about individual cessions provided by the direct writer. The reinsurer uses the information from the direct writer to calculate the net amount at risk (NAAR), reinsurance premiums, allowances, and policy reserves. Periodically, the reinsurer sends the direct writer reports that outline the current status of the reinsurance and bills the direct writer for the reinsurance premiums due. Under this method, the reinsurer has complete information about the risks that it assumes and primary control over the reinsurance administration.

Self Administration

Self administration is a method of reinsurance record administration in which the direct writer maintains detailed records for each ceded policy and sends the reinsurer periodic reports describing the individual risks ceded and reinsurance premiums due for each policy. The reinsurer uses the information provided by the direct writer to manage the risk assumed. The reinsurer also retains the right to monitor the direct writer's handling of the record administration.

For direct writers that cede a large volume of reinsurance, self administration may be more cost-effective than individual cession administration. For certain life insurance and annuity products—such as interest-sensitive, flexible-premium, or variable-benefit products—calculating the NAAR and the reinsurance premium is complex and can be performed more efficiently by the direct writer than by the reinsurer.

Under self administration, the reinsurer may or may not maintain its own records for individual policies. Whereas some reinsurers maintain complete, detailed reports, other reinsurers establish records that include only selected categories of information. Still other reinsurers depend solely on the reports received from the direct writer to provide the information necessary to process the reinsurance.

Bulk Administration

In **bulk administration**, the direct writer periodically submits summarized reports—such as reinsurance premium and policy summaries—to the reinsurer. In addition, the direct writer provides a detailed in-force listing annually. Other than the annual in-force report, the direct writer does not provide detailed information about individual risks reinsured. Similarly, the reinsurer does not manage retention on an individual policy basis. However, the reinsurer uses information related to individual policies to process claims. A high level of trust typically exists between reinsurance partners that use bulk administration.

Many first-dollar quota share reinsurance arrangements employ bulk administration. Bulk administration reduces a reinsurer's recordkeeping responsibilities and, as a result, is less costly than individual cession administration for the reinsurer. However, bulk administration does not provide the reinsurer with adequate information to perform retention management or mortality studies.

The remainder of this chapter discusses agreement provisions related to reinsurance administration. In these sections, we also note provisions that are specific to each type of reinsurance record administration.

Procedures to Begin Reinsurance Coverage

Reinsurance agreements generally include a provision describing the procedures that the direct writer should use to notify the reinsurer of automatic or fac-ob reinsurance liability or to request facultative reinsurance. The provision specifies information the direct writer must send to the reinsurer and the form this information should take.

Notification for Automatic Reinsurance

The **notification for automatic reinsurance provision** specifies (1) the details about each policy that a direct writer must send to a reinsurer to begin automatic reinsurance coverage and (2) how frequently the direct writer must notify the reinsurer of new automatic cessions. Typically, notifications are provided monthly; however, the frequency of notifications can vary widely from agreement to agreement.

The provision states the effective date of the reinsurance. For automatically ceded risks, the reinsurer's liability becomes effective at the same time as the direct writer's liability—even before the reinsurer receives notice that the risk on a policy has been ceded. The provision describes in detail the effects of conditional premium receipts and temporary insurance agreements.

The notification for automatic reinsurance provision also specifies additional conditions that can affect the commencement of reinsurance coverage. The following are examples of such additional conditions:

- Some agreements state that if a direct writer has previously submitted a risk facultatively to any reinsurer, the direct writer cannot cede that risk automatically.

■ If the original reason for submitting the case facultatively is no longer valid, the reinsurer may allow the direct writer to cede automatically a case that was previously submitted facultatively. Situations that might permit such a case to be submitted automatically include those in which

- New underwriting information on a proposed insured has decreased the proposed insured's risk level

- The direct writer has changed its underwriting standards or increased its retention limit

- The reinsurer has increased its automatic binding limits or its jumbo limits

- A specified time period—for example, two years—has passed since the facultative submission of the case

The notification for automatic reinsurance provision may describe the procedure the direct writer should follow if the needed amount of reinsurance exceeds the limits set in the reinsurance agreement. For example, the agreement may require the direct writer to send the reinsurer a special notice or to submit the policy facultatively. Such a provision helps the direct writer find coverage for risks greater than the amounts allowed under the reinsurance agreement while allowing the reinsurer to manage the amount of risk it assumes on each life and to arrange for retroceded coverage when necessary.

Notification Under Individual Cession Administration

For individual cession administration of automatic reinsurance, the notification for automatic reinsurance provision requires the direct writer to send the reinsurer individual cession forms—either paper or electronic—containing considerable detail about each policy, including information the reinsurer needs to calculate the NAAR and the reinsurance premiums. Figure 5.1 shows some of the information typically included in an individual life insurance cession. The reinsurer returns to the direct writer a reinsurance certificate with reinsurance premiums listed and a bill for the first premium.

Sometimes, the reinsurance agreement specifies the format the direct writer should use to submit the notification information. Alternatively, the agreement may include a preprinted notification form. In any case, the document by which information about ceded policies is submitted to a reinsurer is generally known as a ***notice of reinsurance*** or a *reinsurance cession form*.

Notification Under Self Administration

For self-administered reinsurance, the notification for automatic reinsurance provision generally requires the direct writer to send the reinsurer the same information as for individual cession reinsurance, but the form and timing of the required information are different. Instead of sending individual cession notices as the reinsurance is needed, the direct writer notifies the reinsurer of automatic reinsurance liability by periodically—usually monthly or quarterly—sending information for all cessions. Typically, the information is provided in the form of billing statements, statements of transaction details, or bordereaux, which are described in Figure 5.2.

FIGURE 5.1

Information Typically Included in an Individual Life Insurance Cession

Information about the Insured

Name	Sex	Tobacco use status
Birth date	Underwriting classification: preferred, standard, or substandard, etc.	Country of residence

Information about the Insurance Policy

Name of direct writer	Age used to determine direct premium rate	Age to which direct premiums are payable
Direct writer policy number	Joint, single, or multi-life	Medical, nonmedical, paramedical, or guaranteed-issue basis of underwriting
Date of in-force risk	Joint age basis	Mortality table used
Plan type (UL, term, whole life, etc.)	Age to which coverage extends	Mortality rating
Plan description	Jurisdiction of issue	Flat extra rate
Face amount issued by direct writer	Frequency of direct premium payments	Number of years flat extra rate applies
Effective date of policy		

Information about the Reinsurance Agreement and Transaction

Agreement code	Quota share	Zero or non-zero first-year reinsurance premium
Method of reinsurance: YRT, coinsurance, or modco	Face amount ceded to reinsurer	Currency of risk
Facultative, fac-ob, or automatic	Reinsurance premium rate identification	

Source: Jane Lightcap Brown and Jennifer W. Herrod, *Reinsurance Administration* (Atlanta: LOMA, 2000), 118.

Notification Under Bulk Administration

Under bulk administration, the notification for automatic reinsurance provision generally requires the direct writer to send only summary information about the ceded policies. The reinsurer does not receive specific details about each cession, such as those shown in Figure 5.1, because the reinsurer relies on the direct writer to make any calculations for which that information would be needed.

FIGURE 5.2

The Use of Bordereaux

In some self-administration arrangements, the direct writer uses a bordereau—the plural is bordereaux—to notify the reinsurer of cessions. A **bordereau** is a written report that the direct writer regularly sends to the reinsurer to provide current information about ceded risks. Information supplied by bordereaux includes listings of reinsurance premiums due and claims received, as well as quarterly and annual compilations of various statistics. The following are two types of bordereaux:

- A **premium bordereau** provides detailed information about each policy, including its reinsurance premium

- A **claims bordereau**, also called a *loss bordereau*, includes information about the individual claims received and/or paid by the direct writer on reinsured policies and the reinsurer's obligation under those claims

Bordereau service is a direct writer's action of providing a reinsurer with a list of total reinsurance premiums and other information. A reinsurer may choose to receive complete bordereau service or selective bordereau service:

- **Complete bordereau service** includes reports on every case covered by the reinsurer.

- **Selective bordereau service** includes only exceptional cases—large amount policies, those with frequent or large-amount claims, new business, and other specific categories. Selective bordereau service can (1) reduce the volume of information flowing between the reinsurance parties and (2) enable the reinsurer to make faster, more accurate analyses of exceptional cases.

Source: Adapted from Jane Lightcap Brown, *Insurance Administration* (Atlanta: LOMA, © 1997), 320. Used with permission; all rights reserved.

Notification for Facultative-Obligatory Reinsurance

The **notification for fac-ob reinsurance provision** specifies the (1) information the direct writer must provide to notify the reinsurer of risks ceded and (2) maximum time periods allowed for the reinsurance parties to respond to each other concerning capacity available and capacity accepted. The direct writer must send the name of the insured, the insured's date of birth, the face amount of the policy, and the reinsurance amount requested. The provision requires the

- Reinsurer to respond to the direct writer within a certain period of time, such as two business days or 72 hours, concerning available capacity

- Direct writer to respond to the reinsurer with the amount of the reinsurer's offer accepted within a similar amount of time, such as two business days or 72 hours

Notification for Facultative Reinsurance

A direct writer usually submits the following kinds of risks facultatively:

- Risks the direct writer prefers not to cede automatically due to underwriting considerations—for example, the direct writer wants to have the reinsurer's opinion on the risk

- Risks that are outside the parameters of the automatic agreement—for example, risks that exceed the automatic binding limit

The ***notification for facultative reinsurance provision*** specifies the (1) information the direct writer must provide to notify the reinsurer of a request for facultative reinsurance coverage, (2) procedures the reinsurer must follow to make an offer of reinsurance to the direct writer, and (3) procedures the direct writer must follow to accept the reinsurer's offer. The provision usually requires the direct writer to send the reinsurer a copy of the entire underwriting file on the proposed insured along with the application for reinsurance. The provision also may give the reinsurer the right to ask for additional information if necessary.

Some agreements—typically agreements between companies that have long-standing relationships and have developed a high level of trust—may allow the direct writer to send only the information about which it is concerned and for which it needs underwriting assistance. For example, if the direct writer is certain that the risk to be reinsured is a standard health risk, but is uncertain whether the amount of coverage requested is justified, the reinsurer may allow the direct writer to send only the proposed insured's financial statements.

When a reinsurer wishes to accept a risk facultatively, it sends an offer to the direct writer, usually within 12 to 48 hours. The offer may include additional requirements.

> **Example:** The reinsurer may require the direct writer to (1) issue the policy with a specific policy endorsement or rider or (2) retain a larger proportion of the risk (not to exceed the direct writer's retention limit).

If the direct writer chooses to accept the reinsurer's offer, the direct writer must follow certain procedures for the reinsurance to become effective. Generally, the notification for facultative reinsurance provision requires the direct writer to accept the reinsurer's offer during the lifetime of the insured and no later than 90 or 120 days after the date the offer was made. To accept the reinsurer's offer, the direct writer typically must take the following steps:

- Make a dated notation in the underwriting file

- Send the individual cession or a notification of acceptance to the reinsurer

- Include the policy in future reports that are sent to the reinsurer

- Pay the first reinsurance premium at the time the next billing statement is issued

Figure 5.3 compares the information the direct writer must provide the reinsurer to comply with the notification for automatic, fac-ob, and facultative reinsurance provisions.

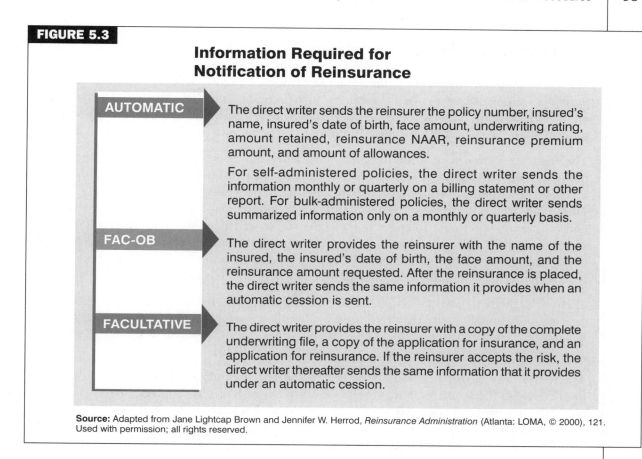

FIGURE 5.3

Information Required for Notification of Reinsurance

AUTOMATIC

The direct writer sends the reinsurer the policy number, insured's name, insured's date of birth, face amount, underwriting rating, amount retained, reinsurance NAAR, reinsurance premium amount, and amount of allowances.

For self-administered policies, the direct writer sends the information monthly or quarterly on a billing statement or other report. For bulk-administered policies, the direct writer sends summarized information only on a monthly or quarterly basis.

FAC-OB

The direct writer provides the reinsurer with the name of the insured, the insured's date of birth, the face amount, and the reinsurance amount requested. After the reinsurance is placed, the direct writer sends the same information it provides when an automatic cession is sent.

FACULTATIVE

The direct writer provides the reinsurer with a copy of the complete underwriting file, a copy of the application for insurance, and an application for reinsurance. If the reinsurer accepts the risk, the direct writer thereafter sends the same information that it provides under an automatic cession.

Source: Adapted from Jane Lightcap Brown and Jennifer W. Herrod, *Reinsurance Administration* (Atlanta: LOMA, © 2000), 121. Used with permission; all rights reserved.

Reasons Why Reinsurance May Not Be in Effect

The agreement provision that addresses the procedures to begin reinsurance coverage also may specify circumstances under which reinsurance will not be in effect. The agreement may state that the reinsurance will not be in effect unless the direct writer issues the policy as agreed.

Example: If a reinsurer requires an aviation exclusion in the policies it reinsures and the direct writer has issued the policy without the exclusion, then the reinsurer may deny liability.

A reinsurance agreement also may state that the reinsurer can deny liability on an automatic case if the direct writer fails to follow its normal underwriting procedures.

Example: In establishing the reinsurance agreement, the direct writer stated that its regular underwriting procedure includes certain medical examinations, conducted according to the amount of insurance applied for and the proposed insured's age. If the direct writer fails to perform the appropriate medical examinations on a proposed insured, it could possibly approve and cede a risk that is unacceptable to the reinsurer under the reinsurance agreement. If the direct writer does not correct the problem and ensure that it conducts such medical examinations as required by the agreement, the reinsurer may be relieved of liability for the affected policies.

Reporting Requirements

The party that administers the reinsurance records must submit periodic reports to the other party. The reports serve as a basis for reinsurance premium and allowance payments, retention management, and financial reporting. The reinsurance agreement specifies the reports to be submitted, the party responsible for submitting the reports, and the timing for each report.

The reports required depend on the method of reinsurance record administration specified in the agreement and the requirements of the financial statements that the companies must file. An arrangement administered on an individual cession basis typically calls for the direct writer to submit individual cessions to the reinsurer and for the reinsurer to submit reinsurance certificates and reinsurance premium billing reports to the direct writer. A self-administered reinsurance arrangement generally requires the direct writer to submit the reports listed in Figure 5.4. We discuss these reports in more detail in Chapter 11. A bulk administration arrangement usually requires similar, but summarized, information, typically on a less frequent basis.

The reinsurance agreement specifies the frequency of the required reports—for example, monthly, quarterly, or annually—and the deadlines for submitting the reports after the end of each reporting period. The reporting provision also states the medium in which the reports should be presented—for example, paper, tape, computer disk, CD-ROM, or electronic file.

The reinsurance agreement also may specify any additional information that the direct writer must report to the reinsurer. For example, the agreement typically requires the direct writer to notify the reinsurer of changes that the direct writer makes to any document it uses if that document could potentially affect the assumed risk. Such documents include the application for insurance, conditional or binding premium receipts, policy rider forms, manuals used in determining premiums and nonforfeiture values, underwriting guidelines, and policy reserve and cash value tables.

FIGURE 5.4

Reports Typically Required by a Self-Administered Reinsurance Agreement

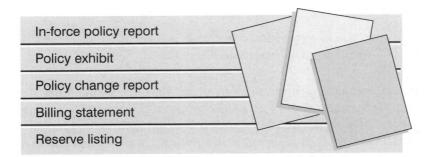

- In-force policy report
- Policy exhibit
- Policy change report
- Billing statement
- Reserve listing

Source: Adapted from Jane Lightcap Brown and Jennifer W. Herrod, *Reinsurance Administration* (Atlanta: LOMA, © 2000), 122. Used with permission; all rights reserved.

Records Inspection

The **records inspection provision** states the rights of each party to inspect the other party's records and documents relating to the reinsurance provided under the agreement. The provision typically limits the right of record inspection by allowing inspection at any reasonable time for any reasonable purpose and at the respective parties' offices during normal business hours. The provision also specifies the minimum advance notice the inspecting party must provide the other party prior to an inspection.

The records inspection provision usually also describes the types of documents that can be examined. Such documents generally include underwriting files, claim files, and billing files. The records inspection provision may require that the inspecting party give the other party advance notice of the documents it wishes to examine.

Provisions for Changes to the Reinsurance

Because reinsurance arrangements may remain in force for years, the reinsurance agreement provides specific instructions for handling changes in coverage on reinsured policies. These changes can include recapture resulting from an increase in the direct writer's retention limits; increases in benefits for reinsured policies; continuations, conversions, and reinstatements of reinsured policies; and reductions and terminations of reinsurance.

An automatic reinsurance agreement addresses most of these changes. As a result, the direct writer is allowed to make changes to a reinsured policy without obtaining the reinsurer's consent, as long as the changes fall within the parameters of the agreement. The direct writer's only obligation is to notify the reinsurer of the changes within a reasonable time.

Under facultative reinsurance agreements, however, the direct writer is required to obtain prior approval from the reinsurer before making many of these policy changes. For changes that increase coverage or reduce underwriting ratings, the direct writer must obtain the reinsurer's approval before making the change to the policy. The reinsurer rarely objects to a change, but it may wish to amend the reinsurance agreement as a result of the change. Note that most risk changes result in an adjustment to the amount of the reinsurance premium payable.

Provisions for Increases in Retention Limits and Recapture

The reinsurance agreement generally permits the direct writer to increase its retention limits. The agreement provision dealing with increases in retention usually states that, if a direct writer chooses to increase its retention limits, the company also can choose to recapture some of the reinsured risk so that the company maintains full retention on the reinsured policies. Keep in mind that recapture of ceded business is typically optional—the direct writer does not have to recapture the ceded business. If the direct writer elects not to recapture, the higher retention limit would apply only to newly issued policies. If a direct writer chooses to recapture business, this recapture results in a reduction of the amount reinsured and, typically, a decrease in the direct writer's total reinsurance costs.

The reinsurance agreement generally requires the direct writer to give the reinsurer written notice of its intention to recapture at least 90 days before the effective date of recapture. Typically, for a policy to be eligible for recapture, the direct writer must have (1) retained its full retention at the time it originally ceded the case and (2) reinsured the case with the reinsurer for a specified period of time (often 10 to 15 years). The purpose of this waiting period is to help the reinsurer recover the initial costs it incurred to reinsure the policy. When the waiting period has passed, the direct writer can recapture the policy on the policy's next anniversary date. Generally, the agreement does not allow the direct writer to cede the recaptured business to another reinsurer.

Reinsurance agreements typically specify that the amount to be recaptured is equal to the difference between the direct writer's current retention limit and the direct writer's retention limit at the time the reinsurance was ceded, as shown in the following equation:

$$\text{Amount to Be Recaptured} = \text{Direct Writer's Current Retention Limit} - \text{Direct Writer's Retention Limit at Time of Cession}$$

That is, the direct writer must recapture enough risk on each policy to increase the total amount of risk it holds up to the amount of its current retention limit.

Example: The Napoli Insurance Company reinsured a $250,000 life insurance policy at an original retention limit of $100,000. Napoli has since increased its retention limit to $150,000 for this type of coverage. If Napoli chooses to exercise its option to recapture, it must recapture $50,000 of the risk under this policy, thereby reducing the reinsurance by $50,000. The amount that Napoli must recapture can be calculated as follows:

$$\$150{,}000 - \$100{,}000 = \$50{,}000$$

If multiple policies are in force on a particular life, recapture starts with the policies ceded first. If a policy is reinsured by more than one reinsurer, the reduction in the risk held by each reinsurer will be proportional to the amount of risk each reinsurer originally accepted.

Example: Napoli has a retention limit of $100,000 on its whole life insurance policies. Napoli has three reinsurance agreements in place for these policies:

- Talbot Reinsurance has agreed to take 25 percent of the excess of retention on Napoli's life insurance products

- Walagora Reinsurance has agreed to take 25 percent of the excess of retention on Napoli's life insurance products

- Jonas Reinsurance has agreed to take 50 percent of the excess of retention on Napoli's life insurance products

Example *continued…*

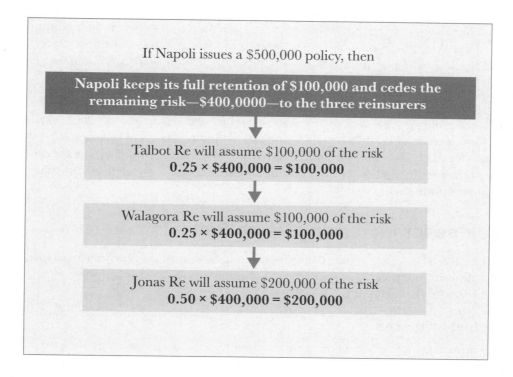

If Napoli issues a $500,000 policy, then

Napoli keeps its full retention of $100,000 and cedes the remaining risk—$400,0000—to the three reinsurers

Talbot Re will assume $100,000 of the risk
0.25 × $400,000 = $100,000

Walagora Re will assume $100,000 of the risk
0.25 × $400,000 = $100,000

Jonas Re will assume $200,000 of the risk
0.50 × $400,000 = $200,000

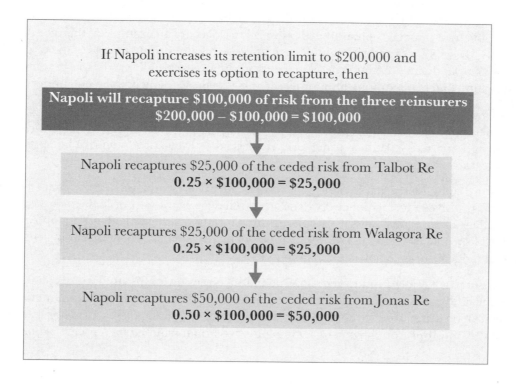

If Napoli increases its retention limit to $200,000 and exercises its option to recapture, then

Napoli will recapture $100,000 of risk from the three reinsurers
$200,000 – $100,000 = $100,000

Napoli recaptures $25,000 of the ceded risk from Talbot Re
0.25 × $100,000 = $25,000

Napoli recaptures $25,000 of the ceded risk from Walagora Re
0.25 × $100,000 = $25,000

Napoli recaptures $50,000 of the ceded risk from Jonas Re
0.50 × $100,000 = $50,000

The provision addressing recapture typically states that, if a policy has a waiver of premium for disability claim in effect, the reinsurance on the waiver of premium coverage will remain in effect until the policy returns to a premium-paying status. The direct writer, however, can recapture the life risk or other risks covered by the policy, just as if no waiver of premium for disability claim were in effect. When the policy returns to premium-paying status, the direct writer can then recapture the waiver of premium risk as well, and the reinsurer will have no further risk on the policy.

Some reinsurance agreements state that a policy with a waiver of premium for disability claim in effect is not eligible for recapture of any risks until the policy returns to premium-paying status. Further, some agreements add a stipulation that if, within two years of the recapture, the waiver of premium for disability claim is resumed as a result of the same disability, the reinsurer will be liable for paying its share of the waived premiums that were paid during the time that the policy was not in premium-paying status.

Provisions for Increasing Death Benefits

Increases in death benefit amounts can be contractual—that is, payable in accordance with the terms of a life insurance policy—or noncontractual—that is, requested by the policyowner, although not payable under the terms of the policy.

Contractual Increases

Some life insurance policies and policy riders provide for a future increase in the amount of the death benefit without requiring additional evidence of the insured's insurability. These insurance policies and riders may give the policyowner the option of increasing the death benefit monthly, annually, or on specified dates, or upon the occurrence of an event such as death (not of the insured), birth, or marriage. Guaranteed insurability riders are an example of this type of feature. Generally, these policies and riders limit each increase to either a percentage of the original face amount or a flat dollar amount. These policies and riders also usually establish a maximum total face amount. Such maximum limits protect the reinsurer—which does not underwrite the increases—from overexposure to risk on any one life.

Other increasing death benefit policies and policy riders provide for automatic predetermined death benefit increases. An increasing term rider is an example of this type of increasing death benefit feature.

In addition, some increasing benefit policies and riders allow increases in the death benefit in conjunction with changes in policy dividend scales, changes in the cost-of-living index, or changes in the values of an equity fund. Examples include inflation riders, dividend option riders, and variable life products. Figure 5.5 shows examples of increasing death benefit features that may be included in life insurance policies and policy riders.

The reinsurer generally must accept contractual increases up to the amount of the reinsurer's automatic binding limits. The reinsurance agreement usually specifies the maximum increase in risk that can be transferred to the reinsurer. The purpose of limiting increases in risk transfer is to prevent the reinsurer from having to assume more risk than planned on a policy. Some reinsur-

FIGURE 5.5

Types of Increasing Death Benefit Features

	EXPLANATION	EXAMPLE
AUTOMATIC INCREASES	The amount of the death benefit automatically increases on specific dates.	The death benefit on a policy will double after the policy has been in effect for 20 years.
OPTIONAL INCREASES	The policyowner has the option to increase the death benefit on specified dates or on the occurrence of a certain event.	A policy allows a policyowner to increase the death benefit on the policy by 20 percent every 10 years.
INCREASES CAUSED BY CHANGES IN SCALES, INDEXES, OR EQUITY FUNDS	The amount of the death benefit changes along with changes in policy dividend scales, the cost-of-living index, or the values in an equity fund.	The death benefit on a variable life insurance policy increases and decreases with the value of the equity fund supporting the policy.

Source: Adapted from Jane Lightcap Brown and Jennifer W. Herrod, *Reinsurance Administration* (Atlanta: LOMA, © 2000), 126. Used with permission; all rights reserved.

ance agreements call for the direct writer to retain any increases for certain types of policies or riders. The reinsurer usually receives an increased reinsurance premium to pay for the increased risk associated with an increase in the amount of a policy's death benefit.

> **Example:** If the increase in the amount of a death benefit results from a guaranteed purchase option, the reinsurance agreement typically requires the direct writer to pay the reinsurer a premium charge per $1,000 in addition to the reinsurance premiums paid on the original risk ceded. However, if the death benefit increase results from a scheduled increase, then a previously established reinsurance premium based on the insured's age at issue may apply.

In a first-dollar quota share agreement, the direct writer and each participating reinsurer usually must share in the increase based on the percentages of the original risk assumed. For the initial cession on increasing benefit products, the direct writer generally applies a reduced retention that will accommodate a proportionate sharing of future increases. The basis for the reduced retention is a predetermined formula mutually agreed upon by the reinsurance parties.

Example: The Intrepid Life Insurance Company issues an increasing benefit life insurance policy with an original face amount of $2,500,000, increasing to a limit of $4,000,000. Intrepid's retention limit for this coverage is $1,000,000, and it reinsures the policy under a first-dollar quota share arrangement. To prevent its amount of retained coverage from *ever* exceeding $1,000,000 throughout the life of the policy, Intrepid will retain only a percentage of the face amount in each year of coverage. Because Intrepid's retention limit is one-fourth (25 percent) of the policy's maximum benefit, Intrepid will retain 25 percent of the policy's face value each year.

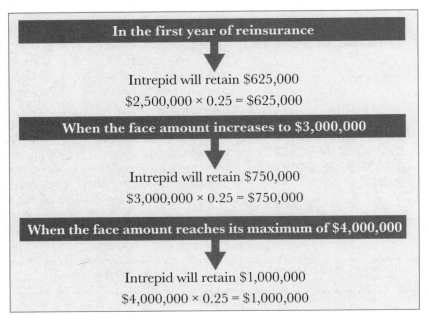

In the first year of reinsurance

Intrepid will retain $625,000
$2,500,000 × 0.25 = $625,000

When the face amount increases to $3,000,000

Intrepid will retain $750,000
$3,000,000 × 0.25 = $750,000

When the face amount reaches its maximum of $4,000,000

Intrepid will retain $1,000,000
$4,000,000 × 0.25 = $1,000,000

Noncontractual Increases

Even if a life insurance policy does not provide for increases in the death benefit, the policyowner may ask the direct writer to increase the face amount. Such noncontractual increases generally require new evidence of insurability. The reinsurance agreement generally requires the reinsurance partners to handle the increased amount like new business, and all the requirements for reinsuring new business apply.

Continuations Provision

A ***continuation*** of an insurance policy occurs either when (1) the provisions of an in-force policy are significantly modified or (2) a policy replaces an existing policy from the same direct writer. Additionally, a continuation of an insurance policy differs from a new policy in at least one of the following ways:

■ The policy is not subject to the direct writer's new business underwriting requirements

- The direct writer does not pay full first-year commissions to the insurance producer
- The policy does not introduce a new suicide exclusion period
- The policy does not introduce a new contestable period

A conversion of a policy usually qualifies as a continuation. We discuss conversion in the next section of this chapter. An internal replacement also can be a continuation, assuming that the replacement policy satisfies one of the preceding conditions. However, an external replacement does not qualify as a continuation because the two policies involved are issued by different companies. The reinstatement of a policy is not a continuation because only one policy is involved and that policy is not modified. The following table shows the types of policy changes that can qualify as a continuation.

Type of Policy Change	Can Qualify as a Continuation?
Conversion	Yes
Internal Replacement	Yes
External Replacement	No
Reinstatement	No

The **continuations provision** in a reinsurance agreement addresses which reinsurer(s) should provide the reinsurance, the amount of reinsurance, and the effective date of reinsurance for continued policies. Figure 5.6 describes the reinsurance treatment of continuations.

Limitations regarding the reinsurer(s) to be used and the amount of reinsurance for continuations protect both parties from antiselection. The direct writer cannot use the continuation as an opportunity to seek lower reinsurance premium rates from another reinsurer, and the reinsurer cannot use the continuation to cancel coverage on a policy that may have become more risky.

If the continued policy is a form of insurance that the reinsurer for the original policy does not currently reinsure, limitations regarding which reinsurer to use may not apply. In such cases, the reinsurer may provide the direct writer a written release. Even under an automatic agreement, the direct writer can then seek reinsurance from another reinsurer.

Occasionally, problems arise when a continuation involves a risk classification that did not exist when the original policy was issued.

Example: The reinsurance agreement that applies to the original policy does not distinguish between smokers and nonsmokers, and the original policy does not specify a tobacco use classification. However, the continued policy is being written as a nonsmoker policy.

Typically, the reinsurance parties negotiate a solution for this type of problem and amend the reinsurance agreement accordingly.

FIGURE 5.6

Reinsurance Treatment of Continuations

- The direct writer must reinsure a continuation with the same reinsurer that reinsured the original policy.

- The amount to be reinsured for a continuation must be in the same proportion as in the original policy, but cannot exceed the amount initially reinsured.

- If more than one reinsurer is involved, the proportions of the risk held must remain the same.

- Reinsurance on the continuation becomes effective immediately after the reinsurer is released from liability on the original policy.

- The dates that apply to recapture and other reinsurance-related issues run from the effective date of the original policy.

- For administrative reasons, the reinsurance agreement may allow the reinsurer to relinquish its right to reinsure the continuation by providing the direct writer with a written release.

Source: Adapted from Jane Lightcap Brown and Jennifer W. Herrod, *Reinsurance Administration* (Atlanta: LOMA, © 2000), 130. Used with permission; all rights reserved.

Conversions Provision

A ***conversion*** is a new policy that is issued on the basis of the policyowner's contractual right to change the policy form, as provided in the original policy. For example, some life insurance policies allow a policyowner to convert á term policy to a whole life policy. Conversions do not require additional evidence of insurability.

The ***conversions provision*** in a reinsurance agreement typically states (1) that the direct writer must continue the reinsurance on converted policies with the original reinsurer unless the reinsurer releases its right to reinsure the policies and (2) any conditions under which the direct writer or the reinsurer can cancel the reinsurance on conversions. If the reinsurer does not give a written release of reinsurance and the direct writer mistakenly cedes the policies to another reinsurer, then the direct writer must send any claims under the policies to the original reinsurer for payment. The direct writer also must make reinsurance premium payments to the original reinsurer and obtain reinsurance premium refunds from the second reinsurer, as appropriate.

Example: If a term life insurance policy reinsured on a YRT basis is converted to a whole life policy reinsured on a YRT basis, the reinsurance terms on the original policy typically apply to the new whole life policy. YRT reinsurance premium rates normally apply if a policyowner converts a coinsured term policy to a whole life policy reinsured on a coinsurance basis, or if a policyowner converts a policy to a plan of insurance that is not covered by the reinsurance agreement.

The agreement usually requires the reinsurance premium due following a conversion to be calculated on the same basis as the original reinsurance premium.

Example: ■ For a conversion of a reinsured policy that is coinsured by the direct writer, the reinsurance on the conversion is typically issued using the YRT premium schedule for the *new* policy form

■ For a conversion of a reinsured policy that is *not* coinsured by the direct writer, the reinsurance on the conversion is typically issued using the YRT premium schedule for the *original* policy form

Reinstatements Provision

Reinstatement is the process by which an insurer puts back into force an insurance policy that has lapsed due to nonpayment of premiums. The **reinstatements provision** in a reinsurance agreement typically specifies that when a reinsured policy lapses for nonpayment of premium, the reinsurance can be reinstated if certain conditions are met. These conditions, which must be consistent with the direct writer's guidelines for reinstatement, usually require that (1) the policyowner must seek reinstatement of the lapsed policy within a certain time period *and* (2) the direct writer must pay to the reinsurer all reinsurance premiums due during the time the policy was lapsed, but only to the extent that the direct writer collected direct renewal premiums for the policy.

For automatic reinsurance, the reinsurer usually accepts any reinstatements the direct writer accepts, according to normal procedures related to reinstatements. That is, the reinsurer automatically reinstates the reinsurance when the direct writer reinstates the policy. For facultative reinsurance, the reinstatements provision generally allows the reinsurer to consider the reinstatement facultatively and then deny or approve the reinstatement of the reinsurance.

The reinsurance agreement also may allow the reinsurer to approve or deny reinsurance on a reinstated policy that was ceded automatically if (1) the reinsurer assumed more than 50 percent of the risk or (2) the time between the policy lapse and its reinstatement exceeds 90 days. The reinstatements provision may require the direct writer to provide the reinsurer with the following information:

■ A copy of the reinstatement form signed by the policyowner

■ The direct writer's reinstatement requirements

■ Any other information the reinsurer needs to make a decision on the reinstatement

Provisions for Reductions and Terminations of Reinsurance

A **reduction of reinsurance** is the process of reducing the amount of reinsurance covering an insurance policy. When a life insurance policyowner reduces a reinsured policy's face amount or exercises a nonforfeiture option that decreases the value of the policy, the direct writer must reduce the reinsurance on that policy or on other policies covering the insured life.

A ***termination of reinsurance*** is the process by which a direct writer cancels the reinsurance covering a policy issued by the company. A termination of reinsurance on a life insurance policy can occur because a reinsured policy expires, matures, is surrendered, or lapses due to nonpayment of premiums or because the insured dies. The reinsurance agreement typically states that the reinsurer's liability ends when the reinsured policy is no longer in effect.

A reduction of reinsurance also can result in a termination of reinsurance. When a policyowner reduces the face amount of a policy or when a policy terminates, the direct writer must reduce or terminate the amount of reinsurance ceded. The direct writer must notify the reinsurer in writing of the change in the amount reinsured. The reinsurance agreement typically states that all involved reinsurers will share in the reduction of reinsurance in the proportion in which they reinsured the original risk. The agreement also defines what payment, if any, is due the direct writer as a result of the change in cash value for the reinsured portion of a coinsured policy.

Reductions and terminations of reinsurance are handled differently depending on the form of reinsurance:

- If a coinsured policy is reduced or terminated, the reduction is handled proportionately.

- YRT reinsurance agreements often allow the direct writer to fill up its retention, thus taking all of the reduction from the amount reinsured. However, a YRT agreement can call for a proportionate reduction, as well.

Reinsurance agreements usually specify a per life basis or a per policy basis for administering reductions and terminations of reinsurance. In either case, the agreement never requires the direct writer to retain more risk than its retention limits allow.

Per Life Basis

The use of a ***per life basis***—sometimes called a *level retention basis*—to administer reductions and terminations of reinsurance (1) potentially affects the reinsurance on every policy the direct writer has in force on an insured and (2) typically requires the direct writer to maintain its full retention on that life. When the agreement provision dealing with reductions and terminations of reinsurance specifies a per life basis, the provision requires that the reinsurance be reduced in the same amount, or in proportionate amounts, as the insurance on the life, and the provision specifies how the reinsurance is to be reduced.

Generally, when reinsurance reductions and terminations are handled on a per life basis, the reinsurance agreement requires that the reinsurance on the reduced or terminated policy be reduced or terminated before any other reinsurance coverage on the insured is reduced or terminated. If the total amount of the reinsurance reduction exceeds the amount of reinsurance on the policy that is reduced or terminated, then the remainder of the reduction needed to fill the direct writer's retention limit is applied to other policies on that life, typically in chronological order— either most recent policy first or oldest policy first. Figure 5.7 presents an example of how a reduction on a per life basis may be handled.

A provision specifying a per life basis also states whether reductions apply to automatic and facultative cessions.

On a per life basis, the reinsurance parties are required to keep track of the cumulative risk represented by all the policies on each life rather than just the risk represented by each policy.

FIGURE 5.7

Example of a Per Life Reduction in Reinsurance

The Sunny Skies Insurance Company currently has a retention limit of $300,000 per life. When the risk on a particular life exceeds this limit, Sunny Skies cedes the excess of retention to the Aero Reinsurance Company. Donald Carter has four life insurance policies with Sunny Skies. The retained and reinsured amounts on these four policies are shown in the following table:

	Face Amount	Date of Policy Issue	Amount of Risk Retained by Sunny Skies	Amount of Risk Ceded to Aero Re
Policy 1	$175,000	June 1985	$175,000	$0
Policy 2	$250,000	August 1990	$125,000	$125,000
Policy 3	$150,000	May 1993	$0	$150,000
Policy 4	$100,000	February 1995	$0	$100,000
Totals:	**$675,000**		**$300,000**	**$375,000**

The reinsurance agreement requires Sunny Skies to apply reinsurance reductions and terminations first to the reduced or terminated policy and then to the remaining policies, oldest policy first.

When Mr. Carter surrendered Policy 2, Sunny Skies' retention on Mr. Carter's life decreased by $125,000:

$$\$300,000 - \$125,000 = \$175,000$$

To maintain its full retention on Mr. Carter's life, Sunny Skies reduced the amount of reinsurance on Mr. Carter's policies by $250,000—the same amount as the reduction in the life insurance coverage. The following table shows the effects of the reduction in reinsurance on the four policies:

Policy Order for Reinsurance Reduction	Amount of Reduction in Reinsurance	Amount of Risk Retained by Sunny Skies	Reinsurance Remaining on Policy
First—Policy 2, the terminated policy	$125,000	0	0
Second—Policy 1, the oldest remaining policy	$0—no change because no reinsurance was ever in effect	$175,000	0
Third—Policy 3, the next oldest remaining policy	$125,000	$125,000	$25,000
Fourth—Policy 4, the most recent policy	$0—no change because the applicable retention limit has already been maintained	0	$100,000
Totals:	**$250,000**	**$300,000**	**$125,000**

Using the per life basis can be even more complex if the (1) direct writer's retention limits vary by product, (2) direct writer increases its retention limits, (3) insured is covered by several different products, or (4) direct writer has ceded some of the risk on the insured to more than one reinsurer.

Per Policy Basis

When reductions and terminations of reinsurance are administered on a ***per policy basis***, only the reinsurance on the policy that is being reduced or terminated is affected. As a result, handling reductions and terminations of reinsurance on a per policy basis is less complicated than handling them on a per life basis. Under an excess-of-retention reinsurance arrangement, the reduction of reinsurance on a per policy basis equals the lesser of the (1) amount of reduction on the reinsured policy or (2) amount of reinsurance on the policy. Under a first-dollar quota share (FDQS) reinsurance arrangement, the amount of a reduction in reinsurance on a per policy basis depends on the proportional shares of risk assigned to the direct writer and the reinsurer.

Example: Under the FDQS reinsurance arrangement that the Maple Insurance Company entered into with the Elm Reinsurance Company, Maple retains 20 percent of the risk on each case and cedes the remaining 80 percent of risk to Elm Re. For a policy with a face amount of $200,000, Maple retains $40,000 of risk and cedes $160,000 of risk to Elm Re, as shown in the following calculations:

Maple's risk: $200,000 × 0.20 = $40,000

Elm Re's risk: $200,000 × 0.80 = $160,000

Suppose that the policyowner requests a $50,000 reduction in the policy's face amount. The new face amount is $150,000; Maple's amount of risk retained decreases to $30,000; and the amount of risk ceded to Elm Re decreases to $120,000, as shown in the following calculations:

New face amount: $200,000 – $50,000 = $150,000

Maple's risk: $150,000 × 0.20 = $30,000

Elm Re's risk: $150,000 × 0.80 = $120,000

Key Terms

individual cession administration
self administration
bulk administration
notification for automatic reinsurance
  provision
notice of reinsurance
bordereau
premium bordereau
claims bordereau
bordereau service
complete bordereau service
selective bordereau service
notification for fac-ob reinsurance provision

notification for facultative
  reinsurance provision
records inspection provision
continuation
continuations provision
conversion
conversions provision
reinstatement
reinstatements provision
reduction of reinsurance
termination of reinsurance
per life basis
per policy basis

Endnote

1.   This chapter represents a revision of of material from Jane Lightcap Brown and Jennifer W. Herrod, *Reinsurance Administration* (Atlanta: LOMA, © 2000), 113–133. Used with permission; all rights reserved.

CHAPTER
6

Claims, Rescission, and Potential Problems

After studying this chapter, you should be able to

- Describe the reinsurance agreement provision related to claim administration

- Describe the reinsurance agreement provision related to rescission

- Describe the reinsurance agreement provision related to errors and omissions

- Describe the reinsurance agreement provision related to arbitration

- Describe the reinsurance agreement provision related to direct writer and reinsurer insolvency

OUTLINE

Claim Administration
The Direct Writer's Authority
to Handle Claims
Claim Procedures

Rescission

**Potential Problems
between a Direct Writer
and a Reinsurer**
Errors and Omissions
Arbitration

Insolvency
Direct Writer Insolvency
Reinsurer Insolvency

The parties to a reinsurance agreement anticipate the occasional occurrence of problems by stating in the reinsurance agreement the procedures the parties agree to use to resolve such problems.

This chapter addresses the arrangements that reinsurance agreements include for administering claims and for handling rescissions of reinsured policies. We also describe agreement provisions designed to resolve problems that may arise during the course of the reinsurance agreement and to protect the parties if one of them becomes insolvent.[1]

Claim Administration

To ensure that the reinsurer pays its share of reinsured claims appropriately and in a timely manner, an indemnity reinsurance agreement contains a ***claim provision***. This provision states the terms and conditions of the reinsurer's liability for claims submitted under reinsured policies. Figure 6.1 summarizes the information typically included in a claim provision.

The Direct Writer's Authority to Handle Claims

Because an insurance policy is a contract between the direct writer and the policyowner, the claim provision in a reinsurance agreement typically states that the direct writer has the authority to make decisions on claims and that the reinsurer is bound by the direct writer's decisions. In some circumstances, however, the reinsurance agreement requires the direct writer to obtain a recommendation from the reinsurer before settling a claim, or else the reinsurer may not be

FIGURE 6.1

Information in a Claim Provision

- The extent of the direct writer's authority to handle claims, including any limits on that authority

- The procedures the direct writer must follow to be reimbursed by the reinsurer for paid claims, including the manner in which claims will be reported to the reinsurer

- How the direct writer and reinsurer will share responsibility for expenses related to claims and adjustments to the benefit amount

- The conditions under which the reinsurer will be liable to share in paying extracontractual damages

Source: Adapted from Jane Lightcap Brown and Jennifer W. Herrod, *Reinsurance Administration* (Atlanta: LOMA, © 2000), 136. Used with permission; all rights reserved.

bound to participate in paying the claim. The direct writer typically must consult with the reinsurer before settling a claim in the following situations:

- A claim occurs during the reinsured life insurance policy's contestable period

- The reinsurer has assumed more than 50 percent of the risk covered by a reinsured policy

- The total amount of a claim or the amount of risk ceded to the reinsurer exceeds the limits stated in the agreement's claim provision

- The direct writer has retained less than its published retention limit on a reinsured policy

- A claim involves an insured's death in a foreign country

- The direct writer suspects that a claim involves fraud

- The reinsured risk was ceded on a facultative basis

In addition, the reinsurance agreement claim provision usually requires the direct writer to provide the reinsurer the opportunity to review the claim file of any claim that the direct writer plans to deny. Examining a potential claim denial allows the reinsurer to

- Review the direct writer's claim philosophy and handling

- Validate or question the direct writer's claim decision

- Offer to assist the direct writer with the administration of the claim

- Gather information about the claim in case the policyowner or beneficiary contests the claim denial

Claim Procedures

After a direct writer pays a claim under a reinsured policy, the direct writer turns to the reinsurer for reimbursement of the reinsured portion of the claim. To obtain reimbursement, the direct writer is obligated to notify the reinsurer promptly after paying the claim. The direct writer notifies the reinsurer by providing the reinsurer with claim-related documents, including proofs of loss documents. The types of proofs of loss documents accepted by the direct writer generally are accepted by the reinsurer.

For life reinsurance, the reinsurance claim provision typically states that, within a specified time period after receiving notice that the direct writer has paid a death claim under a reinsured policy, the reinsurer will pay the reinsurance benefits in a lump sum, even if the reinsured policy calls for a different settlement option.

> **Example:** A life insurance policy beneficiary has chosen a fixed-period benefit payment option, which requires the direct writer to pay the beneficiary the proceeds and interest in a series of equal installments during a specified period. Nevertheless, the reinsurer must pay the direct writer the entire reinsurance benefit as soon as the reinsurer receives notice of the claim and all the required documentation related to the claim.

Reinsurance agreements provide for a settlement option other than a lump-sum payment for some types of policy benefits. For example, a reinsurer sometimes agrees to pay its share of accelerated death benefits as specified in the reinsured life insurance policy's settlement option. Also, for disability income reinsurance or long-term care reinsurance, the reinsurer periodically disburses reinsurance benefit payments to the direct writer throughout the benefit payment period in proportion to the benefit amounts paid by the direct writer.

The reinsurer typically does not share in routine claim settlement expenses, such as the salaries of the direct writer's claim analysts. However, the reinsurance agreement may call for the reinsurer to reimburse the direct writer for a proportionate share of any interest paid to the beneficiary on policy benefits or any unusual claim-related expenses.

Claim Contests

A **contest** of an insurance claim is a court action to determine the validity of the claim. A claim contest generally occurs when an insurer denies liability to pay a claim, and the beneficiary or policyowner files a lawsuit seeking to force the insurer to pay the claim. After a court action is begun, the reinsurer usually has the option of whether to participate in the lawsuit.

Although such a decision is rare, the reinsurer may decide not to participate in a claim contest. In this situation, the reinsurance agreement requires the reinsurer to pay its proportionate share of the full claim amount due and any expenses incurred to date to the direct writer. Thereafter, the reinsurer has no further liability for any other expenses related to the claim. In addition, however, the reinsurer is not entitled to a refund of any amounts paid to the direct writer in such a case.

> **Example:** Assume that a contest of an insurance claim involved a $500,000 claim and that the reinsurer chose not to participate and paid $250,000—its proportionate share of the claim—to the direct writer. The court action resulted in a decision that the insurer was obligated to pay only $250,000 in policy benefits. Although the reinsurer paid more than its proportionate share of the total claim the direct writer was required to pay, the reinsurer is not entitled to be reimbursed for that overpayment.

In most cases, the reinsurer participates in a claim contest. In such cases, the reinsurance agreement generally calls for the reinsurer to send a written notification of its participation to the direct writer. Under some reinsurance agreements, if the reinsurer does not send the direct writer a denial of participation within a certain period of time after it receives the claim file, the direct writer can assume that the reinsurer has joined the contest. By joining the contest, the reinsurer becomes (1) liable for its share of the expenses of the court action and (2) eligible to share in any reduction in the amount of the direct writer's liability for the claim.

The reinsurance agreement specifies which claim expenses the reinsurer will share when it joins a contest. Typically, the reinsurer is liable for claim expenses only up to the amount of risk the reinsurer held on the reinsured policy, and the reinsurer is not liable for any extracontractual damages charged to the direct writer. **Extracontractual damages** are monetary awards that are given to a party to a lawsuit in addition to compensatory damages. In the context of a claim contest, ***compensatory damages***, which are sometimes referred to as *actual damages*, are monetary awards to pay a claimant for damage suffered as a result of an insurer's improper denial of a claim. For example, if a claimant's lawsuit for life insurance policy death benefits is successful, the court usually orders the insurer to pay the claimant compensatory damages equal to the amount of death benefits payable under the terms of the insurance policy. Extracontractual damages generally take the form of ***punitive damages***, which are monetary awards intended to punish or make an example of an insurance company that has committed fraud or acted in a malicious or oppressive manner toward a claimant. ***Fraud*** is an act by which one party intentionally deceives another party and induces that other party to part with something of value or give up a legal right. Chapter 11 provides further discussion of fraud.

Other reinsurance agreements specify that the reinsurer will share proportionately in any extracontractual damages unless the damages are assessed against the direct writer for an act committed solely by that company. Under some agreements, this restriction applies only if the actions of the direct writer involve fraudulent behavior or failure to exercise good faith. ***Good faith*** refers to a party's honesty of intention and avoidance of attempts to deceive or take unfair advantage of another party to an agreement. Generally, the level of the reinsurer's liability depends on the wording in the reinsurance agreement about the direct writer's obligation to consult the reinsurer before denying a claim.

Procedures for Other Claim Situations

The claim provision in a reinsurance agreement typically describes the appropriate reinsurance procedures the parties are to follow for some other claim circumstances.

Claim Investigations

The reinsurance agreement usually grants the reinsurer the opportunity to review the claim file of any claim for which unusual claim-investigation expenses are expected.

> **Example:** A disability income insurance claim often requires a lengthy, detailed series of investigative reports for the insurer to decide whether to pay the claim. The direct writer usually must consult with the reinsurer on such a claim before settling the claim or making a commitment to settle it.

The agreement may stipulate that the reinsurer has a certain period of time—such as 15 days—to correspond with the direct writer about a claim that requires extensive investigation. The agreement also may require the reinsurer to pay a proportionate share of any claim-investigation costs or interest charges accrued during the investigation.

Waiver of Premium for Disability Claims

For waiver of premium for disability claims, the reinsurance agreement generally requires (1) the reinsurer to pay the direct writer its proportionate share of the waived direct premium annually and (2) the direct writer to continue paying the reinsurance premiums.

Misstatement of Age or Sex

If the direct writer discovers a misstatement of age or sex in a life insurance application, the direct writer may increase or decrease—depending on the error—the amount of insurance coverage provided by the policy. Under some types of proportional reinsurance, such as a first-dollar quota share agreement, the reinsurer shares in the increase or decrease in liability in proportion to its total liability on the risk.

Example: A reinsurer covered 75 percent ($300,000) of the risk on a $400,000 life insurance policy through a first-dollar quota share agreement. When processing the claim on the policy, the direct writer discovered that the insured was three years older than was stated on the insurance application. As a result, the direct writer reduced the face amount of the policy by $50,000 to $350,000. The reinsured amount became $262,500, calculated as follows:

$$0.75 \times \$350,000 = \$262,500$$

Suicide During the Exclusion Period

The provisions of a life insurance policy describe the benefit to be paid in the event the insured commits suicide during the suicide exclusion period. Typically, this benefit—known as the ***limited death benefit***—is the amount of the premiums paid for the policy minus any indebtedness owed to the direct writer. When the direct writer pays a limited death benefit following an insured's suicide, the reinsurance agreement typically requires the reinsurer either to refund to the direct writer the reinsurance premiums paid or to pay its share of the limited death benefit to the direct writer.

Rescission

A ***rescission*** is the cancellation of a contract under which the parties are returned to the positions they would have occupied had no contract been created. In an insurance context, an insurance contract that is rescinded is voided from the beginning as if no coverage had ever been in place. Rescission of an insurance policy sometimes occurs when the direct writer determines that it issued a policy based on material misrepresentation or fraud in the application.

A ***material misrepresentation*** is an untrue statement made by one party to a contract which induces the other party to enter a contract that it would not have entered had it known the truth. When a rescission involves a material misrepresentation, the direct writer usually refunds the premiums paid for the policy to the policyowner. However, if the material misrepresentation was fraudulent, the direct writer usually retains the premiums.

A direct writer rescinds a policy only after careful review. The review typically includes consultation with representatives from the company's underwriting, medical, and legal departments and strict adherence to applicable laws regarding unfair claims practices. A thorough review protects the direct writer and its reinsurers from potential legal action alleging ***bad faith***, which means a dishonest motive or an intention to knowingly commit a wrong or fail to fulfill a legal duty.

The **rescission provision** in a reinsurance agreement describes the notification and administrative procedures required when a direct writer rescinds a reinsured policy. This provision generally requires the direct writer to make decisions regarding rescission in good faith and to inform the reinsurer in a timely manner of any rescission of a reinsured policy. The direct writer sends the reinsurer copies of all the documentation supporting the direct writer's decision, including a copy of the rescission letter the direct writer sent to the policyowner. Some facultative reinsurance arrangements require the direct writer to notify—and in some cases, obtain approval from—the reinsurer of a planned rescission prior to rescinding the policy

The rescission provision also requires the direct writer to notify the reinsurer immediately if the policyowner initiates a legal action regarding a rescission. Just as with claim contests, the reinsurance agreement allows the reinsurer to choose whether to participate in a legal action involving the direct writer's rescission of a reinsured policy. If the reinsurer chooses not to participate, the reinsurer generally pays the reinsured amount to the direct writer and then has no further liability for the policy. If the reinsurer chooses to participate, it usually shares in the costs related to the legal action.

When a policy is rescinded, the direct writer and reinsurer must remove the policy reserves they have created for the rescinded policy. Some direct writers prefer to deduct the full liability of a rescinded policy immediately. Other direct writers prefer to wait until after the rescission is accomplished and the premium refund check has been cashed.

Potential Problems Between a Direct Writer and a Reinsurer

The parties to a reinsurance agreement anticipate the occasional occurrence of problems by stating in the reinsurance agreement the procedures the parties agree to use to resolve such problems. These procedures address errors and omissions that may occur in administering the reinsurance agreement and more serious disputes that cannot be solved through negotiation.

Errors and Omissions

Unintentional errors or omissions of information may occur during the administration of a reinsurance agreement. The **errors and omissions provision** of a reinsurance agreement states that if either party to the agreement fails to comply with the terms of the agreement through unintentional mistake or clerical error, then both parties will be restored to the position they would have occupied if the mistake or error had not occurred. The parties must make a good faith effort to correct the error in a way that is fair and that upholds the parties' original intent. Moreover, unintentional errors and omissions will not affect the rights and obligations established by the agreement as long as both parties work to handle errors and omissions appropriately. The errors and omissions provision serves to protect the parties against the consequences of unintentional mistakes and to minimize disagreements between the parties to the reinsurance agreement.

The errors and omissions provision sometimes also specifies that the waiver of any terms of the agreement by either party in one situation should not be interpreted as a waiver of the terms in the future. For example, a reinsurer's acceptance of one facultative case under an automatic reinsurance agreement does not imply that the reinsurer will accept all other facultative cases.

The errors and omissions provision goes into effect only after reinsurance has become effective on a particular policy. For facultative coverage, reinsurance does not take effect until the reinsurer has made an offer to accept the risk and the direct writer has accepted the offer before it expires. The errors and omissions provision does not apply in cases in which the direct writer fails to

- Obtain required facultative reinsurance

- Send a facultative cession

- Send a document that would affect an underwriting decision

- Perform full underwriting or other routine requirements as required by the agreement

The errors and omissions provision typically applies only to clerical errors, not to errors involving decisions that one of the parties deliberately made.

> **Example:** The errors and omissions provision usually covers a situation in which a direct writer inadvertently cedes a health insurance risk on a nonsmoking basis when the insured is actually a smoker.

> **Example:** The errors and omissions provision generally does not apply if the direct writer chooses not to check its records for additional policies covering the life of a proposed insured. If the direct writer issues the applied-for policy and consequently becomes over-retained, the errors and omissions provision will not apply to correct the over-retention. Such an error is considered to be a management decision and not a clerical error.

If the direct writer fails to cede a risk that it is required to cede under an automatic reinsurance agreement, the errors and omissions provision usually requires the direct writer to (1) notify the reinsurer of the oversight as soon as the direct writer discovers it, (2) provide the reinsurer with all relevant information about the cession, and (3) pay all reinsurance premiums due from the date the policy should have been ceded. The errors and omissions provision may require the direct writer to conduct an audit to determine if any other risks that should have been ceded were, in fact, not ceded. The provision also may state that, following the completion of the audit, the reinsurer has no further obligation to assume any risk for policies the direct writer erroneously failed to cede prior to the audit. Figure 6.2 summarizes the steps a direct writer generally must take to correct an error made under a reinsurance agreement.

The errors and omissions provision does not cover policies that the direct writer cedes automatically even though they exceed the reinsurer's jumbo or automatic binding limits. When such an excessive cession is discovered, the direct writer usually submits all relevant information to the reinsurer so the reinsurer can determine if it is willing to assume some or all of the risk. The reinsurer has no obligation to accept the risk if (1) the reinsurer determines that it would have declined the risk, (2) the reinsurer is already fully retained on the life, or (3) the direct writer does not have a facultative agreement with the reinsurer. In such situations, however, the reinsurer may choose to accept the risk as a good will gesture, or the direct writer may try to reinsure the risk facultatively with another reinsurer.

FIGURE 6.2

Steps the Direct Writer Must Take to Correct an Error

1	2	3	4
Advise the reinsurer of the problem and provide relevant information promptly	Identify all cases that involve the same problem	Restore both parties to the positions they would have occupied if the problem had not occurred, including submitting reinsurance premiums on the correct basis	Identify and implement any controls needed to prevent a recurrence of the error

Source: Adapted from Jane Lightcap Brown and Jennifer W. Herrod, *Reinsurance Administration* (Atlanta: LOMA, © 2000), 143. Used with permission; all rights reserved.

Arbitration

Arbitration is a method of dispute resolution in which impartial third parties—known as **arbitrators**—evaluate the facts in dispute and render a decision that usually is binding on the parties to the dispute. Arbitrators for reinsurance disputes are experts from the insurance and reinsurance industry.

Reinsurance agreements usually include an **arbitration provision**, which requires the reinsurance parties to submit disputes that they cannot resolve through negotiation to an arbitration panel rather than to a court of law. The arbitration provision also describes the procedures the parties must use to select arbitrators and to conduct the arbitration process. Arbitration often is preferable to **litigation**—which is the process or act of resolving a dispute by means of a lawsuit—for the following reasons:[2]

- Arbitration helps ensure that the intentions of the parties when the reinsurance agreement was established are taken into consideration.

- The parties to a reinsurance agreement typically view arbitration as a more appropriate way to handle disagreements than litigation because insurance industry experts can more fairly assess the specific technical issues involved than can civil courts.

- Arbitration generally is less costly, faster, easier, and more flexible than litigation. In the United States, many reinsurance agreements base the requirements for the arbitration process on the American Arbitration Association of New York City Rules of Arbitration. These rules allow for more freedom in the procedures and the types of information accepted as admissible than do courts of law.

- Unlike litigation, arbitration allows the parties to keep confidential business information from becoming a matter of public record.

When arbitration is the chosen method of dispute resolution, the reinsurance agreement may include special provisions to make sure that the requirement for arbitration is enforceable. Some jurisdictions assert that the right to a trial before a court is public policy and will not enforce an arbitration agreement. As a result, a reinsurance agreement may explicitly state that the agreement is to be interpreted by the laws of a jurisdiction that will enforce agreements to arbitrate. In the United States, if the parties are located in different jurisdictions, the reinsurance agreement can require the parties to submit the dispute to a federal court if either party refuses to arbitrate. According to federal arbitration laws, the federal courts will require the parties to undergo arbitration.[3]

A party that wishes to begin arbitration proceedings notifies the other party in writing of that intent. The arbitration provision usually requires this written notice to explain the dispute and the notifying party's recommended manner of handling the dispute. Figure 6.3 shows an example of an arbitration notice. The reinsurance agreement typically provides that, after receiving such a notice, the other party has a specific time period within which to reply. The other party's reply may be an (1) attempt to resolve the issue without arbitration or (2) acknowledgement of the initiation of arbitration, including contact information for that company's arbitrator.

The arbitration provision usually specifies that the arbitration process will be conducted by three arbitrators, who will hear the arguments of both of the parties and make a binding decision. Typically, the arbitrators must be current or former officers of insurance companies and can have no present or former affiliation with either party or their subsidiaries. The arbitration provision generally calls for each party to choose one arbitrator, although some agreements require each party to submit a list of arbitrators and allow each party to strike names from the other's list until the two arbitrators are chosen. In both situations, the two chosen arbitrators then select the third arbitrator.

If one party fails to appoint an arbitrator, the arbitration provision may allow the other party to appoint a second arbitrator or may require the parties to ask an impartial arbitration expert—for example, the president of the American Arbitration Association—to appoint a second arbitrator. This latter method also may apply if the two appointed arbitrators cannot decide on a third arbitrator.[4]

The arbitration provision typically specifies that within 30 days of the selection of the arbitration panel, the arbitrators must choose a date and location for the proceedings. Some reinsurance agreements specify the location at which arbitration proceedings will be held.

Each party submits a written statement outlining its version of the facts and arguments to both the arbitration panel and the other party. The arbitration provision requires this statement to be sent within a certain time period, such as 30 days prior to the arbitration hearing date. The reinsurance agreement generally allows the parties to reply to each other's statements, and the agreement usually requires the parties to submit a list of the relevant facts on which they agree prior to the hearing.

Also prior to the hearing, the parties to the reinsurance agreement must exchange all relevant documents and identify all of the individuals they expect to call as witnesses. Such documents may include the reinsurance agreement, billing reports, policy application files, and other

A Notice of Arbitration

LANFORD LIFE INSURANCE COMPANY

June 22, 2005

Mr. Samuel Chadburn
Senior Vice President
Royal Reinsurance Company
1232 Holiday Circle
Anytown, CA 55555

Re: Claim Number 7654321

Dear Samuel:

Pursuant to Article IX of the reinsurance agreement between Lanford Life Insurance Company and Royal Reinsurance Company, we are hereby requesting arbitration of the above referenced claim. We nominate Ms. Angela Noble as our arbitrator. Ms. Noble resides at 1234 Oak Street, Anytown, CA, 55555. Her phone number is 555-555-5555 and her fax number is 555-555-7777. Her e-mail address is Angela.Noble@palmnet.com.

Pursuant to the arbitration clause, have your arbitrator contact Ms. Noble within 30 days of this letter to select the third arbitrator.

Thank you in advance for your anticipated cooperation in this matter.

Sincerely,

Brandon Simms
Second Vice President and Assistant General Counsel
Lanford Life Insurance Company

documents. The arbitrators usually have the authority to exclude documents or witnesses that the parties have not disclosed or identified in a timely manner.

Although the arbitration provision typically states that the hearing need not follow the strict rules of a court trial, many procedures used in court proceedings are used in arbitration hearings. For example, each party is entitled to cross-examine the other party's witnesses and to rebut evidence presented by the other party. The arbitrators are required to base their decisions on their interpretation of the terms and conditions of the reinsurance agreement and on the customs of the insurance industry. The three-person panel must submit its written decision to both parties within 60 days of the hearing, unless both parties agree to some other time period. The majority decision of the three arbitrators is final, and no appeal process is available to the parties. The arbitrators' decision usually is filed with a court having jurisdiction over the parties to the reinsurance agreement, and the court then issues an order that is legally binding on the parties.

The parties to the agreement generally share the expenses that are incurred throughout the arbitration process. Typically, each party pays its own expenses and the expenses of the arbitrator it has chosen. The parties usually share equally the expenses for the third arbitrator and the other expenses of the arbitration process. Some reinsurance agreements allow the arbitration panel to assign any of the winning party's costs to the losing party.

Insolvency

As you learned earlier in this text, insolvency is a condition in which a business is unable to meet its financial obligations on time. When an insurer becomes financially unsound, insurance regulators generally are authorized to intervene in the insurer's operations to protect policyowner interests. The specific remedies that regulators are permitted to apply when an insurer becomes insolvent vary somewhat from country to country.[5]

In the United States, remedies vary somewhat from state to state, depending on applicable state insurance laws. The following NAIC model laws form the basis of such state laws:

Model Law	Authority Granted
The **Model Hazardous Condition Regulation**	Authorizes regulators to order an insurer to take specified actions to improve its financial condition
The **Model Supervision Act**	Authorizes regulators to require an insurer to gain permission from regulators before taking any of a variety of specified actions
The **Model Rehabilitation Act** or, in some states, the **Uniform Insurers Liquidation Act**	Authorizes regulators to take over the operation of an insurance company

State laws based on these NAIC model laws prescribe the following types of corrective actions when an insurer's financial soundness is impaired:

■ Before insolvency occurs, regulators may order an insurer to take specific corrective actions designed to improve the insurer's financial condition. Figure 6.4 lists examples from the Model Hazardous Condition Regulation of actions that regulators may require an insurer to take.

■ Before insolvency occurs, regulators may place an insurer under *administrative supervision*. In such cases, state regulators require the insurer to obtain regulatory permission before taking any of a variety of specified actions. Figure 6.4 lists examples from the Model Supervision Act of actions that may require such regulatory permission.

FIGURE 6.4

Remedial Actions Available to Regulators in Cases of Financial Distress

Model Hazardous Condition Regulation	Model Supervision Act
Authorizes regulators to require the financially impaired insurer to take the following corrective actions:	Authorizes regulators to require the financially impaired insurer to obtain permission from regulators before it can take any of the following actions:
Use reinsurance to reduce its liabilities and obtain surplus relief	Sell or transfer assets or in-force business or use assets as collateral for loans
Limit its new or renewal business	Withdraw funds, lend assets, or invest
Reduce its general and commission expenses by specified means	Incur debt
Increase its capital and surplus	Accept new initial premiums
Suspend or limit dividend payments	Renew policies that are not guaranteed renewable
Limit or divest investments in specified assets	Merge with another company
File reports stating the value of invested assets	Enter into a new reinsurance agreement
Document the adequacy of its premium rates	Pay specified surrender values to customers
	Increase the compensation to its officers or directors

Source: Adapted from Susan Conant, *Capital Management for Insurance Companies* (Atlanta: LOMA, © 2001), 68. Used with permission; all rights reserved.

- When more drastic regulatory action is required, state regulators may place the insurer in **receivership**, also known as *conservatorship*. Receivership is a trust arrangement in which an individual—known as a *receiver* or *conservator*—is appointed by a court to hold and administer an insolvent insurer's assets and liabilities. In receivership, regulators install a team of on-site supervisors who actively monitor the insurer's ongoing operations. Insolvency may be declared concurrently with receivership or may be delayed. Either the insurer or the regulator may seek a declaration of insolvency.

Receivership can have two possible outcomes:

- **Rehabilitation**, in which regulators take over operation of the insolvent company from its management and attempt to restore the company to solvency. In rehabilitation, an impaired insurer continues to operate and to exist, but its sales and marketing activities usually are suspended. If the insurer cannot be rehabilitated, it is placed into liquidation.

■ *Liquidation*, in which the receiver works to close down the business after collecting all assets and settling all obligations. In liquidation, the receiver either transfers all of the insurer's business and assets to other insurers or sells the insurer's assets and terminates its business. A liquidated insurer ceases to exist. Typically, a solvent insurer or several solvent insurers accept a permanent transfer of the insolvent insurer's contractual obligations by means of an assumption reinsurance agreement. The coverage provided to the customers of a failed insurance company under an assumption reinsurance arrangement is known as *continuation coverage*.

In the United States, state guaranty associations provide insurers with financial support for providing this continuation coverage. A *guaranty association* is an agency that is formed by member insurance companies operating in a given jurisdiction and that is responsible for covering an insolvent insurer's financial obligations to customers and ensuring that these customers are treated equitably when the insurer's assets are distributed. Many other countries have a national guaranty association. However, some small countries that do not have a guaranty association may provide a government bailout to protect the customers of insolvent insurers.

The insolvency of either party to a reinsurance agreement can have a significant negative impact on the other party's financial condition. As a result, direct writers and reinsurers must exercise due diligence—that is, conduct a careful investigation of a potential reinsurance partner's assets, liabilities, and future prospects—when entering into reinsurance agreements. One typical component of due diligence for reinsurance is monitoring rating agency evaluations of other insurers. A *rating agency* is an organization, owned independently of any insurer or government body, that evaluates the financial condition of insurers and provides information to potential customers of and investors in insurance companies. An insurer's solvency is one of the primary bases for the quality ratings that it receives. Figure 6.5 lists the number of U.S. life and health insurer insolvencies from 1994 to 2003.

Although the insolvency of either party to a reinsurance agreement is unlikely, reinsurance agreements typically include an insolvency provision to protect the interests of the parties and to protect the insureds, policyowners, beneficiaries, and others who rely on the direct writer's financial strength. In a reinsurance agreement, the *insolvency provision* describes the rights and responsibilities of the direct writer and the reinsurer in the event that either party becomes insolvent. The provision also may state that a party to the agreement will be deemed insolvent if any of the following situations occur:

■ The company applies for or consents to the appointment of a receiver, rehabilitator, or liquidator of its properties or assets

■ The company seeks reorganization or an arrangement with creditors to avoid insolvency or takes advantage of a bankruptcy, rehabilitation, or liquidation law or statute

■ The company becomes the subject of an order to rehabilitate or liquidate

■ The company is adjudicated as bankrupt or insolvent

FIGURE 6.5

**U.S. Life and Health Insurer Insolvencies
Reported by the NAIC, 1994–2003**

Year	Number of Insolvencies*
1994	8
1995	2
1996	4
1997	4
1998	2
1999	7
2000	4
2001	0
2002	1
2003	4

*Does not include insolvencies of small, single-state insurers

Source: Adapted from Insurance Information Institute, "Hot Topics and Issues Update: Insolvencies/Guaranty Funds," February 2005, http://www.iii.org/media/hottopics/insurance/insolvencies (18 August 2005). Used with permission.

Direct Writer Insolvency

The insolvency provision in a reinsurance agreement typically specifies that, upon the insolvency of the direct writer, the reinsurer becomes obligated to pay any amounts owed on reinsured policies immediately upon receiving verification that such amounts are rightfully due. Thus, the reinsurer must pay its reinsurance liability in full, even if the direct writer has failed to pay all or a portion of any claim. The reinsurer pays the amounts due into the trust held by the direct writer's receiver.

In addition, the insolvency provision in reinsurance agreements requires a receiver for an insolvent direct writer to give the reinsurer adequate notice of any pending claims for which the reinsurer has assumed risk. The reinsurer has the right to investigate any claims at its own expense and to deny claims as it deems necessary. The direct writer's share of the reinsurer's expenses in handling such claims may be charged to the direct writer, with the court's approval, as an expense of the rehabilitation or liquidation.

Reinsurer Insolvency

The insolvency provision included in a reinsurance agreement usually requires the reinsurer to notify the direct writer immediately if the reinsurer becomes insolvent and to provide the direct writer with any applicable documentation of its financial situation. The insolvency provision generally gives the direct writer the right to terminate the reinsurance agreement immediately as a consequence of the reinsurer's insolvency and to recapture all reinsured risks within a specified period of time. However, jurisdictional law or the actions of the reinsurer's receiver may negate this right. Some reinsurance agreements allow the direct writer to recapture risk without penalty; other agreements require the direct writer to pay a mutually agreed-upon recapture fee.

The insolvency provision in the reinsurance agreement usually requires the direct writer to notify the reinsurer in writing of its intent to recapture coverage and to specify an effective date for the recapture—generally the date of the reinsurer's insolvency. The direct writer usually arranges for replacement reinsurance before executing the recapture. The reinsurer remains responsible for any payments due prior to the date of recapture. Generally, a reinsurer that becomes insolvent remains liable to pay any benefits associated with reinsurance in force at the time of its insolvency.

Key Terms

claim provision

contest

extracontractual damages

compensatory damages

punitive damages

fraud

good faith

limited death benefit

rescission

material misrepresentation

bad faith

rescission provision

errors and omissions provision

arbitration

arbitrator

arbitration provision

litigation

administrative supervision

receivership

rehabilitation

liquidation

continuation coverage

guaranty association

rating agency

insolvency provision

Endnotes

1. This chapter represents a revision of material from Jane Lightcap Brown and Jennifer W. Herrod, *Reinsurance Administration* (Atlanta: LOMA, © 2000), 135–149. Used with permission; all rights reserved.

2. John E. Tiller and Denise Fagerberg Tiller, *Life, Health and Annuity Reinsurance*, 2nd ed. (Winsted, CT: ACTEX Publications, 1995), 197.

3. Ibid., 198.

4. Ibid., 197–198.

5. Adapted from Susan Conant, *Capital Management for Insurance Companies* (Atlanta: LOMA, © 2001), 67–73. Used with permission; all rights reserved.

CHAPTER
7

Financial Arrangements

After studying this chapter, you should be able to

- Discuss the types of financial exchanges potentially involved in basic coinsurance, modco, funds withheld coinsurance, and yearly renewable term (YRT) reinsurance transactions

- Describe the provisions for changing, reporting, and paying reinsurance premiums

- Describe the types of premium rate tables that may be included in reinsurance agreements

- Describe the treatment of reinsurance allowances

- For coinsurance, modco, and funds withheld coinsurance,

explain the treatment of cash values and policy dividends

- Explain the effects of favorable and adverse risk experience on the reinsurer and direct writer and describe the correct treatment of experience refunds to direct writers

- Describe the treatment of modco reserve adjustments

- Describe the treatment of premium taxes in reinsurance

- Describe the arrangements for currencies to be used in international reinsurance transactions

OUTLINE

Reinsurance Premiums and Allowances

Premium Rate Tables

Reinsurance Premium Reporting and Payment

Paying Premiums for Coinsurance, Modco, and YRT Reinsurance

Nonpayment of Reinsurance Premiums

Reinsurance Premium Rate Changes

Reinsurance Premium Reporting

Allowances

Miscellaneous Other Payments under Coinsurance and Modco

Policy Cash Values

Policy Dividends

Experience Refunds

Modco Reserve Adjustments

Provision for Premium Taxes

Currency for Reinsurance

Currency Fluctuations

Consequences for Late Payment Due to Decreases in Currency Exchange Values

Reinsurance agreements contain financial provisions designed to ensure the accuracy and timeliness of financial exchanges between a direct writer and a reinsurer, who must undertake complex administrative procedures to account for the financial elements of the agreement.

In this chapter, we examine the financial provisions that may be included in a reinsurance agreement.[1] These provisions ensure the accuracy and timeliness of every monetary amount to be exchanged between the direct writer and the reinsurer. Although we have divided the subject matter of reinsurance agreement provisions into separate topics for clarity of our discussion, a reinsurance agreement is a unified document whose parts are interrelated. The financial components of a reinsurance arrangement can be complex and differ from one agreement to another. The parties to an arrangement account for these elements and summarize the elements in the billing records that the companies exchange. The primary financial components that a reinsurance transaction *can* include appear in Figure 7.1 and are described in this chapter.

In this chapter, we describe financial provisions included in four types of reinsurance agreements: coinsurance, modco, yearly renewable term (YRT), and funds withheld coinsurance. First, we explain the typical arrangements for calculating, paying, reporting, and changing reinsurance premiums and agreement provisions relating to allowances. Next, we discuss the provisions relating to cash values, policy dividends, experience refunds, modco reserve adjustments, and premium taxes. We end this chapter by describing the currency used in conducting international reinsurance transactions.

FIGURE 7.1

Financial Components of Reinsurance Transactions

- A transfer of insurance risk from the direct writer to the reinsurer, so that the reinsurer becomes responsible for reimbursing the direct writer for a portion of the benefits paid under a reinsured policy

- Reinsurance premium payments from the direct writer to the reinsurer

- Assignment of responsibility on one or both parties to hold and invest the policy reserves on the reinsured portion of the business

- Designation of which of the parties is entitled to the interest earnings on the invested assets backing reserves, if necessary

- An allowance whereby the reinsurer shares in the direct writer's expenses for generating and maintaining the business

- If applicable, an experience refund from the reinsurer to the direct writer

- In rare instances, considerations addressing the reinsurer's share of policy dividends under reinsured participating policies

- If applicable, a requirement that the reinsurer pay a share of the premium taxes paid on reinsured business

- Designation of a currency in which accounting, recordkeeping, and payments between the parties will be denominated

Reinsurance Premiums and Allowances

A reinsurance agreement specifies the types and amounts of reinsurance premiums and allowances. The agreement states the premium rates for both the primary coverages that are reinsured and any additional benefits or other riders on reinsured policies. The manner in which premiums are determined differs between (1) basic coinsurance and its variations and (2) yearly renewable term (YRT) reinsurance.

In basic coinsurance, funds withheld coinsurance, and modified coinsurance, reinsurance premiums are calculated as a percentage of the *direct premium*—that is, the direct writer's premium on the original policy. Thus, for those plans of reinsurance, the reinsurance premiums are calculated by reference to the direct writer's premium rates, and the reinsurer does not need to develop new premium rate tables. For YRT reinsurance, the reinsurer develops YRT reinsurance premium rates independently from the direct writer's premium rates.

Premium Rate Tables

A reinsurance agreement may refer to a variety of premium rate tables for special purposes. The agreement describes how and when to use the various premium rate tables. A reinsurance agreement typically provides reinsurance premium rates for nonstandard types of coverage—for example, coverage for unusually large face amounts of life insurance or for additional benefits such as waiver of premium for disability or accidental death benefits. The glossary in Figure 7.2 defines many of these special-purpose types of premium rate tables.

Extra premiums (substandard premiums) usually apply when underwriters have classified an insured as a substandard risk. **Substandard risks** are insureds who represent a significantly greater-than-average likelihood of loss within the context of the insurer's underwriting practices. Extra premiums can take the form of a flat extra premium or a substandard extra premium.

A **flat extra premium** is a specified flat monetary amount per $1,000 of insurance that a direct writer imposes for insureds in a substandard risk class. Flat extra premiums apply to only the basic coverage (usually the life insurance benefit) and not to additional benefits, such as the waiver of premium and accidental death benefits. Under coinsurance or modco, a reinsurer collects its proportionate share of the flat extra premium amount and pays a reinsurance commission on the flat extra premium amount. A flat extra premium can be imposed for (1) a temporary period or (2) the duration of the policy's premium-paying period.

■ Normally, **temporary flat extra premiums** are payable only for a specified temporary period after policy issue, such as for 10 years or until the insured reaches age 65. This period usually is the same as the period designated in the reinsured policy. After that period, the extra reinsurance premiums cease to be required. A temporary extra premium compensates for an extra risk that will diminish or end with the passage of time.

Example: Assume that a life or health insured had cancer five years ago but is doing well now. Underwriters could decide that the insured has an additional cancer risk for another five years, but after a total of ten years in remission, any extra risk for cancer is irrelevant.

FIGURE 7.2

Types of Special-Purpose Premium Rate Tables

TYPE OF PREMIUM RATE TABLE	DEFINITION
Gender-specific premium rate table	A premium rate table that shows different premium rates for males and females of the same age
Unisex premium rate table	A premium rate table that shows a single set of premium rates for both males and females
Smoker/nonsmoker premium rate table	A premium rate table that shows different premium rates for otherwise similarly situated smokers and nonsmokers
Aggregate premium rate table	A premium rate table that shows one set of premium rates for all insureds **Example:** A unisex table with no division for smoking or nonsmoking rates
Standard aggregate premium rate table	A premium rate table that shows one set of premium rates for all standard underwritten policies
Large face amount (large FA) of life insurance premium rate table	A premium rate table that shows premium rates for life insurance with face amounts greater than a stated monetary amount
Waiver of premium (WP) for disability benefit rider premium rate table	A premium rate table that shows a premium rate for optional waiver of premium for disability coverage
Accidental death benefit (ADB) rider premium rate table	A premium rate table that shows a supplemental premium rate for optional accidental death benefit coverage

- A **permanent flat extra premium** is a flat extra amount charged for extra risk and continues for the duration of the policy. A permanent flat extra premium typically is assigned for risks that are expected to continue for the duration of the policy, but that are not expected to increase with the passage of time.

A **substandard extra premium**, also called *rating extra* or *table rating*, is an extra premium that continues throughout the premium-paying period for the direct *and* the reinsurance premiums. Substandard extra premiums usually are assigned for risks that are expected to increase as the insured ages. A reinsurance agreement can express a substandard extra premium as a specified additional percentage of mortality risk or by reference to a specially created premium rate table.

Example: The health of a diabetic insured is expected to deteriorate as time passes.

Figure 7.3 presents a glossary of terms for substandard premium rate tables.

Figure 7.4 shows an example of a reinsurance premium rates provision in a YRT reinsurance agreement.

FIGURE 7.3

Types of Substandard Premium Rate Tables

TYPE OF SUBSTANDARD PREMIUM RATE TABLE	DEFINITION
Substandard extra premium rate table	A premium rate table that shows additional premium rates that apply only for substandard risks
Extra-percentage premium rate table	A type of substandard extra premium rate table, designed for application to a constant extra risk, that shows premium rates that are a certain percentage greater than the insurer's standard premium rates
Flat extra premium rate table	A type of substandard extra premium rate table, designed for application to a constant extra risk, that shows a specified extra dollar amount will be added to the standard premium

---

Reinsurance Premium Reporting and Payment

The reinsurance agreement states how often the direct writer must report the reinsurance premium amounts due and how the direct writer must determine the due date of reinsurance premiums. The initial reinsurance premium always is due in the month when the cession occurs.

A *premium payment mode* for insurance policies is the frequency—monthly, quarterly, or annually—at which renewal premiums are payable. One reinsurance premium billing statement can contain several types of premium payment modes. Renewal reinsurance premiums can be due on an annual mode, a quarterly mode, a monthly mode, or on the same premium mode as the reinsured policy, as illustrated in the following table:

	Annual Premium Mode	Quarterly Premium Mode	Monthly Premium Mode	Same Premium Mode as the Reinsured Policy
Renewal reinsurance premiums are due	Annually, in their anniversary month	Quarterly, counting from their anniversary date	Monthly	On the same dates as the premiums for the reinsured policy

FIGURE 7.4

Premium Rates Provision
in YRT Reinsurance

Premiums for the First $3,000,000 of Reinsurance per Life

1. For standard risks under individual cession administration, life reinsurance premiums shall be calculated by multiplying the reinsurance death benefit by the appropriate cost of insurance from the respective schedules attached. Any increases in benefits with evidence of insurability will be treated as a new policy issue. Any increases in benefits without evidence of insurability in accordance with the policy provisions shall be based on the attained age and duration since issue of the original policy.

Schedule A
Sample YRT Premiums per 1000
Age Nearest Male Standard Non-Standard

Issue Age	1	2	3	4	5	6	7	8	9	10	11	12	13	14	15	Ult	Attained Age
...	...	...	...	...	...	...	...	...	...	...	...	...	...	...	...	...	...
35	0.28	0.34	0.45	0.51	0.58	0.63	0.71	0.80	0.90	1.01	1.14	1.26	1.41	1.58	1.77	2.00	50
36	0.29	0.36	0.48	0.56	0.63	0.71	0.80	0.90	1.01	1.14	1.26	1.40	1.57	1.76	1.96	2.21	51
37	0.30	0.38	0.52	0.62	0.71	0.80	0.90	1.01	1.14	1.26	1.39	1.54	1.74	1.94	2.17	2.45	52
38	0.32	0.40	0.55	0.66	0.77	0.86	0.97	1.08	1.22	1.37	1.51	1.69	1.91	2.15	2.40	2.70	53
39	0.33	0.43	0.60	0.72	0.82	0.93	1.05	1.17	1.32	1.47	1.64	1.85	2.10	2.38	2.65	2.97	54
40	0.36	0.46	0.65	0.78	0.90	1.00	1.13	1.26	1.41	1.58	1.77	2.01	2.31	2.62	2.92	3.27	55
41	0.38	0.50	0.72	0.86	0.98	1.09	1.22	1.34	1.50	1.69	1.91	2.19	2.53	2.88	3.20	3.60	56
42	**0.41**	**0.55**	**0.79**	**0.94**	**1.07**	**1.18**	**1.30**	**1.43**	**1.58**	**1.80**	**2.06**	**2.38**	**2.77**	**3.17**	**3.53**	**3.97**	57
43	0.45	0.62	0.86	1.04	1.17	1.30	1.43	1.56	1.72	1.95	2.23	2.57	2.98	3.42	3.83	4.38	58
44	0.49	0.69	0.95	1.13	1.29	1.43	1.56	1.71	1.88	2.12	2.42	2.77	3.22	3.69	4.15	4.84	59
45	0.53	0.77	1.04	1.24	1.41	1.56	1.71	1.86	2.05	2.29	2.61	3.00	3.48	3.98	4.51	5.35	60
...	...	...	...	...	...	...	...	...	...	...	...	...	...	...	...	...	...

Note: This is a portion of the table. An entire table usually covers issues ages from birth to 85.

2. For substandard risks accepted subject to table ratings, life reinsurance premiums shall be calculated by multiplying the corresponding standard reinsurance premiums by the applicable rating factor from the table below:

Table Rating	Rating Factor	Table Rating	Rating Factor
(1) A	1.25	(9) I	3.25
(2) B	1.50	(10) J	3.50
(3) C	1.75	(11) K	3.75
(4) D	2.00	(12) L	4.00
(5) E	2.25	(13) M	4.25
(6) F	2.50	(14) N	4.50
(7) G	2.75	(15) O	4.75
(8) H	3.00	(16) P	5.00

continued on next page

FIGURE 7.4 continued

Premium Rates Provision in
YRT Reinsurance

3. For substandard risks accepted subject to a flat extra premium, life reinsurance premiums shall be calculated using the same flat extra premiums as in the original policy, but applying it to the portion of the death benefit reinsured.

4. If a policy charges flat extra premiums for extra risks, the direct writer will pay the reinsurer the applicable flat extra premium less the following allowances:

Term of Flat Extra Premiums		First Year	Renewal Years
Temporary	5 years or less	10%	10%
Permanent	More than 5 years	75%	10%

We can use the exhibits in the foregoing agreement to calculate the premium for a specified policy, as shown in the following example:

Example: For a $150,000 life insurance policy on a 40-year-old male nonsmoker, the YRT reinsurance premium rate table specifies that the YRT premium rate per $1,000 of reinsurance coverage is $0.36. To calculate the first-year YRT reinsurance premium, multiply the units of coverage by the premium rate per $1,000, as follows:

> Units of Coverage × Premium Rate per $1,000 =
> **150 × $0.36 = $54.00**

Using the same process, we can determine that the renewal reinsurance premium for the second year of coverage is $69.00, as shown:

> Units of Coverage × Premium Rate per $1,000 =
> **150 × $0.46 = $69.00**

Source: Adapted from Jane Lightcap Brown and Jennifer W. Herrod, *Reinsurance Administration* (Atlanta: LOMA, © 2000), 103–105. Used with permission; all rights reserved.

Some reinsurance agreements provide for annual collection of reinsurance premiums, regardless of how often the direct writer collects premiums from policyowners. That is, even if a direct writer collects direct premiums monthly, the annual reinsurance premium is due on the date specified in the agreement. Similarly, a direct writer may report its direct premiums to the reinsurer on a quarterly or monthly basis, even if the direct writer makes the reinsurance premium payments on an annual basis.

In recent decades, it has become common for reinsurance premiums to be payable monthly instead of annually. This arrangement is convenient for the direct writer because most insureds pay their premiums on a monthly mode and, thus, the monthly mode of paying the reinsurance premiums levels the direct writer's cash flows.

Paying Premiums for Coinsurance, Modco, and YRT Reinsurance

Under funds withheld coinsurance, direct writers are not required to pay the full first-year reinsurance premium in advance. For coinsurance, modco, and YRT reinsurance, though, direct writers sometimes must send a payment to cover the annual reinsurance premium in advance. In such situations, when the coinsurance, modco, or YRT reinsurance premium is due, the direct writer will not have collected enough direct premiums to cover the full year's coinsurance or modco reinsurance premium. To reduce the financial impact of the direct writer's paying reinsurance premiums before it has collected the direct premiums on the reinsured policies, the reinsurance parties typically agree to one of the following approaches:

- The direct writer receives an allowance that consists of the reinsurer's refund of a portion of the reinsurance premium. The allowance can take the form of a cash refund or an offset of the amounts that the direct writer remits to the reinsurer.

- An interest adjustment is subtracted from the reinsurance premium to aid the direct writer in matching its cash inflows with its cash outflows. We discuss the modco reserve adjustment later in this chapter.

- The direct writer pays the coinsurance or modco reinsurance premiums quarterly in arrears. This practice enables the direct writer to collect direct premiums before the reinsurance premiums are due.

> **Example:** For reinsurance coverage during the three-month period between January 1 and March 31, a direct writer pays the reinsurance premium on March 31.

Nonpayment of Reinsurance Premiums

A reinsurance agreement typically specifies the consequences of a direct writer's failure to pay reinsurance premiums on time or for its defaulting entirely on reinsurance premium payments. A reinsurance agreement may require the direct writer to pay an interest penalty on the unpaid reinsurance premium amount. Such a penalty typically applies if a reinsurance premium payment is late by more than a stated period, typically 30 to 60 days.

If the direct writer fails to pay, usually the reinsurer sends by registered mail a formal request for payment with interest within a given period, for example 10 days. If the direct writer still does not pay, the reinsurer generally may terminate the reinsurance coverage by delivering to the direct writer a written notice of termination of reinsurance for nonpayment of premiums within a specified period after reinsurance premiums due remain unpaid. The reinsurer sends the notice of termination of reinsurance by registered mail to obtain confirmation that the direct writer has received it. Note that the direct writer is obligated to pay reinsurance premiums for the entire period of coverage, up to the reinsurance termination date.

Reinsurance Premium Rate Changes

Reinsurance premium rates may be guaranteed or nonguaranteed.

- If the reinsurance premium rates are *guaranteed*, neither party acting alone may increase or decrease reinsurance premium rates. Instead, the direct writer and reinsurer must reach a mutual agreement prior to making rate changes.

- If the reinsurance premium rates are *nonguaranteed*, the reinsurer may decide unilaterally to increase the rates, especially for YRT reinsurance. However, usually a reinsurer discusses such a potential increase with the direct writer and increases the reinsurance premium rates only if the reinsured policies provide for nonguaranteed direct premium rates.

Reinsurance Premium Reporting

Every reinsurance agreement specifies which party will be responsible for preparing an accurate premium billing statement and communicating it to the other party in a timely manner. The reinsurance agreement specifies consequences for inaccurate billing statements. The reinsurance agreement also gives the reinsurer the authority to audit the operations of the direct writer to ensure adequate quality control in the direct writer's recordkeeping operations.

Allowances

Generally, reinsurers reimburse a direct writer for a portion of the commissions and expenses associated with an insurance policy by paying an allowance. Recall from Chapter 1 that an allowance is a credit from the reinsurer to the direct writer designed to cover a share of the direct writer's operating expenses. An allowance may be expressed as a percentage of direct premiums, a flat amount per unit of coverage, or a flat amount per transaction. The application of this allowance differs by plan of reinsurance.

- In all agreements that provide for an allowance, the direct writer withholds the allowance from the reinsurance premium payment to the reinsurer.

- In YRT reinsurance, the reinsurer may compensate the direct writer for expenses by charging either (1) a first-year reinsurance premium that is lower than renewal reinsurance premiums or (2) no first-year reinsurance premium at all—an arrangement known as *YRT with zero first-year premium*.

- In basic coinsurance, the reinsurer returns a portion of the reinsurance premium to the direct writer in the form of an allowance.

Miscellaneous Other Payments Under Coinsurance and Modco

Coinsurance, funds withheld coinsurance, and modco reinsurance agreements typically describe the manner, if any, in which the reinsurer will reimburse the direct writer for cash values, policy dividends, and experience refunds. Such provisions ensure the accuracy and timeliness of every monetary amount to be exchanged between the direct writer and the reinsurer. YRT reinsurance agreements typically do not address all of these points because, under YRT, only the mortality risk is transferred.

Policy Cash Values

Three types of reinsurance agreements—coinsurance, funds withheld coinsurance, and modco—typically specify the circumstances and extent to which a reinsurer will reimburse a direct writer for cash values associated with reinsured policies. Agreements generally require the direct writer to inform the reinsurer promptly when reinsured policies terminate and the direct writer has disbursed cash values. YRT reinsurance agreements do not address the treatment of policy cash values, because in YRT only the mortality risk is transferred.

Policy Dividends

Some cash value life insurance policies and annuities, classified as *participating policies*, offer the possibility that the direct writer will declare and pay *policy dividends* from the company's *divisible surplus*.[2] As we noted in Chapter 2, surplus is the amount by which an insurance company's assets exceed its liabilities and capital. Surplus results from a company's profitable operations. The amount of surplus available for distribution to policyholders is known as the **divisible surplus**. A **policy dividend** is a policyholder's share of that divisible surplus. The company's board of directors must declare and approve each distribution of policy dividends. Policy dividend payments are not guaranteed to policyholders, but most insurance companies declare and pay dividends on participating policies that are expected to remain in force over a long term. Participating policies include a dividend options provision that lists the ways in which the policyholder can receive policy dividends. The most common dividend options are the (1) cash dividend option, (2) premium reduction option, (3) accumulation at interest option, (4) paid-up additional insurance option, and (5) one-year term insurance option. Typically, the applicant for a participating policy selects a dividend option when he completes the application for insurance. A policy specifies a default option for dividends if the policyowner does not select one.

On rare occasions, a provision covering policy dividends appears in some reinsurance agreements. When present, a policy dividend provision specifies an equitable method by which the reinsurance parties will share responsibility for paying any policy dividends the direct writer declares on participating policies.

Some reinsurers agree to share in one-year term additions only if the policyowner elected that policy dividend option on the application for insurance—*not* if the one-year additions were later added, unless they were fully underwritten at the later date.

Generally, dividend agreement provisions appear in coinsurance, funds withheld coinsurance, and modco reinsurance agreements, but *not* in YRT reinsurance agreements. For YRT reinsurance, policy dividends do not affect reinsurance premium payments. In some cases, though, a YRT reinsurance agreement is modified to provide for the reinsurer to share in expenses for any paid-up additions or term additions generated by policy dividends.

A direct writer may increase the level of policy dividends it pays after the reinsurance agreement has been formed. Under some reinsurance agreements, the reinsurer must pay a specified percentage of all policy dividend payments, including the direct writer's increases in policy dividends. The situation differs between New York and other jurisdictions, as follows:

- New York law requires reinsurers to participate in the increases in the direct writer's policy dividend payments.

- In other jurisdictions, however, the reinsurer will pay part of any dividends up to a stated maximum amount per insured and will not pay an increased reimbursement unless the reinsurer has approved the increased reimbursement in advance.

Experience Refunds

The actual financial outcome from operations under a reinsurance agreement may be better or worse than the parties anticipated when they entered into the reinsurance agreement.

- *Favorable risk experience* refers to a better outcome from a reinsured product's operations than the outcome the direct writer and the reinsurer assumed when they set the reinsurance premium rates. When reinsured risks show favorable experience, the product's cost to both companies is lower than they initially anticipated.

- *Adverse risk experience* refers to a worse outcome from a reinsured product's operations than the outcome the direct writer and the reinsurer assumed when they set the reinsurance premium rates. When reinsured risks show adverse experience, the product's cost to both companies is higher than they initially anticipated.

Under some reinsurance agreements, when the outcome shows favorable risk experience, the reinsurer reimburses the direct writer for a portion of the reinsurance premium to reflect the reinsurer's reduced cost of providing reinsurance coverage. An *experience refund* is an amount the reinsurer credits to the direct writer as compensation for favorable risk experience. Figure 7.5 shows an example of an experience refund calculation.

Modco Reserve Adjustments

Recall that, under modco, the parties share responsibility for the policy reserve, and the direct writer holds the entire reserve for each reinsured policy; the reinsurer deposits a reserve credit with the direct writer; and both the direct writer's share of the policy reserve and the reinsurer's reserve credit amount are adjusted periodically, usually quarterly. Because the direct writer holds the reserves and the assets that back them, the reinsurer has no control over how these assets are invested. The agreement usually calls for the direct writer to pay interest to the reinsurer on the modco reserves.[3]

To balance the financial impact of the one-sided modco reserve holdings, the parties use a periodic payment known as a *modco reserve adjustment*. The amount of the modco reserve adjustment, typically calculated quarterly, equals the net of (1) interest on reserves payable by the direct writer and (2) the change in the required modco reserve. The modco agreement specifies the interest rate formula for calculating the interest on these required reserves.

FIGURE 7.5

An Experience Refund Formula for Reinsurance

Income		
(1)	Premium income, current period	$305,700
(2)	Reserve for outstanding losses, end of preceding period	0
(3)	Total income	**305,700**
Outgo		
(4)	Claims paid, current period	$20,600
(5)	Reserve for outstanding losses, end of current period	0
(6)	Loss, if any, brought forward from previous period	0
(7)	Expenses of the reinsurer [10% × premium income]	30,570
(8)	Total outgo	**51,170**
Results		
(9)	Gross profit = (3) − (8)	$254,530
(10)	Loss carried forward, current period	0
(11)	Refund to direct writer = 50% × (9)	**127,265**

Source: Adapted from Jane Lightcap Brown and Jennifer W. Herrod, *Reinsurance Administration* (Atlanta: LOMA, © 2000), 109. Used with permission; all rights reserved.

- If the amount of required reserves *increases* during the period, the reinsurer pays the direct writer an adjustment amount equal to the increase in the reserves and the direct writer pays the reinsurer a share of the interest earned on the reserves during the period

- If the amount of required reserves *decreases* during the period, the direct writer pays the reinsurer an adjustment amount equal to the decrease in the reserves plus a share of the interest earned on the reserves during the period

Provision for Premium Taxes

Premium taxes are amounts of tax that governments levy on a direct writer's premium income. The treatment of premium taxes varies by tax jurisdiction and from one reinsurance agreement to another. Typically, a direct writer pays tax equal to 2 to 3 percent of the amount of direct premiums it has collected. In most jurisdictions, reinsurers are not required to pay premium taxes on reinsurance premiums. When a jurisdiction requires a reinsurer to pay premium taxes, the reinsurer is not required to reimburse the direct writer for premium taxes the direct writer has paid. These jurisdictions assume that the direct writer has already paid taxes on the direct premiums.

Agreements usually require the reinsurer to share in the liability for premium taxes by paying a percentage, based on the direct writer's tax rate, of the reinsurance premiums paid. When a direct writer operating in the United States does business in many states, the direct writer usually calculates an average premium tax rate on its business and uses that rate for calculating the reinsurer's reimbursement. Because Canada has only a few potential taxing authorities, companies operating in Canada usually use the exact tax rate that applies to every policy.

The arrangements for a reinsurer to reimburse a direct writer vary from one agreement to another.

- Some reinsurance agreements require the reinsurer to reimburse the direct writer for any taxes the direct writer has paid on the reinsured portion of the direct premium. This arrangement intends to ensure that (1) shares of premium taxes are divided equitably between the parties and (2) the balance of risk and responsibility established at the outset of the agreement is maintained during the life of the agreement.

    Example: Chronos Life Insurance ceded half of a $200,000 life insurance risk to Argo Reinsurance. Chronos has received premiums for the coverage and, therefore, must pay premium taxes. Argo Re is not required to pay premium taxes on the amount of reinsurance premiums it collects from Chronos. Thus, the agreement requires Argo Re to reimburse Chronos for the premium taxes it paid for the $100,000 of ceded coverage.

- Agreements can require the reinsurer to remit directly to the taxing authority a share of the premium taxes. When an agreement requires a reinsurer to pay a portion of the premium taxes directly to the taxing authority, the reinsurer usually is not required to reimburse the direct writer for premium taxes the direct writer has paid.

- Other agreements require the reinsurer to increase the allowance to acknowledge the taxes borne by the direct writer.

Sometimes a reinsurance agreement additionally specifies how the parties will be required to respond if

- Tax rates on premiums increase from one year to the next

- New premium taxes are imposed

Currency for Reinsurance

Because many reinsurance transactions cross national boundaries, these transactions bring together direct writers and reinsurers with different languages and currencies. A reinsurance arrangement that covers an international partnership specifies the currency to be used for all financial transactions under the agreement. Specifying one currency forestalls problems resulting from misunderstandings regarding the amounts to be paid. Generally, the **currency of risk** or *original currency* is the currency in which an insurance policy was issued. The typical reinsurance practice is to maintain all records in the currency of risk and to exchange money in that same currency. However, especially for currencies not having broad acceptance worldwide, the records might be maintained in the currency of risk and transactions settled in another currency—one having broad acceptance, such as U.S. dollars.

The provision that sets a currency for financial settlements may specify any of the following currencies:

- **The direct writer's domestic currency.** If a direct writer is self-administering the reinsurance, using the currency of the direct writer simplifies recordkeeping for the direct writer.

- **The reinsurer's domestic currency.** This approach could enable both the direct writer and the reinsurer to avoid currency fluctuation risk.

- **A currency with broad acceptance worldwide.** For example, an agreement might state that transactions are to be settled using the U.S. dollar.

Currency Fluctuations

Ideally, the currency of risk should be one that maintains a stable value and experiences only a low rate of inflation. In reality, currencies can experience wide swings in value. A country's economy can experience serious inflation that can reduce its currency's worth. When the value of a domestic currency drops, financial exchanges denominated in a foreign currency suddenly involve a larger share of the affected company's resources.

Example: A direct writer domiciled in Neptune and a reinsurance company domiciled in Pluto specified Neptune's currency as their currency of risk. At the time, the value of 1 unit of Neptune's currency was equal to 3 units of Pluto's currency. Under the reinsurance agreement, the reinsurer establishes reserves for the reinsured coverage and agrees to pay allowances to the insurer.

One year after the agreement was formed, Pluto's currency lost value compared to Neptune's currency. Then, 1 unit of Neptune's currency was equal to 4 units of Pluto's currency. After this loss in value, the reinsurer thus must spend a greater share of its resources to establish its share of the required reserves and to pay its share of claims. Also, the direct writer in Neptune must manage its resources according to an understanding that the reinsurer might now be unable to meet some of its financial obligations on time.

Consequences for Late Payment Due to Decreases in Currency Exchange Values

Either party to a reinsurance agreement could fail to make payments due to the other party by the specified due date. As we discussed earlier in this chapter, many agreements specify consequences if one partner, the *debtor*, fails to make any required payments on schedule. These consequences apply equally to the debtor's currency exchange difficulties and to any other financial difficulties. Commonly, if either partner fails to pay balances owed within the allowed time periods, the debtor must pay for any losses resulting from unfavorable currency changes *unless* the creditor is responsible for the delay in payment.

Example: If a delay in payment resulted because the debtor had not received timely notice from the partner concerning amounts due, then the debtor is not responsible for losses resulting from a drop in the value of its currency.

Key Terms

gender-specific premium rate table

unisex premium rate table

smoker/nonsmoker premium rate table

aggregate premium rate table

standard aggregate premium rate table

large face amount (large FA) of life insurance premium rate table

waiver of premium (WP) for disability benefit rider premium rate table

accidental death benefit (ADB) rider premium rate table

substandard risk

flat extra premium

temporary flat extra premium

permanent flat extra premium

substandard extra premium

substandard extra premium rate table

extra-percentage premium rate table

flat extra premium rate table

premium payment mode

divisible surplus

policy dividend

favorable risk experience

adverse risk experience

experience refund

modco reserve adjustment

premium tax

currency of risk

Endnotes

1. This chapter represents a revision of material from Jane Lightcap Brown and Jennifer W. Herrod, *Reinsurance Administration* (Atlanta: LOMA, © 2000), 99–111. Used with permission; all rights reserved.

2. Adapted from Mary C. Bickley, *Principles of Financial Services and Products* (Atlanta: LOMA, © 2004), 129. Used with permission; all rights reserved.

3. John E. Tiller and Denise Fagerberg Tiller, *Life, Health, and Annuity Reinsurance*, 2nd ed. (Winsted, CT: ACTEX Publications, 1995), 87.

CHAPTER

8

Risk Management and Reinsurance

After studying this chapter, you should be able to

- Describe the four basic approaches to risk management

- Explain the risk-return tradeoff and describe how it relates to reinsurance

- Describe the surplus strain that direct writers experience when they issue new business

- Explain how indemnity reinsurance provides surplus relief

- Interpret changes in the value of a surplus relief ratio

- On the basis of a simple example, identify the amount of a direct writer's surplus strain and calculate the amount of surplus relief available from reinsurance

- Describe circumstances in which direct writers might decide to increase or decrease retention limits

- Describe the administrative actions required for a direct writer to increase or decrease its retention limits

- Describe potential limitations of reinsurance operations for direct writers and reinsurers

OUTLINE

Approaches to Risk Management

Balancing Risks and Returns

Leverage
Positive and Negative Leverage Effects
Leverage Ratios

Surplus Strain and Surplus Relief

The Surplus Relief Ratio

Retention Limits: Mechanisms for Redistributing Risks

Types of Retention Limits
Cession Basis and Retention Limits
Retention Limit Corridors

Setting, Monitoring, and Changing Retention Limits
Influences on Retention Limits
Changing Retention Limits

Limitations of Reinsurance
Limitations for a Direct Writer
Limitations for a Reinsurer

Direct writers and reinsurers maintain a balance of risks appropriate for their overall financial capacity. Each company's capacity reflects its financial ability to handle claims, maintain adequate reserves, and maintain adequate surplus.

For insurers, the paramount financial need is to protect the company's financial soundness. Insurers must place more emphasis on safety than they do on earnings. An important component in the appeal of insurance products is the customer's perception of the financial institution's solvency. For financial institutions, successful financial performance consists of an appropriate balance between achieving good returns for the company's owners and maintaining appropriate safety.

Reinsurance is an important tool in the broader context of a company's total system for managing corporate risk. In this chapter, we discuss risk management and its applications to the retention limits of insurance companies. Recall that we discussed retention limits in Chapter 3. We examine a company's attitudes toward risk and how a company's actions with respect to risk affect the company's potential earnings. We also discuss approaches that insurance companies can use to evaluate their levels of risk-taking and the effectiveness of their use of reinsurance in managing risk. Finally, we examine the tactical level of risk management in insurance—a direct writer's underwriting criteria and policies governing its use of reinsurance.

Approaches to Risk Management

Recall that risk is the possibility of an unexpected outcome, such as loss.[1] Risk management provides a set of principles for dealing with risk. **Risk management** is the practice of systematically identifying, assessing, limiting, and otherwise dealing with risk. Insurers can choose any of the following four primary approaches to risk management:

- **Avoiding risk.** One method of managing risk is to avoid risk altogether. For example, individuals can avoid the risk of financial loss in the stock market by not investing in it. Avoiding risk entirely is not a practical option for insurance companies. An insurance company must decide whether it desires to completely avoid a particular risk. Insurers can avoid some risks of financial loss by rejecting applications for insurance; not doing business in a given geographic area; or choosing not to offer a particular product line.

- **Transferring risk.** An insurance company or any other risk manager can transfer to another party the financial responsibility for a given risk, generally in exchange for a fee. The most common way for most individuals and businesses to transfer risk is to purchase insurance coverage. Direct writers transfer a portion of a risk when they obtain traditional indemnity reinsurance.

- **Accepting risk and controlling it.** To accept a risk is to assume all or part of the financial responsibility for that risk. For example, hospitals employ professional risk managers to ensure that the hospital staff takes care to protect the hospital from unnecessary exposure to risks. Insurers accept risk when they sell insurance coverage. Insurers can take steps to prevent or reduce losses even when they accept a risk.

Examples: Most cash value life insurance and annuity contracts impose a surrender charge for the first several years, which helps insurers control the expense risk associated with early withdrawals. A health maintenance organization (HMO) accepts a risk and then attempts to control it by providing preventive health care to HMO members. Automobile insurers sometimes accept drivers with poor driving records but require those drivers to take safe driving courses.

- **Accepting risk and not controlling it.** Some people and businesses consciously choose to accept significant risks, wholly or in part. When insurance companies sell insurance and thus accept risk, they cannot always control the risks they accept.

Example: An employer can elect to bear its employees' medical expenses up to a stated maximum amount—known as a ***self-insured retention limit***—and then buy insurance to cover all benefits in excess of that stated maximum amount.

Balancing Risks and Returns

Many factors contribute to determining whether a direct writer's practices in many areas, particularly with reference to controlling risk and pursuing profits, are conservative, moderate, or aggressive.

- Conservative business practices reflect a low tolerance for business risk.

- Moderate business practices reflect a moderate tolerance for business risk.

- Aggressive business practices reflect a high tolerance for business risk.

Investors generally seek to both earn profit and limit risk. However, in most situations, risk and return exhibit a direct relationship. A ***return*** is any reward, profit, or compensation an investor hopes to earn for taking a risk. All other factors being equal, the greater the risk associated with an investment, then the greater the expected and potential return on the investment. Conversely, the lesser the risk associated with an investment, then the lower the expected and potential return on the investment. The interplay between risk and return is referred to as the ***risk-return tradeoff***. Virtually every financial decision or investment is subject to a risk-return tradeoff. Examples of characteristics that typically are associated with lower or higher levels of risk and return—all other characteristics held constant—are as follows:

Lower Risks and Lower Potential Returns	Higher Risks and Higher Potential Returns
■ Short-term investments	■ Long-term investments
■ Loans to borrowers with good credit	■ Loans to borrowers with poor credit
■ Assets that are easily sold for a fair price	■ Assets that are difficult to sell for a fair price
■ Loans to businesses that have adequate financial resources	■ Loans to businesses that have inadequate financial resources
■ Loans secured by collateral	■ Loans unsecured by collateral
■ Issuing only insurance products that are traditional for the company	■ Issuing new insurance products that are unfamiliar to the company

Leverage

Leverage, also known as the *leverage effect*, is a key concept in the measurement of a corporation's financial risk.[2] Recall that *leverage* can be defined as a financial effect in which the presence of fixed costs—either operating or financing costs—automatically magnifies risks and potential returns to the company's owners. The leverage effect applies to the activities of all types of firms, including insurance companies.

As a company's leverage increases, the company's exposure to risk of loss increases, and the company's earnings potential also increases. Conversely, as a company's leverage decreases, the company's risk of loss decreases, and the company's earnings potential also decreases. In other words, the leverage effect magnifies the risk-return tradeoff.

Example: Ratchet Assurance can borrow money at 8 percent interest. If Ratchet can invest the borrowed money to earn a return of 10 percent, then Ratchet's owners will earn a spread of 2 percent on the borrowed funds. By borrowing the money at 8 percent, however, Ratchet establishes an obligation to meet a fixed interest expense. Thus, leverage has magnified Ratchet's risk.

Leverage also magnifies the risk to Ratchet's owners. If Ratchet's management cannot find a way to invest the money to earn at least 8 percent, Ratchet's owners will lose money every time Ratchet pays loan interest and when Ratchet repays the debt.

Reinsurance premiums constitute a fixed cost in an insurer's product operations. By using reinsurance with a new product, a direct writer replaces unknown or uncertain costs and gains with the known cost of the reinsurance premium and the known risk protection of the reinsurance coverage. Thus, for direct writers, the use of reinsurance introduces leverage to the company's financial profile.

Positive and Negative Leverage Effects

Leverage can be positive or negative, as follows:

- A *positive leverage effect* is the effect of earning a larger profit due to the presence of leverage. If a company can employ fixed operating costs to earn greater profits than before, it is enjoying positive operating leverage.

- A *negative leverage effect* is the effect of earning a lower profit because of the presence of leverage. If a company takes on fixed costs but fails to earn enough operating profits to cover the added costs, then the company will have lower profits than if it had not taken on the fixed costs in the first place.

Leverage Ratios

Leverage ratios are used for comparing the amount of an insurer's obligations with its ability to meet those obligations. A *leverage ratio* is a type of financial ratio used to measure an organization's debt burden relative to the resources available to support the debt burden. The basic leverage ratio for insurers is expressed as:

$$\text{Leverage Ratio} = \frac{\text{Liabilities}}{\text{Owners' Equity}}$$

Recall from Chapter 2 that owners' equity is equivalent to net worth; or capital and surplus; or surplus alone; or capital alone.

In general, the lower the value of an insurance company's leverage ratio, the stronger the insurer's financial position. The value of a company's leverage ratio decreases if the company (1) increases the value of its owners' equity and/or (2) decreases the value of its liabilities. For insurance leverage ratios, liabilities can be defined as (1) contractual reserves alone or (2) contractual reserves plus other miscellaneous reserves and other liabilities.

Example: Argyle Insurance Company has owners' equity of $5 million and liabilities of $50 million. Argyle's leverage ratio is calculated as follows:

$$\frac{\$50,000,000}{\$5,000,000} = 10$$

This result indicates that Argyle's liabilities are 10 times the amount of its capital, or looked at another way, that Argyle's capital is one-tenth the amount of its liabilities.

Surplus Strain and Surplus Relief

Another way of looking at an insurance company's exposure to leverage and the risk-return tradeoff through its reinsurance transactions is by examining surplus strain and surplus relief, which we first discussed in Chapter 2.[3]

■ Surplus strain refers to an insurer's monetary operating loss for a product's first year of operations. The amount of surplus strain associated with a new product equals the capital investment that a direct writer must make in that new product.

■ Surplus relief refers to any arrangement designed to limit surplus strain. The reduction in surplus strain achieved by using reinsurance is a type of surplus relief. The amount of surplus relief from reinsurance is calculated as the sum of the first-year gain that the insurer realizes with reinsurance in force and the first-year loss that the insurer otherwise would have incurred without reinsurance, as shown:

$$\text{Surplus Relief} = \text{First-Year Gain from Product Operations with Reinsurance} + \text{First-Year Loss from Product Operations without Reinsurance}$$

Example: Cameo Insurance is evaluating a proposed reinsurance transaction. Without reinsurance on its new product, Cameo's first-year operating loss—that is, its surplus strain—for that product will be $2.5 million. With reinsurance, Cameo's first-year operating gain from its new product will be $200,000. Thus, Cameo's surplus relief from reinsuring this product is $2,700,000, calculated as follows:

First-Year Gain from Product Operations with Reinsurance	$200,000
First-Year Loss from Product Operations without Reinsurance	+ $2.5 million
Surplus Relief	**$2.7 million**

In the context of surplus relief and surplus strain, *surplus* refers to the cumulative funds invested in the company by its owners. One important potential benefit from using indemnity reinsurance is the opportunity for a direct writer to obtain surplus relief. When a direct writer issues an insurance contract, the direct writer must establish required reserves to support the company's ability to pay its *expected* obligations. To pay any *unexpected* obligations, the direct writer has the options to draw on its surplus or use reinsurance. Reinsurance can help a direct writer avoid spending its surplus to support a new product. Under indemnity reinsurance arrangements, allowances and reserve credits channel needed funds to the direct writer.

A direct writer typically encounters a shortfall of funds in a new product's first year because the first-year premium typically does not cover even the insurer's acquisition expenses. In a product's first year, the insurer must cover both acquisition expenses and reserves for the new product. To make up a shortfall, the insurer must either invest its surplus in the new product or use reinsurance.

Figure 8.1 shows an example of a calculation of a direct writer's (1) surplus strain from new business without reinsurance and (2) surplus relief from indemnity reinsurance on the same new business.

The Surplus Relief Ratio

Financial analysts use ratio analysis on financial statement data to evaluate an insurance company's total financial profile. Not surprisingly, financial analysts use a particular type of financial ratio to evaluate the role of reinsurance in an insurer's total financial profile. An insurer's total financial profile would include reinsurance arrangements entered into over the course of many years. The **surplus relief ratio** compares the insurer's net cost for or net earnings from reinsurance ceded and assumed to the insurer's surplus, as follows:

$$\text{Surplus Relief Ratio} = \frac{\text{Net Cost for or Net Income from Reinsurance}}{\text{Surplus}}$$

FIGURE 8.1

Surplus Strain and Surplus Relief

First-Year Operations without Reinsurance

Without reinsurance, in the first year of a product's operations, the direct writer takes in $600,000 of new premiums, and it must immediately

- Establish a required reserve of $400,000
- Pay acquisition costs of $50,000
- Pay contractual benefits of $200,000

At the end of the first year, the direct writer has a net operating loss of $50,000 from this product. To cover that loss, the direct writer must invest $50,000 of its surplus in the product.

First-Year Operations with Reinsurance

With reinsurance, in the first year the direct writer takes in $600,000 of new premiums, but the direct writer must pay the entire $600,000 to the reinsurer. Under the reinsurance agreement, the reinsurer pays the insurer a reinsurance commission of $150,000 and agrees to cover the new reserve of $400,000 and the benefits payable of $200,000. With reinsurance in force, the direct writer does not have to invest surplus in the new product. At the end of the first year of this new product, the direct writer has a net operating gain of $100,000 from this product.

Surplus Relief Calculation

The following worksheet illustrates surplus strain from new business and surplus relief from applying an indemnity reinsurance arrangement to the new business.

Business Outcomes for the Direct Writer	Surplus Strain without Reinsurance	Surplus Relief with Reinsurance
1. New premiums	$ 600,000	$ 600,000
2. Premiums reinsured	-0-	(600,000)
3. New reserve	(400,000)	(400,000)
4. Reserve credit	-0-	400,000
5. Premiums earned (new premiums – new reserve)	200,000	-0-
6. Reinsurance commissions earned	-0-	150,000
7. Benefits payable	(200,000)	-0-
8. Acquisition expenses	(50,000)	(50,000)
Direct writer's 1st-year gain (strain)	($ 50,000)	$ 100,000

The amount of surplus relief obtained is the sum of the first-year gain that the direct writer realized with reinsurance in force and the first-year loss that the direct writer otherwise would have incurred without reinsurance, calculated as follows:

Net Gain with Reinsurance	+	Net Loss without Reinsurance	=	Surplus Relief Amount
$100,000	+	$50,000	=	$150,000

The reinsurer contributes the $150,000 that provides the surplus relief. The reinsurer expects to recover its $150,000 investment from its profits in years after the first year.

Source: Adapted from Susan Conant, *Capital Management for Insurance Companies* (Atlanta: LOMA, © 2001), 153. Used with permission; all rights reserved.

When a direct writer uses reinsurance, the direct writer may experience either a net cost for the reinsurance or net earnings from the reinsurance. The surplus relief ratio, thus, measures the effectiveness of a direct writer's use of reinsurance. Insurance industry analysts also use other forms of the surplus relief ratio. The surplus relief ratio can take on a positive or a negative value, as follows:

- A *positive* value for the surplus relief ratio typically indicates that the direct writer ceded more insurance coverage than the amount of insurance coverage it issued. A very large positive value for the surplus relief ratio sometimes indicates that the direct writer believes that its capital and surplus is too low or that the risk it has taken on is too large and, thus, the company has obtained an extraordinary amount of reinsurance.

- A *negative* value for the surplus relief ratio indicates that the insurer issued and retained more insurance coverage than it ceded to reinsurers. A very large negative value for the surplus ratio can indicate that an insurer is straining its capital and surplus by issuing and retaining excessive amounts of insurance.

Retention Limits: Mechanisms for Redistributing Risks

Direct writers and reinsurers keep constant watch on their own financial status, and companies take care to maintain a balance of risks appropriate for their overall financial profiles.[4] Each direct writer and reinsurer establishes underwriting retention limits based on its *capacity*, which is the total amount of risk that the company is able to accept. A direct writer's capacity is based on its financial ability to handle claims, maintain adequate reserves, and maintain adequate surplus to provide for growth and company operations.

An insurer's ability to accept risk changes over time, reflecting the company's changing financial status and risk obligations. A direct writer that develops a new product must determine if it can support the predicted sales of the new product by accepting the anticipated level of risk. A reinsurer that considers entering into a new reinsurance agreement must evaluate whether it has adequate financial resources to accept the additional risk for varying volumes of sales.

Types of Retention Limits

Most direct writers establish several types of retention limits. We discussed some types of retention limits in Chapter 3. The following limits are included in indemnity reinsurance arrangements:

- A retention limit for each product

- A jumbo limit for each product

- An automatic binding limit for automatic reinsurance arrangements

- A *corporate retention limit*, also known as a *combined retention*, which is the maximum amount of risk that a group of affiliated companies will retain on any one life. A corporate retention limit is usually lower than the combination of all the other retention limits. The corporate retention limit allows

  - A single direct writer to insure a variety of types of coverage on one insured without exceeding an acceptable total risk retention

  - An affiliated group of insurers to limit their total risk retention on one insured

  Example: The Penguin Life Insurance Company has set the following retention limits:

  - $500,000 product retention limit per insured for its whole life products

  - $300,000 product retention limit per insured for its term life products

  - A corporate retention limit of $700,000 per insured

  A subsidiary of Penguin carries $500,000 in whole life insurance on a particular insured. That same insured has applied for a $300,000 term life insurance policy from Penguin. Penguin's corporate retention limit permits only $200,000 in additional risk for that insured. Thus, Penguin must either (1) decline to issue the extra $100,000 or (2) seek reinsurance to cover the extra $100,000.

Cession Basis and Retention Limits

The form of a retention limit differs according to the case's cession basis—automatic or facultative—as follows:

- Automatic reinsurance arrangements specify monetary limits on the risk amount a reinsurer will accept.

- For facultative reinsurance arrangements, the reinsurer decides on a case-by-case basis how much risk it will accept. For a facultative case, reinsurers might require a direct writer to retain the lesser of its full retention limit or 20 percent of the risk.

Retention Limit Corridors

Insurers sometimes, although rarely, exceed a corporate retention limit. For example, a direct writer could exceed product-line retention limits, but only by a small amount. Insurers sometimes exceed the retention limit for a particular policy by using *corridors*. In this context, a **retention limit corridor** is a monetary amount greater than the company's retention limit that a direct writer is willing to retain to avoid ceding small amounts of coverage. Because small cessions are relatively expensive to administer, direct writers typically use a corridor to limit the number of small cessions and, thus, to make reinsurance more cost-effective.

FIGURE 8.2

Sample Retention Schedule

Underwriting Limits—Term Life Insurance Products
Petaluma Life Insurance Company

For Issue Ages 75 and Younger

Petaluma Life has a flat retention limit of $750,000 on all preferred plus, preferred, standard, and substandard issues through age 75, EXCEPT for a flat retention schedule of $500,000 for Bramble Term Life and Bramble Universal Life.

Petaluma has automatic reinsurance arrangements that allow Petaluma to issue up to $12 million on most issues, EXCEPT for Bramble Term Life and Bramble Universal Life, on which the issue amount is limited to $8 million.

Petaluma Life is subject to a jumbo limit of $20 million.

Petaluma Life can access additional capacity through facultative reinsurance sources.

For Issue Ages 76 through 85

On issue ages 76 through 85, Petaluma Life has a flat retention limit of $250,000 and its automatic reinsurance arrangements allow issues limited to a maximum of $2 million with the following restrictions as to rating class:

Issue Ages	Available for Rating Class A through
76—80	Class H
81—85	Class D

Petaluma Life can access additional capacity through facultative reinsurance sources.

Example: The Walrus Insurance Company has a retention limit of $500,000 on its whole life policies and a retention limit corridor of $25,000. If Walrus issues a policy for an amount greater than $525,000, Walrus retains $500,000 and cedes the remainder. However, if Walrus issues a policy for an amount between $500,000 and $525,000, Walrus retains the entire amount to avoid the expense of ceding a very small amount of coverage.

Generally, a company's retention limits are recorded in a retention schedule, as shown in Figure 8.2. A **retention schedule**, also known as a *table of retention limits*, presents all of an insurer's retention limits, organized by applicable categories such as product, product line, issue age, and underwriting rating.

Setting, Monitoring, and Changing Retention Limits

A direct writer's board of directors has ultimate responsibility for the company's corporate retention limits for each product or line of business. In setting retention limits, insurers generally use complex actuarial projections. A staff team representing several departments generally works together to set retention limits. Actuaries are essential in helping insurers determine optimum amounts of coverage to keep, cede, and accept.

A retention limit reflects a company's attitude toward the risk-return tradeoff. The more insurance risk the direct writer assumes, the greater its potential returns or potential losses. The less insurance risk a direct writer assumes, the lower its potential returns or losses. The higher the direct writer's retention limit, the more risk the insurer keeps. The larger the risks a direct writer retains, the greater the reserves required to pay claims. The lower the direct writer's retention limit, the less risk the direct writer keeps, and the smaller the reserves required to pay claims.

Influences on Retention Limits

Insurance companies consider many of the following factors when setting retention limits:

- **The company's financial position.** A financially strong direct writer may choose to retain risk in order to limit its reinsurance costs.

- **Cost of reinsurance premiums and reinsurance administration expense.** A direct writer must balance the tradeoff between its own business objectives and the fixed cost of reinsurance premiums. A small increase in a direct writer's retention limit can reduce the number of cessions and decrease its reinsurance administration costs. The reinsurer may be able to offer more favorable terms for reinsurance coverage when the direct writer retains a greater percentage of the risk.

- **Conservative or aggressive attitude toward risk.** A company that is relatively conservative in its view of risk may choose a lower retention limit than would a company with a greater risk tolerance.

- **Company expertise.** A direct writer considers its level of experience with underwriting and claims for a given product. If a direct writer has substantial experience with a product, the company can confidently estimate the product's future benefits. Thus, the company could set a higher retention limit for that product.

Reinsurers consider their relationships with retrocessionaires when determining how much risk they can accept. If a reinsurer has an established relationship with a retrocessionaire, the reinsurer knows that it can pass along some of a risk to the retrocessionaire. An experienced reinsurer knows the amount of risk its retrocessionaires generally will accept under various conditions.

Changing Retention Limits

Retention limits are rarely permanent. Direct writers and reinsurers increase or decrease their retention limits as their circumstances change. Direct writers and reinsurers typically use sophisticated software to monitor their product liabilities relative to their retention limits and other pertinent financial factors. To bring about an increase or decrease in retention limits, a direct writer must take the appropriate administrative actions and must communicate with its established reinsurers. Reinsurance agreements may limit the direct writer's option to change retention limits for in-force business covered under a reinsurance agreement without written prenotice to and written preapproval from the reinsurer.

Increasing Retention Limits

Direct writers typically increase their retention limits as their financial positions strengthen; as their information about risks improves; or as their staffs' experience increases. An improved financial position might indicate that the direct writer has the funds available to handle claims volatility and to support new growth. Direct writers increase retention as they become comfortable with an existing, but relatively new, risk. Direct writers may increase retention on a product they are ceasing to issue, because all the insureds are known, so that their experience with that product allows them to evaluate the total risk under the product. Direct writers may increase retention to reduce or even eliminate the expense of reinsurance administration for a small block of business that has dwindled over time.

If a direct writer chooses to increase its retention limits, the direct writer informs the reinsurer and states whether an increase will affect (1) new business only or (2) both new business and in-force business. Upon an increase in a direct writer's retention limit, the direct writer may choose to apply the new retention limit to (1) new business only or (2) new business and recapture in-force business.

Decreasing Retention Limits

Direct writers may decrease the retention limits on a product they no longer offer. If a direct writer chooses to decrease its retention limits, the direct writer must notify its existing reinsurers and request that they accept additional risk on the in-force business. If the existing reinsurers are not interested in increasing their share of the available risks, the direct writer seeks new reinsurers to take the additional risk.

Limitations of Reinsurance

Reinsurance in general has many benefits for the insurance industry. For example, indemnity reinsurance permits direct writers and reinsurers to cede any excess risk to other insurers. The primary purpose of reinsurance is for direct writers to avoid financial jeopardy at the time of a benefit payment. The principal reason for a direct writer to transfer risks to a reinsurer is to minimize the risk from large claims or unexpectedly large numbers of small claims during a specified period. However, reinsurance also has limitations for direct writers and reinsurers.

Limitations for a Direct Writer

A direct writer can experience the following potential limitations of reinsurance:

- Reinsurance premiums constitute an expense. The direct writer might otherwise have spent the same money for other purposes.

- For reinsured business with better-than-expected experience, the direct writer usually gains little or no profits from the reinsured portion of the business. Reinsurance has a leverage effect. Thus, it shields a direct writer from unexpected losses, but it also reduces that company's chances of earning unexpected profits. Using an affiliated reinsurer can help to minimize the impact of this limitation.

Limitations for a Reinsurer

A reinsurer can experience the following potential limitations of providing reinsurance:

- A reinsurer accepts some risks, including the surplus strain of establishing reserves for the portion of insurance coverage assumed. By establishing reserves, the reinsurer may decrease its financial capacity.

- For blocks of assumed business with worse-than-expected experience, the reinsurer shares in the direct writer's losses rather than sharing in the profits.

- Under some types of indemnity reinsurance, the reinsurer assumes some of the insurer's liability for benefit payments and agrees to establish reserves for the reinsured portion of the risk.

Key Terms

risk management
self-insured retention limit
return
risk-return tradeoff
positive leverage effect
negative leverage effect
leverage ratio
surplus relief ratio
corporate retention limit
retention limit corridor
retention schedule

Endnotes

1. The discussion of risk management is adapted from Susan Conant, *Capital Management for Insurance Companies* (Atlanta: LOMA, © 2001), 17–18. Used with permission; all rights reserved.

2. The discussion of leverage is adapted from Susan Conant, *Capital Management for Insurance Companies* (Atlanta: LOMA, © 2001), 40–41. Used with permission; all rights reserved.

3. The discussion of surplus strain and surplus relief is adapted from Susan Conant, *Capital Management for Insurance Companies* (Atlanta: LOMA, © 2001), 100, 152–153. Used with permission; all rights reserved.

4. The discussion of retention limits is derived from Jane Lightcap Brown and Jennifer W. Herrod, *Reinsurance Administration* (Atlanta: LOMA, © 2000), 151–160. Used with permission; all rights reserved.

Part 3:
Reinsurance
Administration

CHAPTER

9

Reinsurance Activities, Staff, and Systems

After studying this chapter, you should be able to

- Describe the activities that typically are performed by reinsurance analysts

- Explain the role that each of the following functional areas within an insurance company plays in the insurer's reinsurance business: marketing, actuarial, underwriting, law and compliance, accounting, auditing, and claims

- Describe the reinsurance-related services provided by reinsurance intermediaries, consumer reporting agencies, and MIB Group, Inc.

- Describe the role of an insurer's information technology department in the insurer's reinsurance business

- Explain how electronic data interchange, electronic commerce, and document management systems facilitate reinsurance business

- Identify the primary security measures that direct writers and reinsurers use to protect the confidentiality and integrity of their information

OUTLINE

Reinsurance Administration Activities

Reinsurance Administration Staff
Reinsurance Analysts
Other Staff Involved in Reinsurance Activities

Reinsurance Communications with Third Parties
Reinsurance Intermediaries
Consumer Reporting Agencies
MIB Group, Inc.

Reinsurance Information Systems
Telecommunications
Document Management Systems
Security for Information Systems

Due to the current volume of reinsurance business and the international nature of the reinsurance industry, computer-based information systems are essential to efficient, effective administration of reinsurance.

From the time a direct writer decides to seek reinsurance to the time that all reinsurance coverage under a reinsurance agreement is ended, employees of the direct writer and the reinsurer perform a wide variety of reinsurance-related activities.[1] Each insurer—whether acting as a direct writer or reinsurer—establishes specific guidelines to ensure that it conducts reinsurance activities efficiently, effectively, and ethically. These organizational guidelines typically address issues such as communication between the reinsurance partners, delivery of services, risk management, compliance with laws and regulations, interaction among employees performing reinsurance activities, and employee training.

This chapter describes the primary activities required to conduct reinsurance business. We also discuss the direct writer and reinsurer staff involved in reinsurance functions and the systems used to facilitate reinsurance transactions.

Reinsurance Administration Activities

Reinsurance administration is similar for business ceded automatically and facultatively. The primary differences between conducting automatic and facultative reinsurance business are (1) which company makes underwriting decisions and (2) whether an ongoing flow of transactions is established, as shown in the following table:

	Automatic Reinsurance	**Facultative Reinsurance**
Underwriting Decisions	The reinsurer accepts risk on the basis of the underwriting performed by the direct writer	The reinsurer performs its own underwriting on business submitted for consideration
Flow of New Transactions	Most automatic reinsurance agreements provide that new business will continue to be ceded automatically until the agreement is terminated	Facultative arrangements may include just one policy or one group of policies and do not necessarily establish a continuing flow of new cessions

Under some reinsurance agreements, the direct writer accepts primary responsibility for administration; under other agreements, the reinsurer accepts the primary responsibility; and in yet others, the reinsurance parties share administrative duties. Generally, the company that is primarily responsible for administering the reinsurance carries out the following tasks:

■ Determining the amount of reinsurance coverage

■ Interpreting and complying with the requirements of existing reinsurance agreements and helping to provide administrative specifications for new agreements

- Handling reinsurance premiums, billing, and payments
- Administering policy changes and policy terminations
- Administering reinsurance claims
- Maintaining comprehensive records and developing reports
- Ensuring quality control and timeliness of all reinsurance administration activities
- Administering reinsurance agreement terminations

Reinsurance Administration Staff

Most insurance companies establish separate functional areas or staff groups to handle certain reinsurance activities, but not every company is organized in the same way. In general, however, a senior manager directs reinsurance analysts and other staff involved in reinsurance administration. We will refer to this functional area of an insurance company as the *reinsurance administration unit*.

Reinsurance Analysts

The staff members who administer reinsurance are known by various titles, such as reinsurance analyst, client administrator, and reinsurance specialist. For consistency in this text, we use the term *reinsurance analyst* to refer to any direct writer or reinsurer employee—except the person holding top leadership responsibility—who is involved in any phase of reinsurance administration. Reinsurance analysts are responsible for handling many of the activities required to conduct reinsurance transactions between reinsurers and direct writers. However, a reinsurance analyst's job duties may vary from company to company and depending on the reinsurance analyst's level of experience. Reinsurance analysts typically perform some or all of the following activities:

- Verifying that the correct reinsurance agreement is used to guide administration of a specified risk and set the effective date of reinsurance coverage
- Researching reinsurance agreements to verify that administrative activities for a given risk meet agreement requirements
- Researching and implementing changes to reinsurance agreements and reinsured policies and determining if billings for such changes are appropriate
- Ensuring that facultative coverage complies with the reinsurer's underwriting decision
- Calculating the portion of each risk that is retained and the portion that is ceded
- Calculating and generating payments for funds due to or from the reinsurance parties
- Reconciling reinsurance bills and payments with company records
- Recordkeeping and preparing detailed reports regarding reinsured policies for use by the reinsurance parties

- Meeting financial and regulatory reporting requirements

- Collaborating with other company staff and outside organizations as necessary

Other Staff Involved in Reinsurance Activities

In addition to the reinsurance administration unit, various other operational units of direct writers and reinsurers perform reinsurance-related activities. Other functional areas typically involved in reinsurance-related activities include marketing, actuarial, underwriting, law and compliance, accounting, auditing, and claim administration.

Marketing

Marketing refers to the processes and activities a company uses to develop, price, promote, and distribute its products and services. The direct writer's marketers often provide input into the selection of reinsurers. In addition, the marketing units of both direct writers and reinsurers consult with reinsurance analysts when estimating the cost of administering a particular client's business.

Some professional reinsurers use reinsurance marketing officers to help them establish reinsurance agreements. A ***reinsurance marketing officer***, also known as a *reinsurance account executive*, is a reinsurer's employee who sells reinsurance and coordinates the marketing process for the reinsurer. Such employees visit the home offices of current and potential clients—usually direct writing companies and other reinsurers—and gather information about new reinsurance arrangements that clients need or adjustments they would like to make to existing arrangements.

In addition to being an employee of a reinsurer, a reinsurance marketing officer also is considered to be an agent of the reinsurer. ***Agency*** is a legal relationship in which one party—known as the ***principal***—authorizes another party—known as the ***agent***—to act on the principal's behalf. When an agency relationship is created, certain legal rights and obligations are imposed on the agent and principal. As a general rule, a principal may do anything through an agent that the principal can legally do for itself. When an agent acts within the scope of the authority conferred on him by the principal, the agent's acts typically are considered to be the acts of the principal.

> **Example:** Assume that the Fulton Reinsurance Company authorized Monica Johnson, a Fulton Re employee, to sell reinsurance and coordinate the marketing process for Fulton Re. In this instance, Ms. Johnson was appointed as Fulton Re's agent and Fulton Re is serving as Ms. Johnson's principal. When Ms. Johnson acts within the scope of her authority as an agent of Fulton Re, her acts are binding on Fulton Re.

Although not required to be licensed as insurance producers, most reinsurance marketing officers have extensive experience in the insurance industry. Typically, direct writers consider reinsurance marketing officers to be valuable sources of information and advice concerning developments in the insurance and reinsurance markets. See Figure 9.1 for an example of a communication about reinsurance marketing.

FIGURE 9.1

A Communication about Reinsurance Marketing

Trip Report

Company Visited: March Life Insurance Company

Date of Meeting: April 11, 2005

Date of Report: April 14, 2005

Prepared by Anthony Briggs

Attendees:

March Life: Carly Timmons, Vice President, Marketing

                  Peter Cavendish, Vice President, Marketing

Sanders Re: Alan Jacobs

                  Matthew Ross

                  Anthony Briggs

An excellent visit with March Life. The purpose of the meeting was to officially introduce Sanders Re and the services we can provide. They seemed very interested in the capacity we can offer.

Their premium target this year is $60 million. They expect that a large part of that will come from large cases. They sell mostly universal life products and their main competitors are Walters Life, Gigantic Life, and Powerful Life. On term insurance, their major competition is with Shoreside Life and Peak Life. Retention is $500,000 for permanent plans and $250,000 for term, graded by age. (It drops to $125,000 at age 60.) Maximum issue age for UL and term is 70.

March has three automatic reinsurance agreements—with Malden Re, Tillson Re, and Michaelson Re. All of these agreements are excess of retention. They seem open to considering first-dollar quota share.

Reinsured volume is $1 billion. Annual average premium for term is $1,000 and face amount is $350,000.

We took the opportunity to talk about our underwriting strengths (large cases and financial), flexibility, and capacity. We also told them we'd send a copy of our client survey.

Our staff will follow with quotes on YRT and facultative.

Source: Adapted from Jane Lightcap Brown and Jennifer W. Herrod, *Reinsurance Administration* (Atlanta: LOMA, © 2000), 64. Used with permission; all rights reserved.

Actuarial

An **actuary** is a technical expert in insurance products and financial instruments who applies mathematical knowledge to industry and company statistics to calculate various financial values. Actuaries who deal with reinsurance calculate appropriate pricing structures and policy reserves for reinsurance ceded and assumed, and they project future business results, such as amounts needed to pay future claims or profits by product line. Actuaries also assist direct writers and reinsurers in setting their retention limits.

Direct writers' actuaries submit requests for proposals for new reinsurance agreements, evaluate the proposals that are submitted, and—with input from employees working in other functional areas of the company—select reinsurers and negotiate reinsurance agreements. In addition, they evaluate new reinsurance products and services.

Reinsurers' actuaries have a complex job because they must calculate policy reserves for multiple products from multiple direct writers. Also, calculating policy reserves for bulk-administered reinsurance typically is challenging because the direct writer provides the reinsurer with only limited information under bulk-administered agreements.

Actuaries of both direct writers and reinsurers assist with the preparation of the companies' periodic financial reports to insurance regulators. Actuaries also perform calculations to create projections of mortality experience. Figure 9.2 shows an example of an actuarial projection. In addition to the categories shown in this figure, actuarial projections also may analyze mortality

FIGURE 9.2

An Example of an Actuarial Projection

Actuarial Analysis of Mortality Experience

	Exposure ($000)	Expected Claims ($000)	Actual Claims ($000)	Actual to Expected	Standard Normal
All Issues	16,047,883	25,454	24,149	94.9%	−0.589
Gender					
Male	10,923,533	18,191	18,002	99.0%	−0.094
Female	5,124,349	7,260	6,146	84.7%	−1.213
Duration					
1st year	6,638,905	7,343,273	7,541,159	102.7%	0.171
2nd year	4,033,684	6,132,316	5,898,572	96.2%	−0.212
Issue Ages					
0-19	450,603	215,392	316,614	147.0%	0.721
20-29	3,397,478	1,877,603	1,978,344	105.4%	0.198
30-39	5,944,088	4,109,584	5,388,841	131.1%	1.409
Underwriting					
Nonsmoker	10,657,476	16,725	14,013	83.8%	−1.545
Smoker	2,674,128	6,645	7,594	114.3%	1.065
Size					
0–25,000	673,205	4,179	4,511	107.9%	1.263
25,001–50,000	2,202,580	5,775	5,090	88.1%	−1.438

experience according to factors such as underwriting classification, single life versus joint-life coverage, type of life insurance plan, quota share versus excess-of-retention reinsurance coverage, coverage under policy riders, and the insured's country of residence.

Underwriting

Underwriting plays an important role in reinsurance for both direct writers and reinsurers. Evaluating the risks associated with policies to be reinsured is the central reinsurance-related task of underwriting. If changes occur to ceded or assumed coverages, or if a direct writer wishes to modify ceded coverage, underwriters for either reinsurance partner may need to underwrite the changes in risk. Underwriters for direct writers and reinsurers also may participate in negotiating reinsurance agreements.

Typically, underwriting is performed by both the direct writer and reinsurer only for those cases that are submitted for facultative reinsurance. The process for obtaining facultative coverage typically includes the following underwriter actions:

- The direct writer's underwriter determines if a particular policy requires reinsurance, and, if so, whether the risk should be ceded automatically or facultatively.

- If the decision is to reinsure the risk facultatively, the direct writer's underwriter cooperates with the company's reinsurance analysts to request reinsurance premium rate quotes from one or more reinsurers on the risk to be ceded. The direct writer's employees are responsible for sending the required underwriting documentation to each reinsurer in a timely manner.

- The reinsurer's underwriter evaluates the proposed reinsurance risk and decides whether to offer reinsurance coverage. The underwriter then submits the reinsurer's decision to the direct writer. Figure 9.3 shows an example of how a reinsurer might submit decisions on facultative cases.

- The direct writer's underwriter evaluates the offers received on the risk to be reinsured, selects a reinsurer, and orders the notification of cession to the reinsurer.

To facilitate the effective underwriting of facultative cases, underwriters sometimes assist reinsurance analysts by providing the reinsurance analysts with information about underwriting administration requirements.

Law and Compliance

Direct writers and reinsurers must comply with all applicable regulatory requirements and their own company guidelines. These regulations and guidelines typically address issues such as company licensing, administration of reinsurance agreements and claims, fulfillment of reporting requirements, and general business conduct.

Direct writers and reinsurers typically have a **law department**—sometimes called the *legal department*—that handles legal matters, such as contracts and litigation, and a **compliance unit** that performs a wide variety of activities to ensure that company operations adhere to applicable laws and regulations and company policies. In some companies, the compliance unit is part of the law department.

The law department helps develop and interpret reinsurance agreement provisions and other documents as needed. Company lawyers provide advice when reinsurance agreement negotiations become particularly complex or when a claim is denied. They also help negotiate other contracts used by the company and either represent the company or supervise outside attorneys in any litigation involving the company.

The compliance unit typically has the following responsibilities:

- Study current and proposed laws to determine their effects on the company's operations

- Educate company employees about applicable regulatory requirements and company compliance policies

- Monitor the conduct of employees and marketers affiliated with the company to ensure they are complying with applicable regulatory requirements and company compliance policies

- Oversee internal control procedures

- Work with insurance regulators when they conduct examinations of the company

---

FIGURE 9.3

Examples of a Reinsurer's Decisions on Facultative Cases

June 17, 2005

To: Andrea Cunningham
       Vice President, Reinsurance Administration
       Calabash Insurance Company

From: Joe Ingram
       Vice President, Underwriting
       Great Plains Reinsurance Company

Re: Decisions on facultative reinsurance requests

Name of Insured	Date of Birth	Amount of Risk Accepted ($ US)	Underwriting Classification	Tobacco Use	Exclusions	Additional Benefits
Peter Davison	01/28/1960	1,000,000	Preferred	Nonuser	Aviation	None
Rafael Sanchez	03/15/1955	500,000	Standard	Nonuser	None	Waiver of Premium for Disability
Geneva Ellis	08/02/1947	Declined	Substandard	User	None	Accidental Death Benefit

Accounting

Accounting is a system or set of rules and methods for collecting, recording, analyzing, summarizing, and reporting financial information. Reinsurance accounting involves (1) maintaining accurate records of the numerous financial transactions associated with administering reinsurance, such as the payment of reinsurance premiums to reinsurers and the payment of reinsurance claim benefits to direct writers, and (2) preparing financial statements and summarizing the companies' reinsurance-related accounts. Figure 9.4 lists some financial statement elements that are related to reinsurance. Each company's accounting unit provides advice to other units within the company about accounting requirements and assists those units in setting up procedures to fulfill the requirements. The accounting requirements may vary by the company's role in a particular reinsurance agreement—direct writer or reinsurer—and by the type of reinsurance arrangement—YRT, coinsurance, or modified coinsurance.

Two general types of accounting are financial accounting and management accounting.

- *Financial accounting* focuses primarily on reporting a company's financial information to meet the needs of the company's external users, such as customers, stockholders, regulatory authorities, taxation authorities, and creditors.

- *Management accounting* is the process of identifying, measuring, analyzing, and communicating financial information so that a company's internal managers can decide how best to use the company's resources.

FIGURE 9.4

Financial Statement Elements Related to Reinsurance

- *Reinsurance recoverables*, which are reinsurance benefit amounts due to the direct writer or owed by the reinsurer

- Reinsurance premiums paid by the direct writer or collected by the reinsurer

- Allowances received by the direct writer or paid by the reinsurer

- Policy reserves on reinsured risks and adjustments to those reserves

- Retrocession-related amounts, such as retrocession recoverables due to the reinsurer or owed by the retrocessionaire, retrocession premiums paid by the reinsurer or collected by the retrocessionaire, allowances received by the reinsurer or paid by the retrocessionaire, and policy reserves on retroceded risks

- Taxes related to reinsurance operations

Management accounting is not a substitute for financial accounting, and it differs from financial accounting in several important ways, as described in Figure 9.5.

The accounting unit can offer assistance to reinsurance analysts as they perform accounting tasks, such as budget planning and control, management information reporting, tax accounting, and maintaining financial records on reinsured business—for example, records of reinsurance premium and claim payments, tax information, and monetary allowances for reinsurance parties. Accountants also work with reinsurance analysts to develop financial accounting reports, such as tax returns and the company's financial reports to regulators.

The accounting unit may (1) advise reinsurance analysts about various methods of payment, such as wire transfers and drafts, (2) provide exchange rates, and (3) track payments made or received by the company. In turn, the reinsurance analysts may help the accounting unit identify the appropriate accounting entries for reinsurance-related transactions or investigate unexpected changes in revenues or expenses.

Auditing

In general terms, an *audit* is an evaluation of a company's records and operations to ensure the accuracy of the records and the effectiveness of the company's operational policies and procedures. In a reinsurance audit, auditors examine the company's reinsurance records and procedures and recommend improvements to those procedures.

FIGURE 9.5

Comparison of Financial Accounting to Management Accounting

FINANCIAL ACCOUNTING	MANAGEMENT ACCOUNTING
Provides information for external users	Provides information for internal users
Is required by law	Is not required by law
Is subject to specific accounting principles	Is not subject to specific accounting principles
Emphasizes precision of information	Emphasizes flexibility and relevance of information for managers
Has a historical focus	Has mainly a forward-looking focus
Reports on the business as a whole	Can focus on the business as a whole or on individual parts of the business
Culminates in the presentation of financial statements and so is an end in itself	Helps managers make decisions and so is a means to an end

Source: Adapted from Miriam Orsina and Gene Stone, *Insurance Company Operations,* 2nd ed. (Atlanta: LOMA, © 2005), 400. Used with permission; all rights reserved.

Figure 9.6 shows a portion of an audit checklist that one reinsurer uses to prepare for a reinsurance audit of a direct writer. We discuss auditing further in Chapter 12.

FIGURE 9.6

An Audit Checklist

☑ **PLANNING**
- Prepare review planning memorandum
- Prepare sample selection memorandum
- Prepare letter of introduction (engagement letter) to direct writer
- Develop pre-review questionnaire
- Review internal correspondence
- Review correspondence with direct writer
- Complete travel arrangements
- Review prior reviews

☑ **PRE-REVIEW ANALYSIS**
- Complete reinsurance agreement summaries
- Review reinsurance premium billings
- Conduct in-force analysis
- Conduct claims analysis
- Analyze issues from prior reviews
- Other analysis (data quality)

☑ **CONTROLS ASSESSMENT**
- Establish business controls objectives
- Request client organizational chart
- Review other information provided by direct writer (such as workflow documentation, Sarbanes-Oxley documentation, direct writer's audit program documentation)

☑ **DETAILED TESTING**
- Reinsurance agreements
- Individual cases
- Claims
- Retention management testing
- Other tests

☑ **FINDINGS**
- Issues list
- One-page summary report
- External report
- Internal notes and memoranda
- Follow-up actions
- Other documents

Claims

Claim administration is the process of evaluating claims and determining the insurer's responsibility for paying those claims. The direct writer's claim analysts notify the company's reinsurance administration unit when a claim under a reinsured policy is received. In some cases, a claim analyst can settle the claim without consulting the reinsurer for a recommendation or an approval. The claim analyst then passes the information about the settlement on to a reinsurance analyst, who prepares reports of claims submitted and paid and sends the reports to the reinsurer to obtain reimbursement for all or a portion of each paid claim.

However, in certain circumstances such as anticipated denials of claims or contestable claims, the direct writer must send the claim documentation to the reinsurer for a claim recommendation prior to settling a claim. Also, the direct writer's claim analyst may contact the reinsurer's claim department for advice on any large or unusual claims. Reinsurers' claim analysts typically have experience with claims submitted under a wide variety of products and complex circumstances. The reinsurer's claim department also may assist the direct writer with claim investigations and contests of claim denials.

Reinsurance Communications with Third Parties

Direct writers and reinsurers often obtain reinsurance-related services and information from third parties. Reinsurance intermediaries, consumer reporting agencies, and, in the United States and Canada, MIB Group, Inc. provide valuable assistance with reinsurance activities.

Reinsurance Intermediaries

As we noted in Chapter 2, the parties to a reinsurance agreement sometimes obtain assistance with reinsurance transactions from a reinsurance intermediary. The parties to an agreement typically use a reinsurance intermediary when the direct writer lacks reinsurance expertise in a particular area. Reinsurance intermediaries usually handle reinsurance for health coverages. Occasionally, they handle life reinsurance, particularly for cases involving very high face amounts, unusual underwriting characteristics, or complex product designs.

Recall the distinction between a reinsurance intermediary—broker, who represents the direct writer, and a reinsurance intermediary—manager, who represents the reinsurer and is an agent of the reinsurer. Globally, the role of the reinsurance intermediary—broker is growing in importance. Figure 9.7 lists some of the services commonly provided by reinsurance intermediaries—brokers. Keep in mind that a direct writer using a reinsurance intermediary—broker may continue to perform some of these functions for itself.

Consumer Reporting Agencies

Reinsurance analysts and underwriters sometimes contact consumer reporting agencies to obtain additional underwriting information. A ***consumer reporting agency*** is a person or organization that assembles or evaluates consumer credit reports and furnishes these reports to other people and organizations in exchange for a fee. A ***consumer credit report*** is a report prepared

FIGURE 9.7

Services Provided by Reinsurance Intermediaries—Brokers

- Determine the insurance risks faced by direct writers and analyze methods of managing those risks

- Determine the reinsurance needs of direct writers using actuarial models and other consultative methods

- Advise direct writers on the specific information that should be provided to reinsurers to place their coverage

- Find and select reinsurers that meet predetermined solvency criteria and legal requirements

- Explain reinsurance agreement standards and practices

- Negotiate reinsurance agreement terms and prices with specific reinsurers, tailoring the agreements to meet the specific risk-management needs of the direct writer

- Provide reinsurance agreement language that clarifies the reinsurance coverage and reduces the probability of disputes and arbitration

- Carry out administrative functions such as (1) paying reinsurance premiums to and accepting claim reimbursements from reinsurers and (2) maintaining policyowner records

- Monitor the contract performance of reinsurers

- Evaluate and monitor a variety of factors affecting reinsurer solvency and warn the direct writer about changes in a reinsurer's financial risks and solvency

- Arbitrate disputes between direct writers and reinsurers

Source: Adapted from Stephen W. Forbes, *The Changing Reinsurance Industry* (Atlanta: LOMA, © 2004), 59–60. Used with permission; all rights reserved.

by a consumer reporting agency that (1) bears on a consumer's credit worthiness, credit standing, credit capacity, character, general reputation, personal characteristics, or mode of living and (2) is used or collected as a factor in establishing the consumer's eligibility for insurance or credit. An ***inspection report*** is a type of consumer credit report that is prepared by a consumer reporting agency for use during the insurance underwriting process. The information collected for an inspection report can include virtually anything about a proposed insured's personal life, occupation, hobbies, health, and financial status. Reinsurance analysts and underwriters use inspection reports to clarify information received from an insurance applicant or other sources.

MIB Group, Inc.

Underwriters in the United States and Canada often request information about proposed insureds from **MIB Group, Inc. (MIB)**, a nonprofit organization established to provide coded information to insurers about impairments that insurance applicants have disclosed or that other insurance companies have detected in connection with previous applications for insurance. MIB maintains information about people applying for coverage with MIB-member life insurance companies. Direct writers and reinsurers that are MIB members may request information to find out whether proposed insureds have significant impairments or other risks that they did not disclose on their current applications for insurance. Insurers report impairment information to MIB as well as obtain information from it.

MIB rules specifically define how MIB information can be used for underwriting purposes. MIB prohibits its member companies from using MIB information as the sole basis for an unfavorable underwriting decision. Any information an insurance company receives from MIB must be kept strictly confidential.

Reinsurance Information Systems

Due to the current volume of reinsurance business and the international nature of the reinsurance industry, computer-based information systems are essential to efficient, effective administration of reinsurance.[2] From the first queries concerning coverage to the last exchange of claim and payment data, direct writers and reinsurers maintain a continuous flow of information between themselves. Negotiating reinsurance agreements, requesting facultative coverage, sending underwriting advice and information, checking agreements for details of implementation, calculating the amount of coverage to be ceded or assumed on a particular case or a group of cases, calculating premium and claim amounts due and paid, producing numerous reports on all sorts of administrative transactions, and checking the quality of every aspect of reinsurance operations—these activities demand rapid, accurate information in a form that can be collected, organized, corrected, modified, and communicated to those who need it.

An **information system** is an interactive combination of technology, people, and processes that collects, manipulates, and disseminates information. A **management information system** (**MIS**) provides information about a company's daily operations and helps employees and managers make decisions and control activities. An MIS allows the system user to request reports with the level of detail appropriate to the user's needs.

Information system technologies—such as word processing and spreadsheet software and database management systems—allow reinsurance analysts to organize, analyze, and report information in almost any configuration desired. Reinsurers in particular need flexible, sophisticated systems to manipulate and report data related to a variety of products provided by a large number of direct writers, each of which has its own information system.

Information technology (**IT**) is the insurance company unit that develops and maintains the company's information systems and oversees information management throughout the company. Setting up and preserving electronic files and records, managing databases, and establishing electronic communications within and outside an insurance company are essential activities of the IT unit.

In some companies, the IT unit also (1) helps to set up and modify decision-making, management reporting, and strategic planning systems for reinsurance, (2) provides technical assistance in evaluating, selecting, implementing, and revising computer-based technologies, and (3) works with reinsurance analysts to interpret and translate electronic data transferred between companies. Further, the IT unit may train staff on how to use the company's information systems to perform reinsurance-related tasks.

Two types of information technology that play major roles in reinsurance are telecommunications and document management systems. The widespread use of such technologies has led direct writers and reinsurers to increase their use of security measures to protect the confidentiality and integrity of their information.

Telecommunications

Telecommunications is the electronic transmission of communication signals that enables organizations to link computer systems into effective networks. A ***network*** is a group of interconnected computers and computer devices, including the telecommunications equipment and computer programming that connect them. Telecommunications technology allows networks to be established among computers that are within close proximity—such as in the same room—or that are in different places around the world. Telecommunications and networks have numerous business applications for reinsurance administration, including voicemail and electronic mail. Telecommunications systems also make electronic data interchange and electronic commerce possible.

Electronic Data Interchange

Electronic data interchange (***EDI***) is the computer-to-computer exchange of data between organizations using a data format agreed upon by the sending and receiving parties. Organizations that agree to exchange data through EDI are called *trading partners* and are said to be part of an *EDI network*. The primary purpose of an EDI network is to allow an organization to transmit data directly from its computers to the computers of other organizations on the network for processing by those organizations. For large amounts of data, EDI generally is a more efficient and cost-effective way of transmitting data than paper documents, tapes, or computer disks.

Direct writers and reinsurers use EDI to transmit data to and from

- Units within each company

- Each other

- Consumer reporting agencies

- MIB

- Reinsurance intermediaries and other providers of reinsurance services

Electronic Commerce

Electronic commerce (***e-commerce***) is the use of the Internet and other computer networks to deliver commercial information and to facilitate business transactions and the delivery of products and services. E-commerce eliminates some of the limitations of traditional commerce, because e-commerce can take place at any time of day and between businesses and people around the world. E-commerce also can increase the speed and decrease the cost of performing certain business activities.

The primary difference between EDI and e-commerce is that EDI involves the transfer of a batch of data—that is, unprocessed facts—to another organization for processing, and e-commerce involves exchanges of information—data that has already been converted into a useful form—back and forth for the purpose of conducting a transaction, performing a service, or solving a problem.

An important application of e-commerce for the reinsurance industry is ***business-to-business (B2B) e-commerce***, which is the electronic transmission of data or information between organizations to perform or facilitate business transactions. B2B e-commerce for reinsurance often involves communication and transactions between

- Direct writers and reinsurers

- Reinsurance parties and reinsurance intermediaries

- Reinsurance parties and vendors, such as consumer reporting agencies

- Reinsurance parties and other financial institutions, such as banks

- Reinsurance parties and regulatory bodies

Document Management Systems

A ***document management system*** is a technology that stores, organizes, and retrieves documents that have been (1) created electronically and converted to digital images by computer or (2) created on paper and converted to digital images through imaging. ***Imaging***, or *scanning*, is a process of converting printed characters or graphics into digital images by using a device called a scanner. The scanner "reads" the characters and graphics on the document and "translates" them into an electronic file, which is then converted to digital images and stored in an information system. After documents are stored in a document management system, document users can search for, view, print, and share the documents by computer. However, most imaging systems do not permit document users to make changes to the digital images.

Document management systems help the reinsurance parties avoid the expense and complicated logistics of having to store and retrieve many thousands or even millions of paper documents. In addition, such systems can increase efficiency, as direct writer and reinsurer employees never have to wait for a paper document to be pulled from a paper file. Document management systems reduce the frustration, delays, and wasted time that result from lost and misfiled paper documents. In addition, these systems facilitate information sharing because several employees in different locations can view the same document at the same time on their computer screens.

Security for Information Systems

Direct writers and reinsurers maintain a great deal of sensitive financial, medical, and personal information about policyowners, insureds, beneficiaries, and other customers. A company's information systems also contain proprietary information belonging to the company and to its reinsurance partners. To protect the valuable information in their information systems, companies must establish security measures. In this context, *security* refers to the physical, technical, and procedural steps a company takes to prevent the loss, wrongful disclosure (accidental or intentional), or theft of information. Many security measures are designed to limit who can use an information system, how the system can be used, and which application programs can be run on the system. For example, access to some information systems and databases is restricted to certain authorized employees. These employees are given appropriate passwords and other procedures that allow them access to the system or database.

Companies that have established their own Internet Web sites limit the public's access to their internal computer systems by installing firewalls. A *firewall* is a combination of computer equipment and programming that creates an electronic barrier between the public and private areas of a company's systems. Only those Web site visitors who know the appropriate security procedures can access the areas beyond the firewall.

The main security measure used by direct writers and reinsurers to protect data and information traveling over a computer network from unauthorized access is *encryption*, which is a technology that encodes data and information so that only an authorized person possessing the required computer equipment and/or programming can decode the data. Another security option used to safeguard data and information carried over the Internet is a *virtual private network* (*VPN*), which is a secure computer network that uses computer equipment and/or programming to act as a "tunnel" through the Internet so that only people in possession of the required technology have access to data and information traveling through the network.

Computer viruses present another significant threat to information security. A *computer virus* is a computer program that attaches itself to other programs and activates itself, often destroying data and programs or disabling computers in the infected system. A virus can severely impair an information system, so direct writers and reinsurers routinely use *antivirus software*, which is a computer application that detects viruses and works to prevent them from infecting a computer and/or helps an infected computer recover.

Another component of information systems security is the duplication of critical data in case the company's original data records are damaged or destroyed by a virus or a fire, flood, or other disaster. To protect the back-up data records from disasters that strike their offices, companies often store these duplicate records in a different location.

Key Terms

marketing

reinsurance marketing officer

agency

principal

agent

actuary

law department

compliance unit

accounting

reinsurance recoverables

financial accounting

management accounting

audit

claim administration

consumer reporting agency

consumer credit report

inspection report

MIB Group, Inc. (MIB)

information system

management information system (MIS)

information technology (IT)

telecommunications

network

electronic data interchange (EDI)

electronic commerce (e-commerce)

business-to-business (B2B) e-commerce

document management system

imaging

security

firewall

encryption

virtual private network (VPN)

computer virus

antivirus software

Endnotes

1. This chapter represents a revision of material from Jane Lightcap Brown and Jennifer W. Herrod, *Reinsurance Administration* (Atlanta: LOMA, © 2000), 55–75. Used with permission; all rights reserved.

2. Much of this section is adapted from Mark Adel and Nicholas L. Desoutter, *Annuity Systems and Administration*, 2nd ed. (Atlanta: LOMA, © 2004), 185–186, 199, and 202–203 and Miriam Orsina and Gene Stone, *Insurance Company Operations*, 2nd ed. (Atlanta: LOMA, © 2005), 219, 309, 315–319, and 322–323. Used with permission; all rights reserved.

CHAPTER

10

Administering New Business

After studying this chapter, you should be able to

- Describe the activities involved in preplacement and placement of reinsurance coverage

- Describe how a reinsurer reviews a request for facultative reinsurance

- Identify appropriate new business records for reinsurance and explain the process for establishing those records

- Explain the process of reserving capacity for requested coverage

- Explain how the process for placing individual new business cessions differs for automatic reinsurance and facultative or fac-ob reinsurance

OUTLINE

Preplacement of Reinsurance

Reviewing a Request for Coverage

Establishing Records and Reserving Capacity

Following Up on Reserved Capacity

Placement of Reinsurance

Facultative and Fac-Ob Cessions

Automatic Cessions

R einsurance admini- stration starts when the direct writer seeks re- insurance for a risk and lasts until the reinsurance is no longer in force.

Reinsurance administration includes all of the day-to-day activities conducted by the direct writer and the reinsurer to process and manage each risk that the direct writer cedes automatically or submits for facultative consideration. Reinsurance administration starts when the direct writer seeks reinsurance for a risk and lasts until the reinsurance is no longer in force. In Chapters 10 and 11, we discuss the administration of indemnity reinsurance arrangements between a direct writer and reinsurer that have entered into a reinsurance agreement.

Reinsurance administration can involve three or all four of the following stages:

- In the *preplacement stage*, the reinsurer reviews the direct writer's request for facultative or fac-ob reinsurance coverage and either offers to reinsure the risk or declines it. If the reinsurer decides to offer coverage, it establishes a reservation for the capacity needed to reinsure the case. As we discuss later in this chapter, preplacement typically is not necessary for automatic reinsurance cessions.

- In the *placement stage*, also known as the submission stage, the direct writer and reinsurer activate reinsurance for automatic, fac-ob, and facultative cessions.

- In the *in-force stage*, the direct writer pays the reinsurance premiums to the reinsurer to keep the coverage in force. The reinsurance parties make adjustments to the reinsurance coverage as changes are made to the reinsured policies. The reinsurer receives claim notices from the direct writer, examines the claims, approves or rejects the claims, and settles valid claims.

- In the *termination stage*, the direct writer notifies the reinsurer of any terminations of reinsured policies, and the reinsurer processes the termination of reinsurance on each case. Termination of reinsurance typically occurs as a result of the payment of a death claim, the lapse or surrender of a reinsured policy, or the recapture of risk on a reinsured policy by the direct writer.

Figure 10.1 summarizes these activities. In this chapter, we describe the first two of the stages in reinsurance administration: the preplacement and placement stages.[1] Chapter 11 addresses the administration activities involved in the final two stages of reinsurance administration: the in-force and termination stages. Because reinsurance administration can vary greatly from one reinsurance agreement to another and from one company to another, the procedures described in this text may be somewhat different from the procedures that your company uses.

Preplacement of Reinsurance

Preplacement is the process by which a reinsurer (1) reviews a direct writer's request for coverage, (2) establishes appropriate records and reserves capacity for the case, and (3) follows up on reservations for capacity that have been inactive for a specified period of time. **Reserved capacity** is the portion of a reinsurer's capacity that the reinsurer sets aside to fund its financial obligations under the anticipated new business. The preplacement process begins when a direct writer requests

---

FIGURE 10.1

Life Cycle of a Reinsurance Case

Preplacement
Reinsurer evaluates case and either offers or declines coverage

Placement
Reinsurer and direct writer activate reinsurance

In-force
Direct writer pays reinsurance premiums; direct writer and/or reinsurer make adjustments to reinsurance; and reinsurer administers claims on reinsured policies

Termination
Direct writer notifies reinsurer when a reinsured policy has been terminated, and reinsurer manages the termination of reinsurance

Source: Adapted from Jane Lightcap Brown and Jennifer W. Herrod, *Reinsurance Administration* (Atlanta: LOMA, © 2000), 164. Used with permission; all rights reserved.

---

coverage, and it continues until either (1) the reinsurance coverage begins, (2) the reinsurer denies the direct writer's request for coverage, or (3) the direct writer withdraws its request for coverage.

As a general rule, preplacement is required only for facultative and fac-ob cases. Preplacement typically is not necessary for automatic cases because the direct writer and the reinsurer have agreed in advance that the direct writer will place certain types of risk with the reinsurer. Thus, administration of automatic reinsurance generally begins at the placement stage. Note that all reinsurance cases, regardless of the basis of submission, go through the stages of placement, in-force administration, and termination.

Preplacement allows the reinsurer to

■ Verify that the request for reinsurance complies with the agreement it has entered into with the direct writer

■ Determine its capacity available to provide the requested coverage

■ Assess the risk

■ Arrange retrocession, if necessary

In this section, we describe how reinsurers perform each of these activities.

Reviewing a Request for Coverage

Under facultative and fac-ob reinsurance agreements, the direct writer requests reinsurance coverage on a particular insured or group of insureds by sending the reinsurer a document known as a ***request for coverage*** or *facultative application*. Figure 10.2 shows an example of a request for coverage. When a reinsurer receives a request for coverage, the reinsurer dates the request, reviews it to ensure it contains all required information, and requests any missing information from the direct writer. When the reinsurer receives all of the required information, the reinsurer establishes the appropriate records.

FIGURE 10.2

Example of a Request for Coverage

Request for Reinsurance

To: Joel Guildan, Syracuse Reinsurance Company

From: Kelly Dawson

Date: 1/19/2005

Name: Tattersall, Marc T.   **Age:** 54   **Sex:** M

Date and Place of Birth: 12/6/1950, NY

Residence: 2247 Main St., East Dalton, NY

Insurance applied for: $500,000 in USD

Insurance retained: $200,000

Reinsurance requested: $300,000

Total insurance in force or applied for with us: $1,000,000

Rating: 100.00 standard

Please reserve your maximum and advise amount. No aviation or avocation concerns. Related papers are enclosed.

Regards,

Kelly Dawson

Kelly Dawson
(555) 555-5555 Fax (555) 555-5556

Source: Adapted from Jane Lightcap Brown and Jennifer W. Herrod, *Reinsurance Administration* (Atlanta: LOMA, 2000), 166. Used with permission; all rights reserved.

For facultative cases, sending a request for coverage to a reinsurer does not guarantee that the direct writer will cede the case to that reinsurer. The direct writer may be *shopping*—that is, submitting cases facultatively to several reinsurers to obtain the best reinsurance coverage for the most competitive price. Thus, sometimes a reinsurer performs preplacement for a case that the direct writer eventually places with another reinsurer. If a direct writer decides not to accept the offered reinsurance coverage, the direct writer either notifies the reinsurer so that the reinsurer can cancel the reservation of capacity or allows the reservation to automatically expire after the date specified in the reinsurer's preplacement offer.

Reinsurance agreements sometimes include time limits to protect a direct writer from the risk resulting from a reinsurer's failure to respond to a request for coverage in a timely manner. However, reinsurers reply to requests for facultative coverage as promptly as possible—usually within two business days—to compete for reinsurance business.

- Typically, a reinsurance agreement for facultative business specifies a maximum number of days the reinsurer has to respond to a request for coverage.

- A reinsurance agreement for fac-ob reinsurance may state that, if the reinsurer does not respond to a request for coverage within a specified time limit, then the direct writer can assume that reinsurance on the policy will take effect.

Establishing Records and Reserving Capacity

A reinsurer establishes a case file for each submitted case. This case file helps the reinsurer

- Track its progress toward placing the case
- Avoid exceeding its own retention limits and the retention limits of its retrocessionaires
- Place a case more quickly after reserving capacity

Reinsurers use status codes—such as those listed in Figure 10.3—to enable them to track the current status of each case. The status code terminology varies from one reinsurer to another. Also, note that some of these codes—*replaced*, *claim*, *paid*, and *terminated*—apply to in-force business rather than to new business.

Example: When a reinsurer makes an offer on a facultative case, the reinsurer codes the case's status as *pending*. If the direct writer subsequently sends a cession, the reinsurer updates the case's status to *placed*, showing that the reinsurance is in force. Alternatively, if the direct writer places the case with another reinsurer, the reinsurer changes the case file's status from *pending* to *not taken*.

In the process of establishing case files and reserving capacity, the reinsurer performs the following activities, which may not always occur in the sequence shown:

- Comparing the request for coverage to the reinsurance agreement
- Checking the reinsurer's retention and financial capacity
- Assessing the risk
- Arranging retrocession as needed
- Placing the reservation of capacity

FIGURE 10.3

Sample Status Codes

- **Reserved** — The reinsurer has set aside reinsurance capacity.

- **Waiting** — The reinsurer has requested additional information from the direct writer. Also known as *pending underwriting* or *outstanding requirements*.

- **Pending** — The reinsurer has made an offer on a facultative case and is waiting for a response from the direct writer.

- **Placed** — The direct writer has ceded the case to the reinsurer. Also known as *active*, *premium paying*, or *in-force*.

- **Declined** — The reinsurer has declined the facultative case.

- **Not Taken** — The direct writer has not accepted the reinsurer's facultative offer. Also known as *withdrawn*.

- **Replaced** — The policyowner has replaced the original policy with or converted the original policy to a different policy.

- **Claim** — The direct writer has notified the reinsurer of a claim filed under the reinsured policy.

- **Paid** — The reinsurer has paid a claim under the reinsured coverage.

- **Terminated** — The policy has lapsed, been surrendered, or otherwise ceased being reinsured.

Source: Adapted from Jane Lightcap Brown and Jennifer W. Herrod, *Reinsurance Administration* (Atlanta: LOMA, © 2000), 167. Used with permission; all rights reserved.

Comparing the Request for Coverage to the Reinsurance Agreement

The reinsurer verifies that the direct writer and reinsurer have a reinsurance agreement for the type of coverage requested and that the agreement is in effect for new business. A direct writer may have many reinsurance agreements in effect with a reinsurer, and each agreement may have different specifications and cover different types of policies. As a result, the reinsurer may need to check extensively to ensure that the reinsurer assigns coverage for a case under the correct agreement.

After locating the correct agreement, the reinsurer determines the types and amounts of reinsurance, if any, it is obligated to provide to the direct writer under that agreement and evaluates whether the request for coverage meets all of the agreement's requirements for risks to be reinsured. These requirements may include

- Age limits and residency requirements for the insured

- The plan of insurance or type of risk

- The amount of coverage to be ceded

- The currency in which the business under the agreement will be transacted

- The underwriting basis of the policy to be reinsured

The term ***underwriting basis*** refers to the amount and type of medical information that the direct writer gathers about a proposed insured to assess the risk the person presents. The four bases for individual life insurance underwriting are medical, paramedical, nonmedical, and guaranteed issue.

- For underwriting on a ***medical basis***, the direct writer has a physician perform a medical examination of the proposed insured and record the results of the examination and the proposed insured's answers to health-related questions on a medical report. The medical report then becomes part of the insurance application. Underwriting on a medical basis often includes specific types of medical tests on the proposed insured, such as laboratory analysis of a blood sample, a chest X-ray, and/or an electrocardiogram (ECG)—a graphic recording of the electrical forces produced by the heart to screen for disease or an abnormality of the heart.

- For underwriting on a ***paramedical basis***, the direct writer has a paramedical examiner perform specified physical examinations of the proposed insured and record the proposed insured's answers to health-related questions on a paramedical report. Although the proposed insured's answers to the health-related questions become part of the insurance application, the physical examination results do not. A paramedical report is much less extensive and less expensive for the direct writer to obtain than a medical report.

- For underwriting on a ***nonmedical basis***, an insurance producer or an underwriter records the proposed insured's answers to a series of health history questions on a nonmedical supplement form, which then becomes part of the insurance application. The proposed insured does not undergo any type of physical examination or medical tests.

- For insurance products offered on a ***guaranteed-issue basis***, the direct writer does not conduct individual underwriting and automatically issues a policy to every eligible proposed insured who applies and meets specified conditions. Eligibility requirements for guaranteed-issue products typically concern the proposed insured's age and the amount of coverage already in force with the direct writer.

If the reinsurer finds an applicable reinsurance agreement and the request for coverage complies with the terms of the agreement, the reinsurer notes on the request the number of the applicable agreement and any related pricing information, such as underwriting classification or mortality rating.

If a reinsurance agreement exists, but the request for coverage does not comply exactly with the agreement, the reinsurer notifies the direct writer so that it can revise the request. If no agreement exists, the reinsurer consults with its pricing actuaries and underwriting staff to determine if the reinsurer can offer the direct writer a reinsurance agreement or a special quote under an existing agreement.

Verifying Retention

The reinsurer checks the amount of its current retention on the insured and, if applicable, the amount of its corporate retention on the insured, to verify that it can provide the requested coverage and to identify cases that may require the reinsurer to retrocede part or all of the risk. Some reinsurers routinely use a retention check form like the one shown in Figure 10.4. A completed retention check form contains the following information:

- The amount of reinsurance applied for in the request for coverage

FIGURE 10.4

A Retention Check Form

Line of Business: Life

Location	Amount in U.S. Dollars	Ceded	Amount in U.S. Dollars
Reinsurer's In Force		Retro/Pool Amount	
Reinsurer's Pending		Excess of Retro/Pool	
Total Pending and In Force ...		Total Ceded	
Confirmed With			
Parent Company In Force		Retro/Pool Amount	
Parent Company Pending		Excess of Retro/Pool	
Confirmed With			
Grand Total In Force & Pending ...		Grand Total Ceded	

Current Application to Reinsurer — **Amount**

Amount Applied For ....
Reinsurer Amount Available ....
Retro/Pool Amount Available ....

Date Checked: _____ By: _____

Source: Adapted from Jane Lightcap Brown and Jennifer W. Herrod, *Reinsurance Administration* (Atlanta: LOMA, © 2000), 170. Used with permission; all rights reserved.

- The amount of reinsurance already in force with the reinsurer on the insured

- The amount of insurance or reinsurance already in force on the insured with any companies affiliated with the reinsurer

- Any amounts that the reinsurer or its affiliates may have ceded to retrocessionaires or retrocession pools

- The amounts of reinsurance available from the reinsurer and its retrocessionaires and retrocession pools on cases of the type being evaluated

The completed retention check form becomes part of the case file.

To complete the retention check form, the reinsurer searches its alpha files using the name, sex, and date of birth of the insured. A reinsurer's **alpha file** is a database that contains information about the amount of reinsurance currently in force and applied for on all insureds, organized by insureds' last names.

The reinsurer then compares the amount of risk already retained on an insured to the retention limits listed in its retention schedules to determine the amount of additional risk it can accept on that case and, if necessary, the amount of risk to cede to a retrocessionaire. Some reinsurance administration information systems automatically perform these calculations for the reinsurer. The calculation of the amount to be retroceded on a case includes the following steps:

■ Determine the amount of in-force coverage on the insured provided by the reinsurer and other affiliated insurers. Add all the in-force coverage to determine the total reinsurance coverage carried on the insured.

■ Review applicable reinsurer and corporate retention schedules for the maximum retention amount allowed for the case.

■ Determine the available corporate retention by subtracting the total in-force coverage from the corporate retention limit. Also, determine the reinsurer's available retention by subtracting the reinsurer's in-force coverage from the reinsurer's retention limit. The lesser of the available corporate retention and the reinsurer's available retention becomes the amount that the reinsurer will retain.

■ Subtract the amount that the reinsurer will retain from the amount applied for to determine the amount, if any, that will be retroceded.

Figure 10.5 reviews this calculation process.

Example: Robert Epstein, a reinsurance analyst at Fairmont Reinsurance, wants to determine the amount that Fairmont Re should retrocede on a request for $2 million in reinsurance coverage from Pickering Insurance Company on the life of Kayla Bruce, a highly paid entertainer. Mr. Epstein checks the Fairmont Re alpha file and discovers that Fairmont Re is currently reinsuring Ms. Bruce's life for $1 million. In addition, Fairmont Re's parent company, Spring Creek Insurance Company, has insured Ms. Bruce for $4.5 million. Mr. Epstein calculates that the total risk—Fairmont Re's in-force risk plus Spring Creek's in-force risk—carried on Ms. Bruce is $5.5 million.

$$\$1,000,000 + \$4,500,000 = \$5,500,000$$

According to the retention schedules established for cases with risk characteristics like those of Ms. Bruce's case, Mr. Epstein determines that Fairmont Re's retention limit is $3 million per life and Spring Creek's corporate retention limit is $6 million per life. Mr. Epstein calculates that the corporate retention available—corporate retention limit minus total in-force risk on Ms. Bruce—is $500,000.

$$\$6,000,000 - \$5,500,000 = \$500,000$$

Mr. Epstein also calculates Fairmont Re's available retention—Fairmont Re's retention limit minus Fairmont Re's reinsurance in force on Ms. Bruce—as $2 million.

$$\$3,000,000 - \$1,000,000 = \$2,000,000$$

By identifying the lesser of the available corporate retention and Fairmont Re's available retention, Mr. Epstein determines that Fairmont Re can retain only $500,000 and, thus, must retrocede $1.5 million of the requested coverage.

$2,000,000 requested – $500,000 retained = $1,500,000 to be retroceded

Assessing the Risk

The first step in assessing a reinsurance risk is determining whether the case requires an underwriting decision. Facultative cases typically require underwriting approval from the reinsurer. Although reinsurance analysts do not assess reinsurance risks, a reinsurance analyst may be responsible for collecting the required underwriting documents and information, organizing those

FIGURE 10.5

Calculation of Amounts to be Retroceded

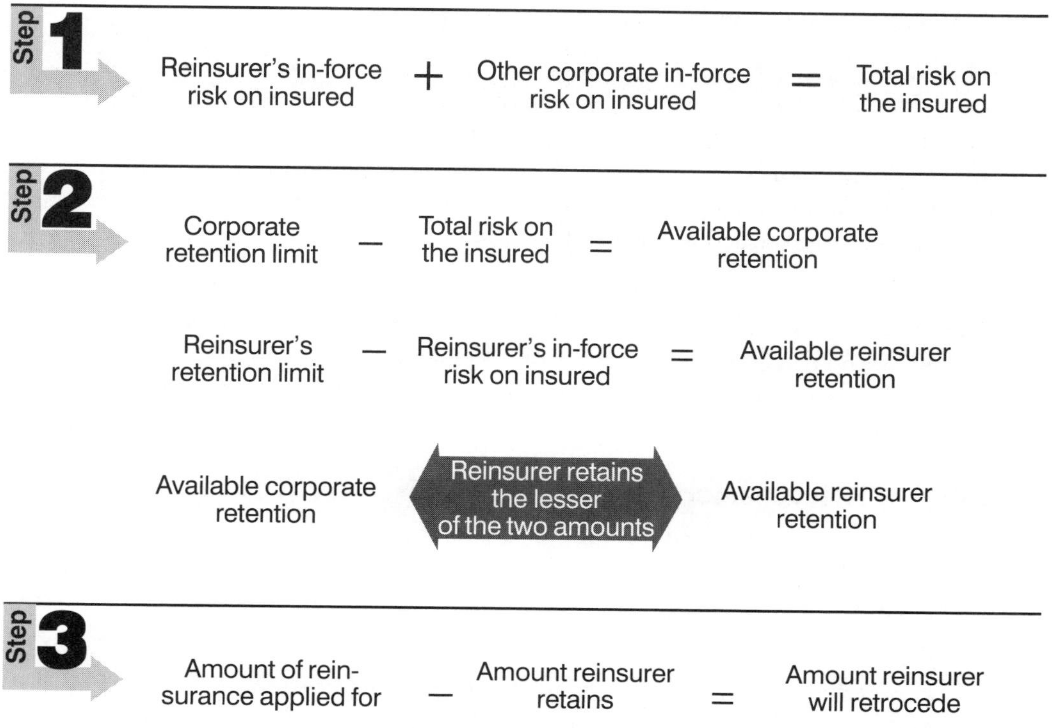

Step 1
Reinsurer's in-force risk on insured + Other corporate in-force risk on insured = Total risk on the insured

Step 2
Corporate retention limit − Total risk on the insured = Available corporate retention

Reinsurer's retention limit − Reinsurer's in-force risk on insured = Available reinsurer retention

Available corporate retention → Reinsurer retains the lesser of the two amounts ← Available reinsurer retention

Step 3
Amount of reinsurance applied for − Amount reinsurer retains = Amount reinsurer will retrocede

documents appropriately in a case file, and referring the file to the reinsurer's underwriters. If any information is missing from the case file, the reinsurance analyst requests the needed information from the direct writer and codes the file as *waiting* until the reinsurer receives all appropriate documents. If the reinsurer previously has declined, dropped, or rated a case or placed that case in force, then the reinsurance analyst attaches files from the previous decision to the current case file.

For each case submitted on a facultative basis, the reinsurer's underwriters evaluate the underwriting documents that the direct writer sends with the request for coverage and decide whether to make an offer, decline the case, or ask the direct writer to provide additional information. This evaluation and decision-making process sometimes is called *facultative reinsurance underwriting*. When a direct writer submits a facultative case to a reinsurance pool, one reinsurer in the pool often acts as the lead reinsurer and performs the underwriting process on behalf of all the pool members.

The reinsurer's underwriter notifies the direct writer of the decision to accept or decline the facultative case. If the underwriter declines the case, the reinsurance analyst or the underwriter changes the status of the case file to *declined*. If the direct writer ever presents the case to the reinsurer again, the underwriter handling the resubmitted case can use the stored case file to learn the circumstances of the previous request.

Typically, a case file includes two types of underwriting-related documents: (1) documents received from the direct writer and (2) documents generated by the reinsurer's information systems. Figure 10.6 provides a list of underwriting-related documents often included in an individual life reinsurance case file. An individual health reinsurance case file includes similar information, plus information on family members covered under the policy to be reinsured.

A reinsurance case file for a group life or health insurance case includes information about the proposed insured group, such as the group's name, size, location, and industry; the scope of coverage; the basis for determining the amount of coverage for each individual; and each group member's sex, date of birth, and salary. Disability income reinsurance case files are similar to life cases for either individuals or groups. However, disability income reinsurance case files also indicate the proposed insured's occupation.

In North America, case files often include information obtained from MIB. Each MIB-member reinsurer has guidelines for obtaining MIB reports. Many reinsurers require MIB reports for all cases underwritten on a medical basis. Other reinsurers may require MIB reports for facultative cases, for fac-ob cases in which retrocessionaires will be used, or for insureds who are over a certain age—for example, 65—or for whom a particularly large amount of reinsurance has been requested.

Arranging Retrocession

Most reinsurers have established multiple automatic and/or fac-ob retrocession arrangements with professional retrocessionaires, other reinsurers, or retrocession pools. A **retrocession pool**, also called a *retro pool*, is a group of two or more professional retrocessionaires or reinsurers that jointly reinsure retroceded risks.

If the amount that the reinsurer needs to retrocede exceeds the amount covered by the reinsurer's established retrocession arrangements, the reinsurer generally refers the case to one of its underwriters. The underwriter examines the case and makes one of four decisions:

■ To pursue retrocession coverage outside the reinsurer's established retrocession arrangements

---

FIGURE 10.6

Underwriting-Related Documents
Often Included in a Case File

Documents Provided by the Direct Writer

- Cover page containing information about the insured and the reinsurance applied for, including the insured's name, residence, date of birth, and underwriting classification, and amount of reinsurance
- Letter from the direct writer to the reinsurer
- Insurance application
- Nonmedical declaration
- Nonmedical questionnaires, such as questionnaires for aviation, scuba diving, and so forth
- Medical questionnaires, such as questionnaires for asthma, tobacco use, and so forth
- Medical or paramedical reports
- Laboratory and x-ray reports
- Physicians' and hospitals' reports
- Results of an electrocardiogram
- Inspection report
- Statements describing the insured's financial position
- Motor vehicle records/driving history
- Correspondence with the proposed insured, applicant, medical personnel, and so forth
- Documentation that the direct writer has confirmed that the insurance applicant is not included on any applicable government lists of suspected terrorists

Documents Generated by the Reinsurer

- Reinsurer's underwriting worksheet
- Documentation of the retention check
- Status code documentation
- Decisions sent to the direct writer and worksheets compiled by reinsurance analysts
- Documentation that the reinsurer has confirmed that the insurance applicant is not included on any applicable government lists of suspected terrorists

Source: Adapted from Jane Lightcap Brown and Jennifer W. Herrod, *Reinsurance Administration* (Atlanta: LOMA, © 2000), 177. Used with permission; all rights reserved.

- To ask retrocessionaires or retro pool members to increase the amount they are willing to accept facultatively

- To accept a smaller amount of the risk and notify the direct writer to seek additional reinsurance

- To decline to reinsure the case (for facultative and fac-ob cases only)

Pursuing Coverage Outside Established Retrocession Arrangements

Each reinsurer sets its own guidelines for arranging retrocession outside its standard retrocession arrangements. Such guidelines may specify that the reinsurer will approach retrocessionaires or retro pools that charge lower retrocession premium rates or provide faster service before approaching those that charge higher rates or provide slower service. Based on those guidelines and the insurance product involved, the underwriter specifies which retrocessionaires or retro pools to approach. The reinsurer sends requests for coverage to one or more retrocessionaires or retro pools and records the requests in the case file. When a retrocessionaire or retro pool responds with an offer, the reinsurer's underwriter determines if the reinsurer should accept the offer. The reinsurer then notifies the chosen retrocessionaire or retro pool of the underwriter's decision. When the reinsurer receives the cession from the direct writer, the reinsurer (1) updates the reinsurance administration system to show the placement of the new business and (2) notifies the retrocessionaire or pool of the *placed* retrocession.

Asking Retrocessionaires or Retro Pool Members to Increase Coverage

To request that retrocessionaires or retro pool members accept additional coverage on a facultative basis, the reinsurer sends a copy of the underwriting file to each retrocessionaire or retro pool member or to a pool leader authorized to make a decision on behalf of the pool members. The reinsurer records any offers for increased coverage in the case file. After the reinsurer has received all of the offers from the retrocessionaires or pool members, the reinsurer's underwriter decides which offers, if any, to accept. The reinsurer notifies the retrocessionaires or retro pool members in writing of its decision to accept or decline their offers.

Accepting a Smaller Amount of the Risk

If the underwriter determines that the reinsurer can accept only a portion of the risk to be ceded, the reinsurer's offer of coverage to the direct writer specifies the amount of the risk the reinsurer will reinsure. The direct writer then has the following options:

- Accept the reinsurer's offer and find coverage for the remainder of the risk by accepting other reinsurers' offers as well

- Decline the reinsurer's offer and seek reinsurance elsewhere

- Retain the entire risk

- Decline to issue the policy

Declining to Reinsure the Case

If the reinsurer decides not to offer coverage on a case, the reinsurer notifies the direct writer of that decision.

Placing the Reservation

If the reinsurer offers to reinsure the case, the reinsurer updates the reinsurance administration information system to reflect the offer and codes the status of the file as *reserved*. This reserved status holds the required capacity for a specified period. The reinsurer assigns the reservation a **date of expiry**—the date on which the reinsurer will cancel the reservation of reinsurance capacity if the reinsurer does not receive a cession or other placement information from the direct writer.

Typically, the date of expiry falls between 90 and 120 days after the date the reservation was made.

Following Up on Reserved Capacity

To keep the maximum capacity available at all times, reinsurers periodically check for reservations that are approaching or have reached their dates of expiry. Follow-up on reserved capacity for facultative submissions helps the reinsurer avoid maintaining reserved capacity that the direct writer does not need. Most reinsurance administration information systems generate lists of outstanding cases—cases for which the direct writer has not sent a cession, a drop notice, or an extension request—that will soon reach their dates of expiry.

■ A **drop notice**, or *close notice*, is a written notification from a direct writer to a reinsurer stating that the direct writer no longer needs reinsurance that it previously requested and asking the reinsurer to cancel the reservation.

■ An **extension request** is a request from a direct writer to a reinsurer to extend the direct writer's reservation of capacity for a specified period so that the direct writer can gather all information needed to move the case from *reserved* to *placed* status.

To follow up on reserved capacity, the reinsurer sends a notice of expiry to each direct writer that has outstanding cases with offers that are due to expire soon. A **notice of expiry** is a document the reinsurer uses to notify the direct writer that an offer to reinsure is due to expire and to request additional information, a cession, a drop notice, or an extension request from the direct writer.

The direct writer marks on the notice of expiry the status of each case listed and returns the notice to the reinsurer, along with any cessions, drop notices, requests for extensions, or requested information. The response from the direct writer allows the reinsurer to take the appropriate action for each case, as follows:

■ If the direct writer no longer requires reinsurance, the reinsurer can release the reserved capacity to make it available for other cases

■ If the direct writer wants to keep the file open and maintain the reservation of capacity, an underwriter must approve the extension of the expiry date

■ If the direct writer intends to send a cession, the reinsurer maintains the reservation of capacity until the cession arrives

Placement of Reinsurance

Placement is a process in which the direct writer and reinsurer activate reinsurance coverage for a new automatic, facultative, or fac-ob cession. Reinsurers generally receive new business from direct writers in one of three ways:

■ Paper cession forms

■ Self-administered lists

■ Diskettes, tapes, or electronic data transfer

Regardless of the way the direct writer transmits new business, a reinsurer generally requires the direct writer to provide it with specified information. Figure 10.7 identifies the information that reinsurers typically require from a direct writer for cession of coverage on an individual life insurance policy.

After receiving a new business cession, the reinsurer (1) reviews the cession, (2) updates the reinsurance administration information system, and (3) sends reinsurance certificates as necessary. The purpose of reviewing the cession is to ensure appropriate and timely handling of the cession. The reinsurer documents the date on which the cession was received and compares the cession with the case file to verify the underwriting basis of the cession.

The reinsurer may send the direct writer a **reinsurance certificate**, which is a document that notifies the direct writer that reinsurance is officially in force. Reinsurers generally send reinsurance certificates only for individual cession reinsurance and not for self- or bulk-administered reinsurance. Figure 10.8 shows an example of a reinsurance certificate.

FIGURE 10.7

Information Required in a New Business Cession for an Individual Life Insurance Policy

- Full name of insured
- Date of birth
- Issue age
- Issue date (for self-administered reinsurance)
- Age basis (last or nearest birthday)
- Sex
- Residence
- Underwriting classification
- Tobacco use/nonuse
- Policy number
- Effective date of policy
- Face amount of policy
- Plan name or code (with a reference list)
- Automatic/facultative indicator
- YRT/coinsurance indicator

- Amount ceded to reinsurer, separated by primary coverage, waiver of premium, accidental death benefit, and so on
- Reinsurance premiums, separated by primary coverage, waiver of premium, accidental death benefit, and so on (for self-administered reinsurance)
- Annual waived premium, if any
- Amount of any allowances (for self-administered reinsurance)
- Extra premium (e.g., $5/1000/5 years) or underwriting rating
- Net amount at risk for the first five years, if not level
- Currency in which reinsurance records will be kept
- Effective date of reinsurance, if different from policy effective date

Source: Adapted from Jane Lightcap Brown and Jennifer W. Herrod, *Reinsurance Administration* (Atlanta: LOMA, © 2000), 183. Used with permission; all rights reserved.

FIGURE 10.8

A Reinsurance Certificate

POLICY NUMBER

CESSION NUMBER

TRANSACTION TYPE

EFFECTIVE DATE

NAME OF INSURED(S)	SEX	S/NS	DATE OF BIRTH	PLACE OF BIRTH	AGE

AGREEMENT NUMBER

PLAN OF PRINCIPAL POLICY	PRELIMINARY TERM	ISSUE DATE	U/W YEAR	RESIDENCY	CURRENCY	ESA	YRT/COINS	AUTO/FAC

	LIFE				
REINSURED AMOUNT					
EXTRA PREMIUM					
RATING					
INIITAL GROSS PREMIUM					
PREMIUM TO BE WAIVED/MONTHLY INCOME					
PREMIUMS PAYABLE UNTIL					
TERMINATION OF COVERAGE (AGE)					

SCHEDULE

DATE	AMOUNT AT RISK	PREMIUMS				COMMISSIONS			
BEGINNING	LIFE	LIFE	CESSION FEE	EXTRAS	BENEFITS	LIFE/CESSION FEE	EXTRAS	BENEFITS	TOTAL ANN. PREMIUMS

Facultative and Fac-Ob Cessions

If a cession on an individual life insurance policy is on a facultative or fac-ob basis, the reinsurer also reconciles new cession data with the reservation data in its reinsurance administration information system. If the information system shows that the reservation has been activated, the reinsurer verifies that the reservation and the cession contain the same data for (1) the life insured's name, date of birth, residence, rating, tobacco use status, and avocations, (2) the currency to be used, and (3) the amount of reinsurance. If the reinsurer finds a discrepancy in the insured's name, date of birth, residence, rating, tobacco use status, or in the currency to be used, the reinsurer contacts the direct writer to determine the correct information. If a discrepancy exists in the amount of reinsurance, the reinsurer generally contacts the direct writer and verifies the requested amount. Then, depending on the type of reinsurance arrangement, the reinsurer takes appropriate actions to ensure the best possible match between the amount of reinsurance requested and the amount of reinsurance approved. Figure 10.9 outlines possible actions that one reinsurer generally takes to handle discrepancies in the reinsurance amount.

When any discrepancies have been resolved, the reinsurer changes the case file status from *reserved* to *placed*. This procedure may be as simple as changing a database entry from *reserved* to *placed* or making a notation in the case file. Sometimes, however, the reservation includes special instructions that require further action. The following are examples of situations that require further action:

- The reinsurer marked the case as a "special quote," which required the reinsurance analyst to enter reinsurance premium rates that differ from the reinsurer's ordinary rates into the reinsurance administration information system.

- The reinsurer indicated that the case needs further underwriting review, which required the reinsurance analyst to forward the case file and the cession to the reinsurer's underwriter.

If a facultative or fac-ob case requires retrocession of risk, the reinsurer verifies that the amount of retrocession coverage indicated on the reservation is the amount the reinsurer actually needs. If the actual amount required is less than the amount reserved, the reinsurer reduces the amount shown in the reinsurance administration information system and notifies the retrocessionaire or the retro pool of the reduction. If the reinsurer no longer needs retrocession coverage, the reinsurer deletes the retrocession amount in the information system and notifies its retrocessionaire or retro pool of this change. When the retrocession amount is accurate, the reinsurer notifies the retrocessionaire or pool when the risk is transferred. In many cases, the retrocession premium paid by the reinsurer serves as the notification to the retrocessionaire or retro pool.

Automatic Cessions

For automatic reinsurance, the reinsurer verifies that each cession is consistent with the applicable reinsurance agreement. Many reinsurers use computer-based information systems to track agreement and cession information and to check factors such as retention, plan and benefit covered, and reinsurance premium. The information system detects mistakes on automatic cessions—particularly automatic cessions reported on a self-administered list—during cession processing, audits, or claim administration. Other reinsurers check agreement compliance using a worksheet similar to the one shown in Figure 10.10.

FIGURE 10.9

Handling Discrepancies in the Reinsurance Amount

If reinsurance amount
listed on the cession is:

	If reinsurance amount listed on the cession is:	
Facultative	**Greater than the amount approved by underwriting**	If the amount on the cession is correct, refer the case to an underwriter for approval. Notify the direct writer of the underwriter's decision. If the increased amount is approved, update the information system to show the additional amount.
		If the amount on the cession is incorrect, ask the direct writer to send a corrected cession. Verify that the reservation is not due to expire and extend the expiry date if necessary.
	Less than the amount approved by underwriting	Notify the direct writer that the excess amount reserved will be released. Update the reservation on the information system to show the decreased amount.
Fac-ob	**Greater than the amount reserved and above fac-ob limits**	If the amount on the cession is correct, check the retention to determine if the requested additional capacity is available. Inform the direct writer that the request exceeds fac-ob limits and, if capacity is available, that the reinsurer will consider the case facultatively. Refer the case to an underwriter. Notify the direct writer of the underwriter's decision. If the increased amount is approved, update the information system to show the additional amount.
		If the amount on the cession is incorrect, ask the direct writer to send a corrected cession. Verify that the reservation is not due to expire and extend the expiry date if necessary.
	Greater than the amount reserved but still within fac-ob limits	Check the retention to determine if additional capacity is available. Inform the direct writer of what additional amount, if any, the reinsurer will accept.
	Less than the amount reserved	Notify the direct writer that the excess amount reserved will be released. Update the reservation on the information system to show the decreased amount.

FIGURE 10.10

Reinsurance Agreement Compliance Worksheet

Agreement code: _____ Agreement Name: _____

Effective Date
of Agreement: _____ Date Received: _____ Payment Received: _____

Life Insured	Sex	Smoking Status	Mortality Rating

Risk Level

	From Cession	Agreement States	Comments/Follow-ups
Underwriting Basis			
Client's Retention			
Age Limits			
Joint Age Calculation			
Mortality Limit			
Automatic Binding Limit			
Quota Share/Excess			
Effective Date of Agreement			
Direct/Retro			
Joint/Single Life			
Benefits Included			
Territory			

Premium Rates

Policy Year	NAAR	Expected NAAR	NAAR Matches	Expected Rate/M	Expected Premium	Expected Substd Rate	Actual Rate/M	Actual Premium	Actual Substd Rate	Premiums Match?

Allowances

Policy Year	Expected Comm Rate	Expected Comm	Expected Substd Comm Rate	Expected Substd Comm	Actual Comm Rate	Actual Comm	Actual Substd Comm Rate	Actual Substd Comm	Comm Match?

Premium Mode: _____ As per agreement? _____
Reporting Mode: _____ As per agreement? _____
Currency: _____ As per agreement? _____

The reinsurer notifies the direct writer or its own product management, reinsurance agreement, and pricing areas of any apparent inconsistencies between the agreement and the cession received so that the inconsistencies can be resolved. After correcting any discrepancies, a reinsurance analyst enters the cession information into the reinsurance administration information system.

Key Terms

reinsurance administration
preplacement
reserved capacity
request for coverage
underwriting basis
medical basis
paramedical basis
nonmedical basis
guaranteed-issue basis

alpha file
retrocession pool
date of expiry
drop notice
extension request
notice of expiry
placement
reinsurance certificate

Endnote

1. This chapter represents a revision of material from Jane Lightcap Brown and Jennifer W. Herrod, *Reinsurance Administration* (Atlanta: LOMA, © 2000), 161–185. Used with permission; all rights reserved.

CHAPTER

11

Administering In-Force Business and Terminations of Reinsurance

After studying this chapter, you should be able to

- Describe five types of reinsurance reports

- Describe the procedures followed to administer

  - Changes in reinsurance coverage
  - Reinsurance premiums and other amounts included on a billing statement
  - Policy reserves
  - Mergers and acquisitions
  - Terminations of reinsurance

- Explain the function of a claim file

- Describe the steps a reinsurer takes to examine, approve, and settle a claim submitted under a reinsured policy

- Describe how reinsurers submit claims to retrocessionaires

OUTLINE

**Administering
In-Force Business**

Reports Used to Administer
In-Force Business

Processing Changes in
Reinsurance Coverage

Processing Billing Statements

Recording Policy Reserves

Administering Mergers and
Acquisitions

**Administering
Terminations of
Reinsurance**

Administering Claims

Establishing the Claim File

Examining the Claim

Approving the Claim

Settling the Claim

Notifying Retrocessionaires of
a Claim

To provide information related to changes in risk, revenue, expenses, and policy reserves, the reporting party typically prepares five types of reports: the in-force policy report, policy exhibit, policy change report, billing statement, and reserve listing.

Chapter 11 continues our discussion of indemnity reinsurance administration by describing how reinsurers record and manage information related to changes in risk, premiums, expenses, and reserves for reinsured policies.[1] Next, we describe how reinsurers process various reinsurance-related transactions; administer changes to reinsurance coverage, premiums, and policy reserves; and administer changes resulting from mergers and acquisitions. Finally, we explain how reinsurers administer terminated policies and handle claims submitted under reinsured policies.

Administering In-Force Business

As we discussed in Chapter 5, the party administering the reinsurance records provides the information needed for in-force administration through a variety of reports. For simplicity, this chapter refers to the reinsurance party that administers the reinsurance records and reports as the *reporting party*. The reinsurance parties use the information in reinsurance reports to

- Verify that reinsurance transactions comply with the terms of the applicable reinsurance agreement

- Prepare statements and reports for financial and management accounting

- Produce policy reserve reports for various regulatory and accounting bodies

- Study lapse experience

- Detect unusual trends involving data integrity problems

- Conduct profitability and mortality studies

- Maintain historical data to use for future pricing

Reports Used to Administer In-Force Business

Although the format of reinsurance reports varies from agreement to agreement, the information included in such reports generally is the same. The reporting party typically prepares five types of reports to provide information related to changes in risk, revenue, expenses, and policy reserves. These reports are the in-force policy report, policy exhibit, policy change report, billing statement, and reserve listing.

In-Force Policy Report

An ***in-force policy report*** is a reinsurance report that lists all in-force reinsured policies as of a given date and provides detailed information about each policy. The in-force policy report allows the direct writer and reinsurer to verify that they are keeping accurate, parallel records. For self-administered reinsurance, the direct writer typically provides the report to the reinsurer monthly, quarterly, or annually.

For an individual life insurance policy, the information on an in-force policy report usually includes the policy number; insured's name, sex, and date of birth; issue age; effective date; plan of insurance; underwriting rating and/or class; tobacco use status; face amount of the policy; type of cession (automatic, facultative, or fac-ob); amount or proportion of risk reinsured; and amount of reinsurance in force. Figure 11.1 shows a section of an in-force policy report. Note that an actual in-force policy report would include additional columns for the underwriting rating or class, tobacco use status, plan of insurance, face amount of the policy, and proportion of risk reinsured.

For group life insurance, the in-force policy report includes the policy number; effective date; plan of insurance; information about the group, such as the group name, number of insured group members, amount of coverage for each member subgroup; total insurance coverage provided by the policy; the amount or proportion of risk reinsured; and the amount of reinsurance in force.

FIGURE 11.1

Portion of an In-Force Policy Report

Individual In-Force Report

Agreement	Cession	Insured	Effective Date	DOB	Issue Age	Sex	Auto/ Fac	Reinsurance NAAR ($)
200300	12334	Rosen, David	05/05/1998	11/02/1944	53	M	F	200,000
200300	12546	Dorian, Louise	08/15/1999	10/29/1936	62	F	F	169,284
200500	14558	Cooper, Jalen	12/12/2000	03/22/1945	55	M	A	75,000
200500	14611	Abrams, Martin	10/01/2000	07/10/1960	40	M	A	16,161
200500	14701	LaRocca, William	11/13/2000	10/31/1950	50	M	A	29,855
300200	16199	Nalibotsy, Sophie	12/13/2001	05/05/1955	46	F	A	200,000

Source: Adapted from Jane Lightcap Brown and Jennifer W. Herrod, *Reinsurance Administration* (Atlanta: LOMA, © 2000), 190. Used with permission; all rights reserved.

Policy Exhibit

A *policy exhibit* is a reinsurance report that summarizes and reconciles the changes that have occurred in reinsured policies during the reporting period. Such changes may include new business, increases and decreases in coverage, conversions, lapses, deaths, terminations, and reinstatements. The policy exhibit usually presents a beginning total policy count and reinsured risk amount, any increases or decreases in the policy count and reinsured risk amount, and a final total policy count and reinsured risk amount for that reporting period. A portion of a policy exhibit is shown in Figure 11.2.

Policy Change Report

A *policy change report*, also known as a *transaction report*, is a reinsurance report that shows details for all policies that have changed during the reporting period in a way that affects the amount of the reinsurance coverage, the reinsurance premium, or the allowance. Terminations due to death or policy lapse, increases or decreases in the face amount, and reinstatements are examples of changes typically listed on a policy change report. Figure 11.3 shows a portion of a policy change report. A policy change report also may show any changes in reinsurance premiums associated with the policy changes.

Billing Statement

A *billing statement* is a reinsurance report that lists the amounts owed by and due to each party to the reinsurance agreement. (The policy change report also may show this type of information.) The billing statement usually separates the amounts owed and due into categories such as first-year and renewal premiums, first-year and renewal allowances, premium refunds, policy dividends, and cash surrender value reimbursements. The reporting party typically uses a separate statement to bill amounts that are calculated on a collective basis rather than per policy. Such amounts include modco reserve adjustments and experience refunds.

If the reporting party owes money to the other reinsurance party, the reporting party usually sends payment of the amount owed along with the billing statement. If the nonreporting party owes money to the reporting party, the billing statement notifies the nonreporting party of the amount that it owes. A portion of a simplified billing statement is shown in Figure 11.4. Note that an actual billing statement (1) divides reinsurance premiums and allowances into first-year and renewal amounts and (2) includes information about premium refunds, policy dividends, and cash surrender value reimbursements.

Reserve Listing

A *reserve listing* is a reinsurance report that shows all policies reinsured and the reserve held for each policy. The reserve listing helps the parties determine the appropriate amount of reserves to maintain for the reinsured portion of each policy in force at the end of the reporting period. Figure 11.5 shows a portion of a reserve listing.

FIGURE 11.2

Portion of a Policy Exhibit

Reinsurance Policy Exhibit
Ceded to: Mid-state Reinsurance Company
For the Period of: 04/01/04–06/30/04
Agreement #:   24653

	Count	Reinsured Amount ($)	Risk Amount ($)	Reinsurance Premium ($)
Beginning In-force	15	8,320,000	8,320,000	90,231.38
New Business	2	350,000	350,000	4,885.11
Reinstatements	0	0	0	0
Conversions On	0	0	0	0
Other Increases	0	0	0	0
Deaths	0	0	0	0
Maturities	0	0	0	0
Expiries	0	0	0	0
Surrenders	0	0	0	0
Lapses	1	100,000	100,000	598.50
Conversions Off	1	500,000	500,000	5,120.00
Recaptures	0	0	0	0
Rescissions	0	0	0	0
Other Decreases	0	0	0	0
Ending In-force	15	8,070,000	8,070,000	89,397.99

Source: Adapted from Jane Lightcap Brown and Jennifer W. Herrod, *Reinsurance Administration* (Atlanta: LOMA, © 2000), 191. Used with permission; all rights reserved.

FIGURE 11.3

Portion of a Policy Change Report

Policy Changes for February 1, 2004 to February 29, 2004

Reinstatements

Agreement	YRT/ COI	Insured	DOB	Plan	Cession Number	Auto/ Fac	Policy	Change Date	Amount ($)
100	COI	Kennison, Gary	6/26/1962	XX	32334	A	59959934	2/13/2004	300,000
100	COI	Lapcevich, Alvin	1/25/1956	XY	32699	A	60259887	2/24/2004	200,000
200	YRT	Prince, Dawson	4/30/1940	XZ	32788	A	60265888	2/14/2004	240,000

Lapses

Agreement	YRT/ COI	Insured	DOB	Plan	Cession Number	Auto/ Fac	Policy	Change Date	Amount ($)
200	COI	Cook, Demetrius	5/22/1955	XX	32445	A	60001242	2/20/2004	280,000
300	COI	Sehra, Azad	9/23/1948	XY	33699	A	600025458	2/02/2004	135,000

Terminations

Agreement	YRT/ COI	Insured	DOB	Plan	Cession Number	Auto/ Fac	Policy	Change Date	Amount ($)
100	COI	Thayer, Alyssa	9/10/1950	XX	31454	A	60000112	2/06/2004	250,000

Decreases

Agreement	YRT/ COI	Insured	DOB	Plan	Cession Number	Auto/ Fac	Policy	Change Date	Amount ($)
300	YRT	Sanchez, Guillermo	2/12/1957	XF	35799	F	60021450	2/07/2004	8,000
400	YRT	Baker, Gretchen	8/02/1960	XJ	36002	A	60001234	2/05/2004	12,000

FIGURE 11.4

Portion of a Billing Statement

Policy	Insured	Date	Cession	Initial Amount ($)	NAAR ($)	Reinsurance Premium ($)	Allow-ances ($)	Net Amount Owed to the Reinsurer ($)
10201	Hanson, Emily	1/08/2005	23454	200,000	200,000	230.00	46.00	184.00
10324	Best, Kyle	1/18/2005	23535	240,000	240,000	691.20	138.24	552.96
10402	Nagpal, Sailesh	1/20/2005	25699	400,000	400,000	848.00	135.68	712.32
10498	Strausser, Joan	1/29/2005	25780	90,000	90,000	574.20	765.68	(191.48)

Source: Adapted from Jane Lightcap Brown and Jennifer W. Herrod, *Reinsurance Administration* (Atlanta: LOMA, © 2000), 193. Used with permission; all rights reserved.

Processing Changes in Reinsurance Coverage

A policy change report documents changes in a block of reinsurance business—that is, a group of reinsured policies—since the last reporting period. Certain changes in reinsured policies can increase or decrease the amount of risk assumed by the reinsurer. New business, recapture, increases in the face amount, claims, reductions, terminations, surrenders, lapses, reinstatements, conversions, and maturity are all examples of changes that can affect the amount of risk covered by reinsurance.

Other changes—such as corrections to an insured's identification information—may not affect the amount at risk under a reinsured policy, but such changes still require administration. Accurate information about changes in risk and insureds' identification information is essential to activities such as retention management, verification that a policy is in force at claim time, production of policy exhibits and billing statements for retrocessionaires, and reserve valuation.

FIGURE 11.5

Portion of a Reserve Listing

Statutory Reserves

Policy	Plan Code	Effective Date	Attained Age	Age	Sex	Name	Face Amount ($)	Ceded Amount ($)	NAAR ($)	Factor	Amount Reserve ($)
122467	XX	5/15/1996	37	46	F	Howell	100,000	94,242	44,272	4.45	8.21
122678	XZ	8/25/1997	43	51	M	Ryan	500,000	370,555	320,555	9.19	122.75
123566	XX	1/14/1998	31	38	M	Hemphill	100,000	95,768	45,768	3.42	6.52
134562	XX	1/101998	30	37	M	Muir	150,000	143,974	93,974	3.16	12.37
137892	XX	1/28/1998	41	48	F	O'Bryan	63,264	59,627	9,627	5.48	2.20

Source: Adapted from Jane Lightcap Brown and Jennifer W. Herrod, *Reinsurance Administration* (Atlanta: LOMA, © 2000), 193. Used with permission; all rights reserved.

The reinsurance analyst generally is responsible for updating reinsurance administration records to reflect changes to a policy and for notifying the appropriate staff at both the direct writer and the reinsurer about inconsistencies or other problems in the information. The analyst may need an underwriter's approval before recording certain types of risk changes to policies reinsured on a facultative basis. Examples of such changes that may require an underwriter's approval are reinstatements, changes from smoker to nonsmoker status, or reinsurance increases not specified in the reinsurance agreement. The analyst also may need to verify that the agreement provides for certain types of changes, such as recaptures, policy reductions, and conversions. For an increase in the face amount of a reinsured policy, the reinsurance analyst checks the reinsurer's retention to determine if the reinsurer needs to retrocede some of the additional risk to avoid becoming over-retained.

After checking all of the relevant information, the reinsurance analyst accesses the appropriate reinsurance administration records, verifies that the beginning amount of in-force risk on the policy exhibit matches the prior period's ending in-force amount, and updates the information for each case involving a risk change. The analyst then verifies that the ending in-force amount in the reinsurer's records matches the ending in-force amount on the policy exhibit. The analyst investigates and resolves any discrepancies in the in-force amounts and calculates the adjusted reinsurance premium for the policies. The reinsurer's next payment or billing statement to the direct writer includes such adjustments.

For bulk-administered business, instead of entering changes for each policy, the reinsurance analyst enters a summarized total change in the amount of risk for the block of policies. The analyst also verifies that (1) the ending amount of in-force risk on one policy exhibit matches the beginning in-force amount on the next policy exhibit and (2) the applicable changes equal the ending in-force amount.

Processing Billing Statements

Billing statements usually involve the receipt or payment of funds. The reinsurer produces billing statements (1) for reinsurance arrangements in which the reinsurer is the reporting party and (2) for retrocessionaires to whom the reinsurer cedes business. The reinsurer also processes billing statements from direct writers that self-administer their business.

When a reinsurer receives a self-administered billing statement from a direct writer, a reinsurance analyst enters the first-year and renewal reinsurance premium and first-year and renewal allowance information from the statement into the reinsurance administration records. Depending on the reinsurer's practices, the reinsurance analyst may enter information for each individual policy or only summarized information for blocks of policies. Figure 11.6 provides more information about recording financial information.

FIGURE 11.6

Recording Accounting Entries

Reinsurance analysts often are responsible for recording accounting entries for financial transactions such as the payment or receipt of reinsurance premiums and allowances. An *accounting entry* is a record of a monetary transaction made in a *journal*, which is an accounting document that contains all of the original chronological records of a company's financial transactions. Each accounting entry affects two or more of a company's accounts. An *account* is the basic tool that a company uses to record, group, and summarize similar types of financial transactions. The following are the primary categories of accounts:

- An *asset account* shows the monetary values of items that a company owns. For example, cash and investments are asset accounts.

- A *liability account* shows the monetary values of a company's debts. An insurer's largest liability account usually is its policy reserve account.

- A *capital and surplus account* represents a company's value and shows the difference between the company's assets and its liabilities.

- A *revenue account* shows the sources of a company's income. For example, an insurer records premiums it receives in a revenue account. The receipt of revenues increases the value of the insurer's cash account.

- An *expense account* shows the uses of a company's funds. For example, a direct writer records the payment of reinsurance premiums in an expense account. The payment of such expenses in cash reduces the value of the insurer's cash account.

Recall the basic accounting equation we described in Chapter 2. According to that equation, a company's assets equal the sum of the company's liabilities and its capital and surplus. To maintain the accounting equation in balance, each accounting entry must have at least two parts, including at least one debit and one credit, which are changes made to the monetary value of an account.

- A *debit* is a specified change made to the monetary value of an account that (1) increases the value of asset accounts and expense accounts and (2) decreases the value of liability accounts, capital and surplus accounts, and revenue accounts.

- A *credit* is a specified change made to the monetary value of an account that (1) increases the value of liability accounts, capital and surplus accounts, and revenue accounts and (2) decreases the value of asset accounts and expense accounts.

FIGURE 11.6 *continued*

Recording Accounting Entries

The sum of the debits in an accounting entry must equal the sum of the credits in the same entry. Each accounting entry lists debits first, with credits indented underneath.

Example: The Surfside Life Insurance Company issued a $100,000 life insurance policy with an annual direct premium of $1,200. Surfside then ceded 60% of the risk on a coinsurance basis to the Mountaintop Reinsurance Company. Mountaintop Re agreed to provide a first-year allowance equal to 75% of the first-year reinsurance premium to Surfside. The amount of risk ceded to Mountaintop Re was $60,000.

> Face amount of policy × Percent ceded
> $100,000 × 0.60 = $60,000 ceded

The first-year reinsurance premium owed by Surfside was $720.

> Annual direct premium × Percent ceded
> $1,200 × 0.60 = $720

The first-year allowance owed by Mountaintop Re was $540.

> First-year reinsurance premium × Percentage of allowance
> $720 × 0.75 = $540

The allowance owed by Mountainside Re partially offset the reinsurance premium owed by Surfside, so the actual cash exchanged was $180.

> First-year premium – Allowance
> $720 – $540 = $180 paid by Surfside

To record the transaction for the reinsurance premium and allowance, Surfside's reinsurance analyst made the following accounting entry to the company's expense account:

> Reinsurance premium $720
>   Allowance $540
>   Cash $180

For the same transaction, Mountaintop Re's reinsurance analyst made the following accounting entry to its revenue account:

> Allowance $540
> Cash $180
>   Reinsurance premium $720

If a payment accompanies a billing statement, the reinsurance analyst verifies that the amount due according to the statement matches the amount of the direct writer's payment. If the reinsurer owes money, the analyst verifies that the amount requested by the direct writer is appropriate.

> **Example:** If the amount owed by the reinsurer is a premium refund for reinsured policies that have been terminated, the reinsurance analyst verifies that the direct writer has paid to date any earned premiums on those policies. The analyst then requisitions the payment for the premium refund and sends it to the direct writer.

If a billing statement indicates that the reinsurer owes amounts for premium tax refunds, experience refunds, or cash value or policy dividend payment reimbursements, the reinsurance analyst takes additional actions to process the statement.

Premium Tax Refunds

If a billing statement requests the reinsurer to pay a premium tax refund, the reinsurance analyst confirms that the reinsurer has agreed in the reinsurance agreement to reimburse the direct writer for premium taxes on the portion of the reinsurance premiums paid to the reinsurer. Based on the agreement, the direct writer calculates the reimbursement as either an exact percentage based on the premium taxes the direct writer actually paid or as an estimated percentage specified in the agreement. A reinsurance analyst confirms the accuracy of the amount requested by the direct writer, requests payment to the direct writer, and updates the reinsurance administration records to reflect the payment.

Experience Refunds

Experience refunds allow the direct writer to share in a portion of the profits that the reinsurer earns on reinsurance premiums. If the reinsurance agreement provides for payment of experience refunds to the direct writer, the agreement also specifies the formula for calculating the refund. The reinsurance analyst confirms that the applicable agreement specifies experience refunds and that the direct writer has used the specified formula to calculate the refund. After verifying the accuracy of the amount requested, the analyst requisitions payment for the direct writer.

Cash Value and Policy Dividend Payment Reimbursements

A *cash value reimbursement* is an amount the reinsurer pays to a direct writer under a coinsurance or modco reinsurance agreement when a life insurance policyowner surrenders a reinsured policy in exchange for the policy's cash value. The result of this surrender is termination of the reinsurance on the policy. The reinsurance agreement also may require the reinsurer to reimburse the direct writer for policy dividend payments made to the policyowner. In general, under a coinsurance or modco agreement, the reinsurer participates in cash value and policy dividend payments, whereas the reinsurer in a YRT agreement does not.

After receiving a request for cash value or policy dividend payment reimbursement, the reinsurance analyst verifies that the agreement calls for reinsurer participation in cash value and policy dividend payments and, for cash value reimbursements, verifies the accuracy of the amount requested. The reinsurance analyst then requests that payment be issued to the direct writer and records the reimbursements paid. In the case of cash value reimbursements, the analyst also terminates the corresponding policy records in the reinsurer's information system.

Recording Policy Reserves

- When a reinsurer receives policy reserve calculations from a direct writer that self-administers its business, or when the reinsurer's actuaries calculate reserves for business that the reinsurer administers, the reinsurance analyst is responsible for updating the information in the reinsurance administration records. The analyst first verifies that the amount reported on the reserve statement seems reasonable in comparison to the existing amount of policy reserves. If the amount on the statement seems unreasonable, the analyst investigates the discrepancy. If the amount seems reasonable, the analyst updates the reinsurer's records by replacing the prior period's reserve information with the new information. The reinsurer periodically updates the reserve changes reported on the reserve listing.

Administering Mergers and Acquisitions

A **merger**, also known as an *amalgamation*, is a transaction wherein the assets and liabilities of two companies are combined. One of the companies survives as a legal entity and the other company ceases to exist. An **acquisition** is a transaction wherein one company gains a controlling interest in another company, resulting in a linkage between formerly independent corporations. A **controlling interest** is ownership of enough voting shares of stock in a company to control company policy.

Generally, a merger or an acquisition does not terminate a reinsurance agreement. Instead, the reinsurance parties add amendments, known as **novation amendments**, to the agreement to describe the new entities involved in the agreement and to specify the date on which the reinsurer becomes liable for any additional risk resulting from the merger or acquisition. Thus, although the names of one or more of the companies may have changed, the terms of the reinsurance agreement do not change. Typically, the reinsurance analyst handles a merger by changing the direct writer or reinsurer number and name on the reinsurance records.

When one reinsurer acquires another reinsurer, the acquiring reinsurer may assume additional risk in the form of blocks of business from the acquired reinsurer. In this case, the novation amendment to the reinsurance agreement states a date on which the acquiring reinsurer will assume responsibility for the additional risk. Prior to that date, the business remains the responsibility of the acquired reinsurer.

The reinsurance analyst employed by the acquiring reinsurer adds the acquired business into the reinsurer's records as in-force business. After the effective date specified in the novation amendment, the acquiring reinsurer administers the reinsured policies.

Administering Terminations of Reinsurance

Reinsurance coverage can be terminated as a result of recapture; lapse, surrender, or expiration of the reinsured policy; and, for life insurance, the death of the insured. We discuss terminations through recapture, lapse, surrender, and expiration in the following paragraphs. We address life reinsurance terminations due to death of the insured later in this chapter when we describe the administration of claims.

The process for terminating reinsurance is similar for terminations due to recapture, lapse, surrender, or expiration. However, terminating reinsurance coverage due to recapture requires an extra administrative step. If a reinsurer receives notice that a direct writer wishes to recapture part or all of a reinsured risk, the reinsurance analyst first must verify that the reinsurance agreement allows recapture at that time. If the agreement does not allow the recapture, the reinsurance analyst arranges for approval of the request for recapture before terminating the reinsurance on the reinsurance administration records.

For terminations due to recapture, lapse, surrender, or expiration, the analyst verifies the effective date for the termination of reinsurance; the policies included in the termination; the current net amount at risk; any premium refund that may be applicable; and—for any case involving coinsurance or modco reinsurance—allowances, policy dividends, or cash value. For recaptures, the analyst also determines whether the direct writer owes any recapture fee.

For all types of terminations, the reinsurance analyst also ensures that (1) the direct writer has transferred all reinsurance premiums and information due, (2) the reinsurer has processed all statements from the direct writer, and (3) the direct writer's current in-force listing matches the reinsurer's records. The reinsurance analyst then terminates the reinsurance administration records for the affected policies, refunds any unearned reinsurance premium to the direct writer, and deletes any in-force and policy reserve amounts that may remain in the records.

Administering Claims

Although the reinsurer's claim analysts are responsible for investigating and approving claims submitted under reinsured policies, reinsurance analysts at many reinsurers are responsible for administering and accounting for claims. A reinsurer's reinsurance analysts and claim analysts collaborate to

- Ensure that the reinsurer pays only valid claims that are reinsured under a valid reinsurance agreement

- Respond to claims promptly, accurately, and professionally by meeting all internal guidelines and all external legal and regulatory requirements

- Ensure that the reinsurer records accurate information for claims and processes claim payments in an accurate and timely manner

As we noted earlier in this text, the reinsurer sometimes has the right to make a recommendation to the direct writer on whether to pay a claim or to deny it. However, the reinsurance agreement may limit the amount of time the reinsurer has after it receives the claim to make a recommendation. Therefore, prompt handling of all claims is essential. However, the reinsurer must balance its desire to pay claims quickly with its desire to pay only those claims for which it is genuinely responsible. If a reinsurer pays claims that are not legitimate, the cost of reinsurance rises for all the reinsurer's clients.

For most reinsurers, a reinsurance analyst has the following responsibilities in administering claims:

- Establishing a claim file

- Examining the claim

- Securing approval for the claim

■ Settling the claim (in some companies)

The reinsurance analyst also may notify the retrocessionaire of a claim on which the reinsurer has retroceded a portion of the risk. Note that the reinsurance analyst is not responsible for investigating claims and for making decisions to pay or not to pay claims. Instead, a reinsurer's claim analysts are responsible for handling these duties. At some reinsurers, claim analysts handle some of the responsibilities we assign to reinsurance analysts.

Establishing the Claim File

The claim administration process begins when the direct writer submits a claim notice to the reinsurer. Figure 11.7 provides an example of a typical reinsurance claim notice.

A reinsurance analyst checks the reinsurer's claim administration records to confirm that the direct writer has not previously submitted the claim. If a record of the claim does not already exist, the reinsurance analyst establishes a claim file for the claim. The *claim file* is an organized collection of all the information relevant to a claim. For example, an individual life insurance claim file typically includes the following information:

■ Insured's name, sex, and date of birth

■ Date of the insured's death, if known

■ Direct writer

■ Policy number assigned by the direct writer

■ Name of and contact information for the person at the direct writer who can provide further information about the claim

■ Date the reinsurer received the claim

The claim file also must include the following documents:

■ A copy of the claimant's statement filed with the direct writer by the claimant—usually the beneficiary of the policy

■ A copy of the proof of loss—typically a death certificate or a funeral director's statement for a life insurance policy

■ A copy of the proof of claim payment, if the direct writer has already paid the claim

Figures 11.8 through 11.10 show examples of a claimant's statement, proof of loss statement, and proof of payment statement.

The reinsurance analyst makes notes in the claim file about any claim activities in progress or completed. Many reinsurers require reinsurance analysts to maintain in each claim file a *claim worksheet*, which is a standard form that a reinsurance analyst uses to document the progress and results of the claim administration process. For example, the claim worksheet typically contains information about (1) the applicable reinsurance agreement, (2) the reinsured policy, (3) the payment of reinsurance premiums, and (4) any amounts of risk retroceded. The claim worksheet also indicates whether the direct writer received a life insurance claim during the policy's

FIGURE 11.7

Example of a Reinsurance Claim Notice

DAHLONEGA REINSURANCE COMPANY
Reinsurance Death Claim Notice

This form should be completed by the ceding company and forwarded to Dahlonega Re, along with copies of proofs of death, claimant's statements, and other papers needed to establish a claim for reinsurance.

Name of insured: _____ Date of birth: _____

List all policies you have issued on this life, whether or not reinsured with Dahlonega Re. Show the date of termination if the policy was not in force on the date of death.

Policy No.	Date of Issue	Face Amt. Issued Life	Face Amt. Issued ADB	Face Amt. Reinsured Life	Face Amt. Reinsured ADB	Reinsurer
Total Issued						
Less Total Terminated						
In Force						

If any policies were reinstated within two years of—or terminated prior to—death, please give dates and other pertinent details in the Comments section.

Date of death: _____ Premium paid to date: _____

Cause of death: _____

Include details of any premium adjustment or interest payment included in the settlement in the Comments section.

Has your claim been approved for payment in full?

Has payment been released to the beneficiary?

Are you awaiting our approval before settlement?

Comments:

Payment is requested on the following:

Policy Number	Cession No.	Life NAAR	ADB Amount	Total

Direct Writer: _____

Date: _____ Completed by: _____ Title: _____

Source: Adapted from Jane Lightcap Brown and Jennifer W. Herrod, *Reinsurance Administration* (Atlanta: LOMA, © 2000), 202. Used with permission; all rights reserved.

FIGURE 11.8

A Claimant's Statement

WEBBER INSURANCE COMPANY
Claimant's Statement

Policy No: 123432252

Deceased's Full Name: Elizabeth Manson   Date of Birth: 11/13/1966   Date of Death: 1/03/2005

Residence: 10012 Abercrombie Court, Destin, MA 12345

Occupation: Physician   Date last worked: 1/03/2005   Cause of death: Car Accident

Accidental Death Benefit Involved? ☐ Yes ☒ No

If policy not returned, who has possession of it?

If policy cannot be found, check here: ☐

Capacity in which you claim proceeds: Spouse beneficiary

Is estate being represented? ☐ Yes ☐ No

Names and addresses of all physicians who attended the deceased and/or all hospitals or institutions where he or she was treated during the last illness and during five years prior thereto. (This section needs to be completed only if the policy is 2 years old or less, was reinstated within the last 2 years, or accidental death benefits are being claimed.)

Name	Address	Dates of Attendance	Disease or Condition

Names of other companies with which insured carried insurance: _____

Authorization to obtain information for: _____

The undersigned authorizes any physician, medical or dental practitioner, hospital, clinic, pharmacy, other health facility, consumer reporting agency including the Social Security Administration, MIB Group, Inc., insurance and reinsurance companies, or employers to release any and all medical and nonmedical information in its possession about the above to Webber Insurance Company or its local representatives. Medical information means all information in the possession of or derived from providers of health care regarding the medical history, mental or physical condition, alcohol or drug abuse information, HIV infection, HIV testing and AIDS-related illnesses or treatment of the above. This authorization also covers, but is not limited to, other insurance claims and coverage, occupational information, and financial information pertaining to the above.

These and all other papers called for by the company shall be made part of the proofs of death. The furnishing of this form or any supplemental forms shall not be considered that there was any insurance in force on the life of the person in question nor a waiver of any of the company's rights or defenses.

Upon request, a copy of this authorization will be furnished to the undersigned.

For two and one-half years, a photocopy of this authorization shall be as valid as the original.

Any person who knowingly and with intent to defraud any insurance company or other person files an application for insurance or statement of claim containing any materially false information, or conceals for the purpose of misleading, information concerning any fact material thereto commits a fraudulent insurance act, which is a crime, and shall also be subject to a civil penalty not to exceed five thousand dollars and the stated value of the claim for each such violation.

Print claimant's name: _____   Claimant's Signature: _____

Date of birth: _____   Date Signed: _____

Taxpayer ID number: _____   Claimant's Address: _____

Source: Adapted from Jane Lightcap Brown and Jennifer W. Herrod, *Reinsurance Administration* (Atlanta: LOMA, © 2000), 205. Used with permission; all rights reserved.

A Proof of Loss Statement

Proof of Death Certification

Name:	Elizabeth Manson
Date:	1/03/2005
Place:	Destin, MA
Age:	38
Marital Status:	Married
Next-of-Kin:	Richard Manson, spouse
Physician:	Dr. Harlan Jacoby
Interment/Cremation:	Interment, Flanders Cemetery

Dated at this 6th day of January, 2005
Z. T. Erickson and Son Funeral Directors
21 Willow Drive, Destin MA
Per _____

Source: Adapted from Jane Lightcap Brown and Jennifer W. Herrod, *Reinsurance Administration* (Atlanta: LOMA, © 2000), 206. Used with permission; all rights reserved.

contestable period. Having this information allows the reinsurer to make sure that it pays only legitimate claims. Figure 11.11 shows an example of a claim worksheet.

Examining the Claim

After establishing a claim file and beginning a claim worksheet, the reinsurance analyst—or, in some cases, a claim analyst—examines the claim. During the examination process, the reinsurance analyst typically performs the following activities:

- Verifying the policy status and the existence of a valid reinsurance agreement that applies to the policy

- Verifying that reinsurance premiums were paid

- Verifying that the claim complies with the applicable agreement

- Reviewing the nature and proof of the loss

- Determining whether the claim is fraudulent or contestable

- Determining the reinsurer's claim liability

FIGURE 11.10

A Proof of Payment Statement

Webber Insurance Company
3312 Webber Blvd, Sweetwater, TX 10029

1234231
February 1, 2005

THE SUM OF FIVE HUNDRED THOUSAND DOLLARS
Pay to the order of: Richard Manson
10012 Abercrombie Court
Destin, MA 12345

$500,000
Payable in US dollars for face
amount through Triumphant
Bank, Middleton, TX

Sandra Gillison

WEBBER
Insurance Company

23904972 394092 590923 8493 390 2903
▼ *(Please detach before depositing check.)* ▼

February 1, 2005	Webber Insurance Company	$500,000
Invoice Reference 1231-2348-231	Invoice No 23283	Payment Amount $500,000
Deceased: Manson, Elizabeth	Policy No: 123432252	Life: $500,000

Attn: Danae Baynes, Reinsurance Dept.
Regards, Joelle Dubiac, Individual Claims

Source: Adapted from Jane Lightcap Brown and Jennifer W. Herrod, *Reinsurance Administration* (Atlanta: LOMA, © 2000), 207. Used with permission; all rights reserved.

Verifying the Policy Status and the Reinsurance Agreement

The reinsurance analyst verifies

- That a reinsurance agreement covers the policy under which the claim was submitted

- That the policy and the reinsurance on the policy were in force at the time of the loss

- Whether any policy changes—such as reinstatements and increases—affected the cession in the past two years

The reinsurance analyst then determines whether the reinsurer has reinsured other policies from any direct writer on this case. If the reinsurer is covering other policies for the same case, the analyst notes these policies and direct writers in the claim file. The reinsurance analyst also checks for any amounts retroceded on the case. If the claim involves retroceded coverage, the reinsurance analyst creates a **retrocession claim file**—that is, a file containing all the information relevant to the claim, plus information about the retrocession—to use when the reinsurer notifies its retrocessionaires of the claim.

FIGURE 11.11

A Claim Worksheet

Claim Worksheet

Claim Number: _____   Reinsurer: _____

Name: _____

Sex: _____

Date of birth: _____

Date of death/disability: _____

Notice received by: _____

Direct writer name: _____

Direct writer policy #: _____

Direct writer contact: _____

Contact phone: _____

Contact fax: _____

Date: _____

Claim type: ☐ Death ☐ Disability ☐ Diswv ☐ Dismem ☐ ADB

In Force: ☐ Yes ☐ No

Premiums paid to date: ☐ Yes ☐ No

Reported: ☐ Individual cession ☐ Bulk

E & O: ☐ Yes ☐ No

If E & O, comment: _____

In Force verified by: _____

Date _____

Agreement #: _____

Pricing information: _____

Bulk id: _____

Right of recommendation: ☐ Yes ☐ No

Agreement verified: ☐ Yes ☐ No

Agreement description: Q/S _____ % ☐ NB ☐ Excess

Effective date: From _____ to _____

Retroceded: ☐ Yes ☐ No

Retroceded to: _____

Retroceded amount: _____

Verified by: _____

Direct Writer	At Issue	Current
Total Line		
Total Face Amount		
Amount Applied for		
Published Retention		
Retention on Claim		
Total Reinsurance/Retro		
Reinsurer's Share		

Policy effective date:

Mortality _____ %   Impairment _____

U/W basis _____

Smoker status: ☐ Yes ☐ No   Preferred ☐ Yes ☐ No   Conversion ☐ Yes, original pyd _____

Reinstated ☐ Yes, give date _____ ☐ No

Evidence of insurability ☐ Yes ☐ No

Contestable ☐ Yes ☐ No   MIB attached ☐ Yes ☐ No

Residence _____   Occupation _____

Cause of death/disability _____

Occasionally, the reinsurance analyst receives a claim for a case covered by a new reinsurance agreement that the reinsurer has not yet added to its reinsurance administration records. The reinsurance analyst works with staff in the reinsurer's reinsurance agreement and pricing areas to establish appropriate records as quickly as possible.

Verifying Payment of Reinsurance Premiums

The reinsurance analyst checks the direct writer's billing statement and the reinsurer's records to confirm that the direct writer has paid the reinsurance premiums on the case. If no additional reinsurance premiums are due, the analyst adds the premium-related information to the claim file. At many reinsurers, if any reinsurance premium on the case is outstanding, the reinsurance analyst refers the case to a claim analyst, who usually deducts the amount of the unpaid reinsurance premium from the amount of policy benefits due to the direct writer. The reinsurance analyst also calculates any premium refunds due if the reinsurance coverage terminates as a result of the claim.

Verifying Claim Compliance with the Reinsurance Agreement

The reinsurance analyst confirms that the claim meets the criteria set forth in the applicable reinsurance agreement. The analyst typically determines whether the claim complies with the following agreement specifications:

- Type of policy
- Underwriting basis of the policy
- Underwriting classification of the insured
- Effective date of the policy
- Allowable coverage
- Maximum amount of risk to be ceded per policy
- Jumbo limit
- Quota share

The reinsurance analyst also determines whether any special instructions or arrangements govern the policy. For example, the reinsurance analyst notifies the claim analyst if the claim is contestable or if the reinsurer has the right to review the claim and offer its opinion to the direct writer on whether to pay the claim, known as the *right of recommendation*. If all aspects of the claim comply with the applicable agreement, the reinsurance analyst records the agreement terms on the claim worksheet. If not, the reinsurance analyst refers the case to a claim analyst for further examination and determination of the reinsurer's obligation under the claim.

Reviewing the Nature and Proof of the Loss

The reinsurance analyst verifies that the direct writer has provided a proper proof of loss to the reinsurer. For a life insurance claim, the direct writer typically submits a copy of the claimant's statement along with a death certificate, doctor's statement, or funeral director's statement. For a disability income insurance claim, the direct writer submits the claimant's statement plus a physician's statement that confirms the disability. If the direct writer has already paid the claim, the direct writer sends the reinsurer proof of that claim payment.

The reinsurance analyst reviews the proof documents and confirms that they apply to the insured, records the information from the proof documents on the claim worksheet, and adds the proof documents to the claim file.

Determining Whether the Claim Is Fraudulent or Contestable

Both reinsurance analysts and claim analysts look for signs of fraudulent claims. **Claim fraud** is an action by which a person intentionally uses false information in an unfair or unlawful attempt to collect benefits under an insurance policy. Any person who is in a position to influence a claim decision or benefit from an approved claim can commit claim fraud. Such a person might be an insured, a beneficiary, a health care provider, an insurance producer, or an employee of the insurance company. Figure 11.12 provides some of the warning signs of a fraudulent claim.

The reinsurer also checks each life insurance claim to determine if it is contestable. A **contestable claim** is a claim for life insurance policy proceeds following the death of an insured during the policy's contestable period. Life insurance policies specify a time period following policy issuance or reinstatement—typically two years in the United States—known as the **contestable period**, during which the insurer has the right to rescind the policy if the application for insurance contained a material misrepresentation.

To determine if a claim is contestable, the reinsurance analyst calculates the length of time that the policy has been in force—that is, the length of time between the effective date of the policy and the date of the insured's death. The effective date of the policy generally is the date on which the direct writer issued the policy; if the policyowner paid the initial premium with the application for the policy, the effective date of the policy may be the date of the application. However, changes to the policy—for example, a reinstatement, conversion, or coverage amount increase—can change the effective date. If the number of years that the policy has been in force is less than the length of the contestable period, then the claim is contestable.

If a claim is not contestable, the reinsurance analyst refers the claim to the claim analyst for approval. If a claim is contestable, the reinsurance analyst notes the number of years the policy has been in force, checks MIB records if the reinsurer is a member of MIB, and sends the claim to the claim analyst for further investigation.

In most U.S. states, after the contestable period has expired, the insurer cannot contest the validity of the policy on the basis of a material misrepresentation in the application for insurance. In some other jurisdictions, an insurer may contest the validity of an insurance policy after the end of the contestable period if the company can demonstrate that the material misrepresentation was made for the purpose of defrauding the insurance company.

Determining the Reinsurer's Claim Liability

For coinsurance or modco reinsurance, the reinsurance analyst uses the information found in the reinsurance agreement and reinsurance administration records to calculate the reinsurer's net amount at risk (NAAR), which generally is the amount of the reinsurer's claim liability. For YRT reinsurance, the schedule in the administration records shows the reinsurer's NAAR. The rein-

FIGURE 11.12

Warning Signs of a Fraudulent Claim

The insurance coverage seems excessive for the risk.

The claim lists a subjective diagnosis, such as stress or fatigue.

The handwriting on the claimant and physician information documents seems to be the same.

The symptoms or length of treatment for a diagnosis appear extreme.

The insurance producer who submitted the application for coverage also submitted the applications for other cases that involved questionable claims.

The format of medical statements provided by a health care provider is not consistent.

The claimant names the same employer, physician, and attorneys as other claimants who have submitted questionable claims.

The claimant does not sign the statement authorizing the insurer to obtain additional information from medical caregivers, MIB, and others.

The claimant provides a post office box instead of a street address.

The claim form submitted is a photocopy, not an original.

Put Money Here

Claim Documentation

The medical information on a series of claim forms is exactly the same.

Without a logical reason, the claimant consults health care providers who do not practice in the claimant's geographic area.

The claimant provides suspiciously detailed or suspiciously vague information and documentation concerning the claim.

White-outs, typeovers, or erasures suggest that the claim form has been altered.

The life insurance coverage is in the contestable period.

Information in the reinsurer's claim file is omitted or differs from information in the insurer's file.

Medical terms are misspelled or inconsistent with the diagnosis or treatment.

Instead of actual medical records, the proof of loss documents provide only a very general statement of diagnosis and treatment.

In an alleged emergency, the claimant insisted on seeing his own physician instead of going to a hospital for treatment.

The claimant exhibits unusual knowledge about medical procedures, insurance coverage, and claim processing.

The attending physician's statement contains a rubber stamp of the physician's signature or is a photocopy.

Source: Adapted from Jane Lightcap Brown and Jennifer W. Herrod, *Reinsurance Administration* (Atlanta: LOMA, © 2000), 211. Used with permission; all rights reserved.

surance administration records for a policy reinsured under quota share reinsurance also may provide the reinsurer's NAAR. If not, the analyst calculates the reinsurer's NAAR by multiplying the direct writer's NAAR by the quota share percentage.

Example: If the direct writer has $200,000 at risk under a policy, and the reinsurer has reinsured the policy using a 60 percent quota share, the reinsurer's NAAR on the policy is $120,000, calculated as follows:

$$\$200,000 \times 0.60 = \$120,000$$

The reinsurance analyst compares the reinsurer's calculated NAAR with the reinsured claim benefit amount specified on the direct writer's claim notice or on the proof of payment sent with the claim form if the direct writer has already paid the claim. If the two amounts are the same, the reinsurance analyst updates the claim worksheet with the reinsurer's NAAR. If the two amounts are not the same, the reinsurance analyst refers the case to the claim analyst for investigation of the discrepancy. The reinsurance analyst also verifies any applicable interest or expense amounts and includes them in the claim benefit amount payable.

Approving the Claim

Each reinsurer establishes guidelines specifying which staff can approve various amounts and types of claims. In some companies, reinsurance analysts have the authority to approve claims up to certain amounts under particular circumstances. However, the same reinsurance analyst that examined a claim generally cannot approve that claim. In other companies, only claim analysts have the authority to approve claims. For simplicity, this text assumes that the person responsible for approving or denying a claim is a claim analyst.

After approving a claim, the claim analyst either settles the claim or instructs a reinsurance analyst or another claim analyst to settle the claim. After denying a claim, the claim analyst generally notifies the direct writer of the decision and advises the reinsurance analyst who examined the claim how to update the reinsurance administration records.

Settling the Claim

The reinsurance analyst or claim analyst settling the claim usually prepares and obtains approval of appropriate forms for payment, communicates the amount of the payment to the direct writer, and sends payment to the direct writer. A reinsurance analyst then updates the reinsurance administration records to reflect the settlement. If the settlement is for a life insurance claim, the reinsurance analyst also terminates the reinsurance records for the policy and updates the reinsurance administration system to reflect changes in the amount of in-force risk and policy reserves.

Some bulk-administered reinsurance arrangements allow the direct writer to net off claims from billing statements. *Netting off* is a process by which a direct writer subtracts the claim amount owed to it by a reinsurer from the amount that the direct writer owes the reinsurer for premiums. If the reinsurance agreement allows netting off, the direct writer notifies the reinsurer of a claim through the billing statement, which shows claim amounts that the direct writer has netted off.

When a reinsurer receives a billing statement that contains netted-off claims, a reinsurance analyst confirms that the applicable reinsurance agreement allows netting off of claims; verifies that the reinsurer has received the claim notice, proof of loss, and other claim documents; and records the claim on the reinsurance administration records. The analyst verifies that the direct writer has paid all reinsurance premiums for the applicable policy, solicits approval from a claim analyst for the claim, and updates the reinsurance administration records to reflect the claim settlement. The claim analyst does not request payment for the claim because the direct writer has already netted off the settlement amount from the billing statement.

Notifying Retrocessionaires of a Claim

As noted earlier in this chapter, the reinsurance analyst determines if the reinsurer retroceded a portion of the risk for a claim to a retrocessionaire. If so, the reinsurance analyst sets up a retrocession claim file in the reinsurance administration records and examines the claim, secures approval for the claim, and settles the claim as we have described. In addition, the reinsurance analyst notifies the retrocessionaire of the claim. If the reinsurer has not yet received all required information, the notice sent to the retrocessionaire states that the reinsurer is awaiting further information. If the reinsurer has received and reviewed all of the claim information and made a decision on the case, the reinsurer sends the retrocessionaire a copy of the proof of loss, the claimant's statement, and the proof of its payment to the direct writer, along with a request for payment from the retrocessionaire. The retrocessionaire then examines the claim, secures approval for the claim, and settles the claim with the reinsurer.

Key Terms

in-force policy report
policy exhibit
policy change report
billing statement
reserve listing
accounting entry
journal
account
asset account
liability account
capital and surplus account
revenue account
expense account
debit

credit
cash value reimbursement
merger
acquisition
controlling interest
novation amendment
claim file
claim worksheet
retrocession claim file
right of recommendation
claim fraud
contestable claim
contestable period
netting off

Endnote

1.   This chapter represents a revision of material from Jane Lightcap Brown and Jennifer W. Herrod, *Reinsurance Administration* (Atlanta: LOMA, © 2000), 187–214. Used with permission; all rights reserved.

CHAPTER 12

Quality Control in Reinsurance

After studying this chapter, you should be able to

- Define quality control and explain the importance of quality control in reinsurance administration

- List and discuss five control principles

- List four types of process controls and describe the use of these process controls in reinsurance administration

- Distinguish among internal audits, external audits, and desk audits as they are used in reinsurance administration and describe the purposes of each type of audit

- Describe typical external audit procedures used in reinsurance administration

- Describe and distinguish among a policy audit questionnaire, a desk audit report, an external audit report, and an exception report

OUTLINE

Principles of Quality Control
Segregation of Duties
Execution of Transactions as Authorized
Recording of Transactions as Executed
Safeguarding of Assets
Physical Comparison of Recorded Amounts

Control Requirements of the Sarbanes-Oxley Act

Quality Control Approaches

Process Controls
Suspense Account Reconciliation
Data Integrity Checks
Trend Analysis
Checking Overdue Reports

Audits
Internal Audits
External Audits
Desk Audits
Comparison of Internal Audits, External Audits, and Desk Audits

Because much reinsurance business is self-administered, reinsurers conduct periodic external audits of direct writers to verify the direct writer's compliance with the reinsurance agreement.

Effective management of a reinsurance arrangement depends upon the careful handling of a multitude of details within an atmosphere of trust between the direct writer and the reinsurer. To ensure that the parties are following appropriate processes, direct writers and reinsurers undertake a variety of quality control activities.[1]

Quality control is the process of ensuring that an organization accomplishes its objectives and follows its standards. A **standard**, also referred to as a *performance standard*, is a statement of either (1) minimum acceptable levels of performance or results, (2) outstanding levels of performance or results, or (3) the acceptable range for levels of performance or results. Organizations set objectives both to measure their own performance and to guide their activities. Periodically, organizations evaluate their activities to see how well their performance meets their objectives. If an organization is not meeting its objectives, then the organization can determine the causes and can implement changes to improve its performance.

As part of a company's control cycle, the company must create written documentation of its policies and procedures. These written documents give employees clear guidance on how the company's management wants its administrative tasks to be approached and accomplished. The documents also provide a basis for auditors to use in checking whether employees correctly followed established procedures.

An organization can carry out quality control reviews on a variety of levels and can examine a variety of processes. For example, an organization can use quality control reviews to evaluate the work of an individual employee, a group of employees, a department, a division, or the entire company. An organization can perform quality control reviews by using automated systems, management personnel, a special internal audit team, or external auditors. Quality control reviews can be ongoing, periodic, or one-time events, and they can occur at predetermined intervals or upon request. Quality control reviews also can be broad to examine a variety of operations or functions, or they can be focused to evaluate one specific area only.

Organizations try to conduct quality control reviews as cost-effectively as possible. An organization generally uses a sampling process to limit the scope and expense of reviews. Examining a statistical sample usually provides adequate insight into the effectiveness of a process while limiting the cost of the review. For example, if a reinsurer needs to evaluate the accuracy and completeness of its information on reinsurance reservations, the reinsurer typically examines a selected sample of the forms and files, rather than every single reservation processed within the specified period.

The results of a quality control review can be summarized in the form of a **quality control ratio**, which is the ratio of the number of files meeting a specific standard to the number of files reviewed for that standard, as follows:

$$\text{Quality Control Ratio} = \frac{\text{Number of Correct Records}}{\text{Total Number of Records}}$$

Example: A reinsurer reviews 200 files to determine whether they properly record reservations of capacity. If 194 files show correct information and 6 files show incorrect information, then the quality control ratio for this standard is 194/200 or 0.97. In other words, the staff had properly recorded 97 percent.

Principles of Quality Control

In this section, we describe some widely recognized principles that support the proper handling of financial transactions within an effective quality control system.[2]

Segregation of Duties

According to the principle of **segregation of duties**, also known as the principle of *dual control*, an employer designs jobs so that incompatible functions are assigned to different individuals. In this context, **incompatible functions** are job duties in the normal course of employment that, when combined, place an employee in a position where he or she could commit an illegal act or could conceal errors or irregularities. Segregating incompatible functions among employees provides a framework that enables a company to safeguard its assets by quickly detecting and correcting errors and irregularities.

Generally, an effective internal control system separates the custodial, authorization, and accounting tasks associated with a company's assets. In this context, *custodial tasks* include the physical or electronic handling of assets.

Execution of Transactions as Authorized

No financial transaction should occur without some form of official authorization. **Execution of transactions as authorized** is a control principle that concerns the delegation of authority to perform specified tasks and the communication of that authority. A specified employee authorizes each financial transaction at the appropriate authorization level. An **authorization level** is the maximum monetary amount that a company employee has the official power to approve on behalf of the company.

Example: A new underwriter may have to obtain authorization from a supervisor for all transactions in excess of $200,000, whereas a more experienced underwriter may have to obtain authorization from a supervisor for all financial transactions in excess of $500,000.

Recording of Transactions as Executed

The **recording of transactions as executed** means that a company records all completed transactions in the correct accounting period, in the correct accounts, in the correct physical units, and in the correct monetary amounts. In this way, the company can correctly summarize all transactions for that accounting period in its current financial statements.

Safeguarding of Assets

The *safeguarding of assets* is an internal control principle that consists of activities designed to protect the organization against the risks of theft, destruction, waste, and deterioration. The following are activities designed to safeguard assets:

- Maintaining written policies about the proper control of company assets

- Limiting unauthorized physical or electronic access to offices, documents, and records

- Maintaining written business disaster recovery plans and off-premises storage of back-up files for all critical records

- Investigating the integrity of employees hired to fill sensitive positions

Physical Comparison of Recorded Amounts

Internal control requires the *physical comparison of recorded amounts,* which means that a company regularly counts its assets, revenues, and expenses and compares this independent count to the amounts in its accounting records. The staff must reconcile its internally generated inventory against information provided to it by third parties. A common method of reconciliation, known as *reconciliation by exception*, involves investigating only those accounting entries that do not match or are out of balance; all other entries are assumed to be correct.

Control Requirements of the Sarbanes-Oxley Act

Public companies in the United States, including insurance companies, must comply with the control provisions of the Sarbanes-Oxley Act of 2002. The *Sarbanes-Oxley Act of 2002* is a U.S. federal law that requires public companies in the United States to take specific precautions related to corporate governance, effective internal controls, and preventing and detecting fraudulent behavior on the part of management and external auditors. The Act addresses the composition of the board of directors; the role of the audit committee; the selection and conduct of external auditors; and the adequacy of a company's internal financial control systems.

Under the internal control provisions of the Sarbanes-Oxley Act, each annual report of a public company must contain an annual internal control report.[3] The internal control report is required to specify the following information:

- Management's responsibility for establishing and maintaining adequate internal control over the company's financial reporting

- The framework management used to evaluate the effectiveness of its internal controls

- Management's assessment of the effectiveness of its internal control system as of the end of the company's most recent fiscal year

- That the company's auditor has issued a report supporting management's assessment of its internal controls

Quality Control Approaches

Direct writers and reinsurers typically use two main approaches to reinsurance quality control: (1) process controls and (2) audits.

- A **process control** is a procedure that allows an organization to monitor the accuracy of its processes on a regular, ongoing basis. Organizations use process controls to check the accuracy and effectiveness of their administrative procedures.

- An audit is a periodic appraisal of a company's objectives, procedures, personnel, controls, and records. Both direct writers and reinsurers conduct audits. Each company audits its own operations. In addition, a reinsurer has the right to audit a direct writer with which it does business.

The primary difference between process controls and audits is that companies use process controls more frequently than they conduct audits. The purpose of process controls is to maintain the effectiveness of the organization's processes, whereas the purpose of audits is to examine the effectiveness of interrelated objectives, procedures, personnel, controls, and records. Figure 12.1 summarizes the various types of process controls and audits that we discuss in the remainder of this chapter.

Process Controls

In this section, we describe four important process controls in reinsurance administration: (1) suspense account reconciliation, (2) data integrity checks, (3) trend analysis, and (4) overdue reports checks.

Suspense Account Reconciliation

Direct writers and reinsurers use temporary accounts known as **suspense accounts** to monitor accounting activities involving different units or different time periods.

FIGURE 12.1

Approaches to Quality Control

PROCESS CONTROLS	AUDITS
Suspense account reconciliation	Internal audit
Data integrity checks	External audit
Trend analysis	Desk audit
Overdue report checks	

Example: A reinsurer receives a reinsurance premium payment check, but the staff is not able to process the billing statement immediately. However, the reinsurer immediately deposits the check and the accounting staff records the deposit in a suspense account. When the staff is able to process the billing statement a few days later, the accounting staff will be able to clear the suspense account and move the funds to a reinsurance premium payment account. However, if for some reason the suspense account is not cleared properly, the suspense account will remain open.

The reinsurance staff must regularly investigate unresolved items in suspense accounts and must resolve longstanding suspense account items. A reinsurance analyst may reconcile the unresolved accounts by correcting keying errors or processing transfers of funds to correct the accounting errors.

An ***exception report*** is an internal management report that selects data on the basis of very specific rules for identifying process exceptions. Many automated reinsurance administration systems produce (1) monthly exception reports listing the suspense accounts that remain open and (2) daily exception reports showing accounts that have not been resolved properly. Daily exception reports are often classified as 30 days uncleared; 31 to 60 days uncleared; 61 to 90 days uncleared; and over 90 days uncleared.

Data Integrity Checks

A ***data integrity check*** is a periodic review of electronic data designed to determine whether data in a company's various databases has been duplicated, improperly deleted, or incorrectly linked. For example, an insured's name may appear in case files, claim files, the alpha file, and other administration records. Before insurers produce their periodic financial reports, they typically perform a data integrity check to detect data errors that could cause problems with their reports.

A data integrity check performed on reinsurance administration databases helps a company determine whether any data requires correction. The company's information technology unit typically designs the computer programs needed to perform a data integrity check. If the check identifies problems, the staff investigates each problem and corrects any errors. Typically, the staff should enter any corrections into the company's system before the system produces reports of the company's financial results for the period.

Example: Insurers perform data integrity checks to identify situations in which one segment of a case file appears more than once; an insured's file is missing or contains inconsistent data; or a case file is not correctly linked to related files.

Trend Analysis

A ***trend*** is a change that occurs over time. ***Trend analysis***, also known as *time-series analysis*, is a type of financial analysis that involves assessing numerical patterns to identify changes over time. Trend analysis requires calculating percentage changes in financial statement items over several successive periods. Trend data typically is collected on a daily, weekly, monthly, quarterly, or annual basis.

Statistical tools used in trend analysis include the following types of averages:

■ An **average**, or *arithmetic mean*, is a statistic found by first summing the values of a set of data points and then dividing that sum by the number of data points in the set. For trend data, an average is the sum of the values from a number of periods divided by the number of periods.

■ A **moving average**, or *rolling average*, is an average of the values of a variable over several time periods used to show trends for the latest period. The average for the new period includes the most recent data point and excludes the oldest data point. For a moving average, the trend analyst drops the oldest period each time a new period is added to the analysis.

■ A **weighted average** is a type of average in which the members of a set of data points are assigned different weights before the average is calculated. Data points that are of greater significance are assigned greater weights.

■ A **weighted moving average** is a type of moving average in which the data points are assigned different weights before the average is calculated, with greater weight being assigned to the most recent data points and lower weight assigned to the oldest data points.

A *trend analysis report* displays trends in the organization's experience. Insurers and reinsurers undertake trend analysis to help explain significant variations in their financial results. A company establishes a normal range for each type of data, and an analyst investigates any result that falls outside of the normal range. Reinsurers develop trend analysis reports on a weekly, monthly, or quarterly basis. Figure 12.2 shows examples of changes that could be revealed by trend analysis.

To investigate unexpected trends, an analyst compares the data from the trend analysis report with the information in the company's databases, and then identifies and corrects any data entry errors. If an unexpected change in a trend still exists, the analyst investigates and attempts to identify a reason for the change.

The following events could trigger a trend analysis investigation by a reinsurer:

■ The face amount of or reinsurance coverage on a block of policies changes by more than 10 percent in a specified period

■ The average lapse rate exceeds 15 percent in a specified period

■ The change in the average reinsurance premium is below $3 or above $8 per thousand of total in-force reinsurance

■ Claims exceed 40 percent of the reinsurance premium

Checking Overdue Reports

An **overdue reports check** is a process control in which an employee investigates the status of periodic administrative reports that are late in being delivered. For example, under a self-administered reinsurance agreement, the direct writer must provide the reinsurer with a billing statement, a policy exhibit, a policy change report, a reserve listing, and an in-force policy report at regular intervals. When a report appears to be overdue, a company employee verifies that the reinsurer has not received the report and then makes inquiries of the direct writer. The employee also confirms the receipt of the outstanding report from the direct writer.

FIGURE 12.2

Examples of Changes That Trend Analysis Could Reveal

- A large percentage decrease in the current face amount of a block of policies, indicating an unexpectedly high level of terminations

- An unusual change in the average premium rate per $1,000 of face amount for a block of policies

- A change in the average amount of new business reported

- A change in total claims or average claim size

Source: Adapted from Jane Lightcap Brown and Jennifer W. Herrod, *Reinsurance Administration* (Atlanta: LOMA, © 2000), 220. Used with permission; all rights reserved.

Each company sets its own guidelines as to when the employee should follow up on outstanding reports.

Audits

Typically, auditing functions are separate from the duties of the reinsurance administration department, because audit and control staff must maintain a high degree of independence and objectivity. To support this objectivity, the audit function reports to the company's board of directors through its audit committee. An **audit committee** is a standing committee of a company's board of directors charged with supervising audits of the company's operations.

Audits may be conducted by company staff or outside entities. An **internal audit** is a systematic review of a company's operations conducted by company employees. An **external audit**, sometimes known as a *consulting engagement*, *risk assessment*, or *due diligence review*, is an on-site inspection of a company's procedures, controls, and records conducted by independent third parties who are not employed by the company being audited.

For reinsurance purposes, direct writers and reinsurers use internal and external audits to systematically inspect their reinsurance administration processes. Typically, both direct writers and reinsurers conduct internal audits of their own staff's work and their own processes. In addition, reinsurers conduct external audits of most direct writers with which they do business. A direct writer may do business with more than one reinsurer, and a direct writer is subject to a separate audit by each reinsurer with which it does business. Thus, participation in external audits can be a recurring activity for both direct writers and reinsurers.

Internal Audits

Direct writers and reinsurers conduct internal audits to ensure that their own processes are meeting expectations and to assess the performance of the company's employees. The purpose of an internal audit is to verify that the company's staff are meeting service standards; recording accurate, complete, and current data in the company's files; and following established procedures as defined by the company and its reinsurance agreements. Auditors review the reinsurance department's procedural documentation and select cases to test whether the company's staff followed documented procedures. Internal audits can help to identify any potential shortcomings and opportunities in a company's process controls.

An internal audit may be limited to an audit of reinsurance administration activities involving only one reinsurance unit or function, such as claims or underwriting. In such a limited audit, the internal auditor closely examines a sampling of files to evaluate the accuracy of data entry, maintenance of service standards, and effectiveness of controls. In reviewing each file, the auditor typically examines the accuracy, timeliness, completeness, and consistency of the data maintained by the reinsurance administration unit.

Alternatively, an internal audit may be broad in scope. For such a full internal audit, the internal auditor verifies the accuracy of the following data elements:

- Premiums
- Allowances
- Net amounts at risk
- Reserve amounts
- Cession amounts
- Retention amounts
- Policy numbers
- All dates
- Spellings of names
- Underwriting ratings

If the reinsurance administration process uses electronic databases, the internal auditor may examine how the databases are linked. The linkages should be designed to prevent duplication of data or inconsistent data on the different systems, particularly in the linkage between systems for assumed and ceded business. After an internal audit is completed, the auditor summarizes the audit findings in a report.

Example: The auditor verifies that
(1) the files were organized in accordance with company procedures,
(2) all required information is present,
(3) required approvals were obtained from the correct people (such as underwriters),
(4) the files were handled promptly, and
(5) process controls were effective.

External Audits

External audits are conducted primarily for the benefit of interested third parties, including a company's board of directors, stockholders, policyowners, creditors, regulators, and others who rely on the information contained in the company's financial statements. Companies undergo specific types of external audits in the following circumstances:

- Public companies must hire an independent public accounting firm to perform an annual external audit and to prepare an audit statement for inclusion in the corporate annual report.

- Companies must undergo a *due diligence* type of external audit when they are considering a merger.

- Insurers undergo periodic examinations by regulatory examiners, as described in Chapter 2

- Reinsurance agreements typically grant the reinsurer the right to conduct periodic external audits of the direct writer. Reinsurers typically conduct such external audits of a direct writer every two to three years. The audits provide information for the reinsurer and the direct writer, and the results are not made public.

Our main interest here is a reinsurer's audit of a direct writer, which is very different from other types of external audits. For instance, the reinsurer conducts an audit purely for its own interest, not for public disclosure. Reinsurance agreements contain an **access to records provision**, which gives the reinsurer the authority to examine the direct writer's records related to the business conducted between the companies. Because much reinsurance business is self-administered, reinsurers need a way to verify a direct writer's compliance with the reinsurance agreements and to evaluate how direct writers handle risks that fall outside the parameters of the applicable agreement.

In a reinsurer's external audit of a direct writer, the reinsurer's representatives visit the direct writer and examine various aspects of the direct writer's operations, documents, and data. An external audit may consist of interviews, examination of records, observation of operations, calculation of various values, and review of procedures manuals. An external audit also typically involves negative testing. In this context, **negative testing** is the process of ensuring that the direct writer ceded all of the policies that met the qualifications specified in the reinsurance agreement and no policies that were not covered by the agreement.

Typically, the reinsurer's audit team focuses on the following tasks:

- Understanding the direct writer's operations, workflows, and procedures
- Evaluating the direct writer's administrative processes
- Identifying weaknesses in the direct writer's control systems
- Confirming the direct writer's compliance with the reinsurance agreement
- Reviewing cases to verify the accuracy of amounts retained and reinsured, reinsurance premiums charged, policy terminations and lapses, and billing
- Evaluating the timeliness of the direct writer's reporting
- Reviewing the direct writer's information systems

Both the direct writer and the reinsurer have a right to request additional unscheduled external audits of the direct writer, as follows:

- The direct writer may request an external audit to obtain the reinsurer's objective opinion about any aspect of the direct writer's reinsurance operations. For example, the direct writer may be considering updating its information systems or developing procedures to handle an increase in business volume.

- The reinsurer may request an unscheduled external audit if it discovers irregularities in reinsurance administration by the direct writer. Figure 12.3 presents circumstances in which a reinsurer might request an unscheduled external audit of a direct writer.

FIGURE 12.3

Indications for an Unscheduled External Audit of a Direct Writer

- Complicated reinsurance agreements, plans, or benefits that require special administration procedures
- Large volume of reinsurance that has substantial financial impact on the reinsurer
- Difference in the experience of the reinsured business from what was predicted or from that of the direct writer
- Consistently late, incomplete, or erroneous reports or documents
- Large number of errors and omissions detected at claim time
- Inconsistencies in reporting
- Frequent adjustments to previously reported data
- Problems resulting from systems conversions or personnel changes
- Change in the direct writer's underwriting philosophy and guidelines
- Frequent submission of late claims by the direct writer
- Apparently inadequate investigation of contestable claims by the direct writer
- Negotiation of a new reinsurance agreement that will involve a significant increase in business
- An extensive, recently implemented recapture program
- A recent or an imminent merger or acquisition

Source: Adapted from Jane Lightcap Brown and Jennifer W. Herrod, *Reinsurance Administration* (Atlanta: LOMA, © 2000), 228. Used with permission; all rights reserved.

External audits generally involve four steps: (1) planning and design; (2) gathering information and reviewing records; (3) evaluating audit findings and documenting the audit; and (4) following up after the audit.

Step 1—Planning and Designing the External Audit

When an audit is warranted, the reinsurance audit team begins by contacting the direct writer to schedule the audit. Generally, the audit team tries to give the direct writer two to three months' notice to allow both companies enough time to prepare for the audit.

The reinsurer sends the direct writer an introductory letter that typically describes when the audit will take place, who will be conducting the audit, the purposes of the audit, and the needs of the audit team. Figure 12.4 shows an example of an introductory letter used by one reinsurer. Note that, for some audits, the audited company sends information in advance to the examining company.

The reinsurer's audit team chooses a sample of reinsured cases to examine. The selected cases typically reflect a wide range of types and amounts of coverage. The number of cases sampled varies depending on the situation. The following are examples of factors that may affect the number of cases selected for sampling:

- The number of reinsurance agreements between the direct writer and the reinsurer → The larger the number of agreements, the larger the sample

- The number of reinsured policies in a block → The larger the reinsured block, the larger the sample

- The reinsurer's level of concern about the direct writer's quality control → The greater the reinsurer's concern, the larger the sample

- The variety of plans having a significant volume of business → The larger the volume of business, the larger the sample

The audit team next prepares a policy audit questionnaire for each policy included in the audit sample. A **_policy audit questionnaire_** is a document that allows an audit team to examine the accuracy and timeliness of the data about insureds, compliance with the reinsurance agreement, premium verification, rates and accuracy, and other elements to be examined by comparing the reinsurer's data with the direct writer's data. External auditors complete a policy audit questionnaire for each examined policy. Figure 12.5 lists the topics that typically are addressed in a policy audit questionnaire.

Step 2—Gathering Information and Reviewing Records

The direct writer's staff instructs the external audit team on how to use the computer system to access needed files. The direct writer's staff may demonstrate policy administration work flow, including intake of new business and determining what portion of that business to cede; their billing process; and controls to monitor timeliness, accuracy, and completeness of data.

FIGURE 12.4

Introductory Letter for an External Audit

=== NEW HORIZONS REINSURANCE COMPANY ===

1234 Oak Drive
Cornelius, PA 11111
(555) 555-1111
July 10, 20xx

Mr. Charles Matthews
Vice President, Administration
Luna Life Insurance Company
19 Luna Court
Oberlin, NY 22222

Dear Mr. Matthews:

This letter is to confirm our forthcoming visit to Luna Life. The dates that we have agreed upon are from Wednesday, October 6 to Friday, October 8, 20xx.

The following staff members will be visiting your office:

- Courtney L. Ahn, Manager, Reinsurance Administration
- Kimya Brown, Supervisor, Reinsurance Administration
- Darren P. Levesque, Audit Director

We would like for you to make the following arrangements:

1. An Opening Conference. The opening conference is an opportunity to make any further introductions, summarize the objectives and scope of our review, and outline a schedule for the visit.

2. Sample Cases. We have selected a list of cases for review. We are sending that list under separate cover. We request that files and status reports for these cases be made available for our review.

3. System Access. We would appreciate having some form of inquiry access to your computer system. A brief set of instructions on how to make online inquiries would be helpful.

4. Documentation of Processes and Controls. We would like to review any procedural and workflow documentation that covers the processing of your business. Please demonstrate your workflow for individual cessions and self-administered cessions, including your procedures for

- Billing
- Monitoring timeliness, accuracy, and completeness of your data
- Your reinsurance information management system

5. Amounts Ceded to New Horizons Re and Retention Management. We would also appreciate your describing the methodology for determining the amounts ceded to New Horizons Re and the controls and procedures you have for retention management purposes.

6. Audits. We would appreciate a copy of any formal audit reports from the last two years. If possible, we would like to receive these prior to our arrival.

7. Closing Conference. After our audit, we would like to briefly discuss our overall findings with your staff.

We are looking forward to our visit.

Sincerely,

Courtney L. Ahn

Courtney L. Ahn
Audit Team Leader

Source: Adapted from Jane Lightcap Brown and Jennifer W. Herrod, *Reinsurance Administration* (Atlanta: LOMA, © 2000), 231. Used with permission; all rights reserved.

FIGURE 12.5

Policy Audit Questionnaire

Insured's Information	Identification Numbers	Direct Policy Information
Name _____	Reinsurer's policy number _____	Mortality rate/ mortality charge _____
Age at time of issue _____	Direct writer's policy number _____	Policy issue date (Date the policy became effective) _____
Date of birth _____	Cession number _____	
Smoking class _____	Reinsurance agreement number _____	
Underwriting basis _____		
Sex _____		

Reinsurance Agreement Compliance

Is the cession within the automatic limit outlined in the agreement? _____

Is the cession within the reinsurer's retention? _____

Has the direct writer kept its full retention? _____

Is the insured within the age limit set in the agreement? _____

Is the insured within the mortality rate set out in the agreement? _____

Is the policy effective date within the effective date of the agreement? _____

Are all plans and benefits applied for covered under the agreement? _____

Premium Verification

Net amount at risk _____

Face amount of policy _____

Year being audited _____

The reinsurance premium rate per thousand of in-force in the reinsurance agreement _____

The annual premium calculated based on NAAR and rates in the reinsurance agreement _____

The substandard premiun rate per thousand per investigation _____

The commission rate in the reinsurance agreement _____

The premium calculated based on the reinsurance agreement _____

The expected net premium _____

The rate per thousand used by the direct writer _____

The annual premium calculated by the direct writer _____

The substandard rate per thousand calculated by the direct writer _____

The substandard premium calculated by the direct writer _____

The direct writer's commission rate _____

The commission calculated by the direct writer _____

The actual net premium _____

continued on next page

FIGURE 12.5 *continued*

Policy Audit Questionnaire

Rates and Accuracy

Is the cession administered on the premium rates
  in the reinsurance agreement?

Is the reinsurer's calculation of the premium the
  same as the direct writer's?

Was the correct quota share applied?

When was the reinsurance premium paid?

Comments and Follow-Up

Do the auditors need to know anything else
about this case to understand it?

Does anything about this case need to be
discussed with the direct writer during the audit?

Source: Adapted from Jane Lightcap Brown and Jennifer W. Herrod, *Reinsurance Administration* (Atlanta: LOMA, © 2000), 232. Used with permission; all rights reserved.

Next, the external audit team reviews the selected sample files, investigates any special circumstances it encounters, and examines the direct writer's retention management, audit processes, and technology. At this point, the external audit team follows the audit plan and uses the policy audit questionnaire.

The external audit team audits the direct writer's underwriting administration by interviewing the direct writer's underwriters to determine whether underwriters

- Understand automatic binding limits, jumbo limits, and other constraints, so that the underwriters assign cases to appropriate reinsurers

- Understand retention limits and follow appropriate procedures for determining cession amounts

- Follow appropriate procedures for updating files and other system records

In an audit of a direct writer's claim administration, the external audit team ensures that the direct writer's procedures for administering claims are timely, accurate, and properly documented; that the direct writer's staff applies claim procedures consistently; that the direct writer has guidelines for contestable claims; and that the direct writer's staff follows the guidelines for contestable claims. The external audit team also evaluates the expertise of the claim staff.

The sample files used for auditing claims generally include files of contestable claims, uncontested but large claims, foreign claims, claims involving errors and omissions, claims involving conversions and reinstatements, and any other unusual claims. Types of claims audited include life claims, disability claims, and critical illness claims, as appropriate.

At the end of the audit visit, the audit team meets with the direct writer's staff and presents the audit team's initial findings and recommendations. The audit team may help the direct writer solve problems or improve its processes.

Step 3—Evaluating the Audit Findings and Documenting the Audit

To document its findings, the audit team prepares a written **audit report** that includes the following types of documentation:

- **An analysis of problems.** A brief description of the problems uncovered; an assessment of the severity of each problem; whether the problem is a one-time error or a systemic error; the estimated financial impact of the problem; and the proposed resolution for each problem

- **An internal trip report.** A detailed review of the audit, intended for the reinsurer's management team

- **The audit report.** A document created for the direct writer, communicating the audit's significant findings and recommendations

- **Direct writer's management response.** The direct writer's action plan documenting corrective steps the direct writer has agreed to take

Step 4—Follow-Up after the External Audit

During follow-up, the direct writer and the reinsurer complete actions agreed to during the audit and correct data and processes as needed. During this step, the direct writer and the reinsurer collaborate to solve problems.

Desk Audits

In reinsurance, a **desk audit** is a reinsurer's systematic review of the quality of the direct writer's reinsurance administration, performed by the reinsurer's staff at the reinsurer's own offices. Desk audits verify that the information a reinsurer has received from a direct writer is accurate and timely and complies with the applicable reinsurance agreements. A desk audit allows a reinsurer to review a direct writer's procedures without the reinsurer's incurring the large costs associated with a more extensive external audit. The desk audit is limited in scope because the reinsurer does not actually examine the direct writer on site, nor does the reinsurer examine information on risks that the direct writer retained. Reinsurers conduct desk audits in a variety of situations. Whereas some very detailed one-time desk audits may be conducted to address concerns about a particular direct writer, other desk audits are ongoing, and yet other desk audits may be repeated at regular intervals. A desk audit may be conducted in preparation for an external audit. Figure 12.6 shows the types of verification that are part of a desk audit.

Details Checked in a Desk Audit

The reinsurer obtains copies of case files that cover a mix of policy types. Typically, the reinsurer samples cases representing standard and substandard underwriting classifications; insureds of both sexes and various ages; various coverages; facultative and automatic cessions; YRT and coinsurance plans of reinsurance; and new business, in-force business, and terminations.

During such a desk audit, the reinsurer usually checks for accuracy of the following information:

- Reinsurance premium rates, allowances, age, and duration of coverage
- Calculation of joint age
- Calculation of reinsurance premium
- Amounts retained and ceded, and quota share applied
- Effective date of policy
- Allowable products
- Calculation of allowance
- Experience refund

- Automatic binding limit and jumbo limit
- Coverage of cession under the reinsurance agreement
- Age exclusion
- Allowable conversions and reinstatements
- Recapture
- Reserve valuation
- New business close date

Auditors report the findings of a desk audit in detail to the direct writer, including suggestions for correcting noted errors or checking policies needing investigation. Figure 12.7 presents examples of possible findings of a desk audit.

Comparison of Internal Audits, External Audits, and Desk Audits

Audits in reinsurance administration focus on verifying the quality of the direct writer's administrative processes. Thus, in reinsurance administration, internal audits, external audits, and desk audits focus on the direct writer rather than the reinsurer.

Whereas an internal audit of reinsurance administration involves the direct writer's evaluation of its own administration, the reinsurer performs the desk audit and the external audit of the direct writer.

Desk Audit Report

The audit sampled 90 policies.

■ All sample policies reflect the correct quota share percentage.

■ Policy dates of all policies fall within the reinsurance agreement's effective date.

■ Retention for all policies is correct.

■ Average lapsed time between reinsurance premium due date and payment received date was approximately 109.5 days.

Reinsurer's Policy Number	Insured's Name	Comments and Corrections
1132313231	Patel, Violet	Renewal premiums equal zero. Follow up with client.
13245456342	Brown, Maxwell	Change joint equal age of 44 to a single life age of 48.
12455553423	Wallace, Matthew	Cession form shows Mexico as the country of residence; in-force report shows residence as Colombia. Follow up with client.
12985435465	Dennis, Hillary	Commission rate used should be 25% versus 30% for this plan. Screen all policies in this plan and adjust.
12446970596	Hansen, Nathaniel	According to the in-force report, the insured has a substandard underwriting classification. Facultative underwriting decision is a standard classification. Check the discrepancy and correct.

Key Terms

quality control
standard
quality control ratio
segregation of duties
incompatible functions
execution of transactions as authorized
authorization level
recording of transactions as executed
safeguarding of assets
physical comparison of recorded amounts
reconciliation by exception
Sarbanes-Oxley Act of 2002
process control
suspense account
exception report
data integrity check

trend
trend analysis
average
moving average
weighted average
weighted moving average
overdue reports check
audit committee
internal audit
external audit
access to records provision
negative testing
policy audit questionnaire
audit report
desk audit

Endnotes

1. This chapter represents a revision of material from Jane Lightcap Brown and Jennifer W. Herrod, *Reinsurance Administration* (Atlanta: LOMA, © 2000), 215–235. Used with permission; all rights reserved.

2. Adapted from Elizabeth A. Mulligan, *The Accounting Function and Management Accounting in Life Insurance Companies* (Atlanta: LOMA, © 2002), 63–66. Used with permission; all rights reserved.

3. U.S. Securities and Exchange Commission, "SEC Implements Internal Control Provisions of Sarbanes-Oxley Act," 27 May 2003, http://www.sec.gov/news/press/2003-66.htm (4 December 2003).

GLOSSARY

access to records provision.
A reinsurance agreement provision that gives the reinsurance company the authority to examine the direct writer's records related to the business conducted between the companies. [12]

accidental death benefit (ADB) rider premium rate table.
A premium rate table that shows a supplemental premium rate for optional accidental death benefit coverage. [7]

account.
The basic tool that a company uses to record, group, and summarize similar types of financial transactions. [11]

accounting.
A system or set of rules and methods for collecting, recording, analyzing, summarizing, and reporting financial information. [9]

accounting entry.
A record of a monetary transaction made in a journal. [11]

accredited reinsurer.
A reinsurance company that is not licensed in the ceding company's jurisdiction, but meets specified financial and reporting requirements of that jurisdiction and holds a license in and is domiciled in at least one other jurisdiction. [2]

acquisition.
A transaction wherein one company gains a controlling interest in another company, resulting in a linkage between formerly independent corporations. [11]

acquisition expenses.
A direct writer's costs that are directly attributable to developing, marketing, and issuing new business. [1]

actual damages.
See **compensatory damages**.

actuary.
A technical expert in insurance products and financial instruments who applies mathematical knowledge to industry and company statistics to calculate various financial values. [9]

ADB rider premium rate table.
See **accidental death benefit rider premium rate table**.

administration expense.
See **maintenance expense**.

administrative supervision.
A legal condition under which regulators require an insurer to obtain regulatory permission before taking any of a variety of specified actions. [6]

admitted assets.
For an insurer, assets whose full value can be reported on the assets page of the U.S. Annual Statement. [2]

admitted reinsurer.
See **authorized reinsurer**.

adverse risk experience.
A worse outcome from a reinsured product's operations than the outcome the direct writer and the reinsurer assumed when setting reinsurance premium rates. *Contrast with* **favorable risk experience**. [7]

agency.
A legal relationship in which one party—the *principal*—authorizes another party—the *agent*—to act on the principal's behalf. [9]

agent.
In an agency relationship, the party that is authorized to act on behalf of another party, the *principal*. [9]

aggregate premium rate table.
A premium rate table that shows one set of premium rates for all insureds. [7]

agreement effective date.
The date on which a reinsurance agreement takes effect. [4]

allowance.
In reinsurance, an amount granted by a reinsurer to a direct writer and designed to recognize the direct writer's acquisition, maintenance, and other costs. Also known as *expense allowance, reinsurance allowance, ceding commission,* or *reinsurance commission*. [1]

alpha file.
A database that is maintained by a reinsurer and that contains information about the amount of reinsurance currently in force and applied for on all insureds, organized by the insureds' last names. [10]

amalgamation.
See **merger**.

Annual Statement.
A financial report that every insurer in the United States must file at least annually with the National Association of Insurance Commissioners (NAIC) and the insurance regulatory organization in each state in which the insurer conducts business. Regulators use the information in the report to evaluate an insurance company's solvency and its compliance with insurance laws. [2]

antivirus software.
A computer application that detects viruses and works to prevent them from infecting a computer and/or helps an infected computer recover. [9]

arbitration.
A method of dispute resolution in which impartial third parties—known as *arbitrators*—evaluate the facts in dispute and render a decision that usually is binding on the parties to the dispute. [6]

arbitration provision.

A reinsurance agreement provision that requires the reinsurance parties to submit disputes they cannot resolve through negotiation to an arbitration panel rather than to a court of law and that describes the procedures the parties must use to select arbitrators and conduct the arbitration process. [6]

arbitrator.

An impartial third party who evaluates the facts in a dispute and renders a decision that usually is binding on the parties to the dispute. [6]

arithmetic mean.

See **average**.

article.

A relatively standard provision found in reinsurance agreements. [4]

asset account.

An account that shows the monetary values of items that a company owns. [11]

asset risk.

For an insurance product, the risk that the assets supporting the product will lose value or will fail to earn at least the rate of return used in the product design. [3]

assets.

All the things of value owned by a company, such as cash, financial securities, buildings, furniture, and land. *Contrast with* **liabilities**. [2]

association examination.

An on-site regulatory examination that conforms to the procedures outlined in the *Examiners Handbook* published by the National Association of Insurance Commissioners (NAIC). *See also* **financial condition examination**; **market conduct examination**. [2]

assumption certificate.

An insurance certificate issued to an insurer's existing policyowners to show that a reinsurer has assumed from the issuing company all of the risk under the policies. *See also* **assumption reinsurance**. [1]

assumption reinsurance.

A type of reinsurance that involves the total and permanent transfer of risk from the issuing company to a reinsurer. In assumption reinsurance, a reinsurer purchases a block of in-force insurance, creating contractual relationships with all insureds and assuming responsibility for policy administration and all liabilities. Also known as *portfolio reinsurance*. *Contrast with* **traditional indemnity reinsurance**. [1]

Assumption Reinsurance Model Act.

A sample law sponsored by the National Association of Insurance Commissioners (NAIC) in the United States to provide for the regulation of the transfer and novation of insurance contracts by way of assumption reinsurance. Defines the rights and responsibilities of policyholders, regulators, and the parties to assumption reinsurance agreements. [2]

attachment point.

In a reinsurance arrangement, the specified monetary limit at which a direct writer's obligation transfers to the reinsurer. [3]

audit.

An evaluation of a company's records and operations to ensure the accuracy of the records and the effectiveness of the company's operational policies and procedures. A periodic appraisal of a company's objectives, procedures, personnel, controls, and records. [9, 12]

audit committee.

A standing committee of a company's board of directors charged with supervising audits of the company's operations. [12]

audit report.

A written report prepared by an audit team to document the findings of an external audit. [12]

authorization level.

The maximum monetary amount that a company employee has the official power to approve on behalf of the company. [12]

authorized reinsurer.

A reinsurance company that is licensed or otherwise recognized by the insurance department in the jurisdiction of a direct writer. Also known as an *admitted reinsurer*. [2]

automatic binding limit.

Under an automatic reinsurance arrangement, the maximum monetary amount of risk the reinsurer will obligate itself to automatically accept on a given policy or case without making an independent underwriting assessment. The reinsurer is obligated to automatically accept the entire ceded risk on all policies when that risk does not exceed the automatic binding limit. [3]

automatic reinsurance.

A reinsurance cession basis in which a direct writer agrees in advance to cede and a reinsurer agrees in advance to assume all cases meeting the specifications in the reinsurance arrangement. Automatic reinsurance allows a direct writer to *automatically* bind a reinsurer to a risk without first providing the reinsurer with underwriting evidence for the case and without asking the reinsurer's approval in advance. *Contrast with* **facultative reinsurance; facultative-obligatory (fac-ob) reinsurance.** [3]

average.

A statistic found by first summing the values of a set of data points and then dividing that sum by the number of data points in the set. Also known as an *arithmetic mean*. [12]

B2B e-commerce.

See **business-to-business e-commerce**.

bad faith.

A dishonest motive or an intention to knowingly commit a wrong or fail to fulfill a legal duty. Also known as *malfeasance*. [6]

balance sheet.
   A financial document that lists the values of a company's assets, liabilities, and capital and surplus as of a specific date. A financial statement that shows a company's financial condition or position as of a specified date; summarizes what a company owns (assets), what it owes (liabilities), and its owners' investment in the company (capital and surplus or owners' equity) on a specified date. [2]

basic accounting equation.
   A mathematical formula which states that assets equal the sum of liabilities and owners' equity; forms the basis of a balance sheet. [2]

billing statement.
   A reinsurance report that lists the amounts owed by and due to each party to the reinsurance agreement. [11]

binding premium receipt.
   An insurance premium receipt that provides temporary insurance coverage from the time the applicant receives the receipt. Also known as a *temporary insurance agreement* (*TIA*). [4]

boiler and machinery insurance.
   A type of property insurance that covers losses incurred to boilers and machinery as a result of boiler explosions, electrical malfunctions, and machinery breakdowns. [1]

bordereau.
   In some self-administered reinsurance arrangements, a written report sent regularly to the reinsurer to provide current information about ceded risks. [5]

bordereau service.
   A direct writer's action of providing a reinsurer with a list of total reinsurance premiums and other information. [5]

bulk administration.
   A method of reinsurance record administration in which the direct writer periodically submits summarized reports, such as reinsurance premium and policy summaries, to the reinsurer. [5]

business income insurance.
   A type of property insurance that covers losses resulting from the suspension of business operations, including loss of net income, expenses that continue during suspension of business operations, and extra expenses incurred to avoid or minimize business interruption. [1]

business-to-business (B2B) e-commerce.
   The electronic transmission of data or information between organizations to perform or facilitate business transactions. [9]

Canadian Reinsurance Conference (CRC).
   An annual meeting of Canadian insurance companies and reinsurance companies that provides a forum for current life and health insurance and reinsurance issues. The CRC establishes the Canadian Reinsurance Guidelines. [2]

Canadian Reinsurance Guidelines.

A set of common reinsurance principles, established by the Canadian Reinsurance Conference (CRC), that can be voluntarily used as a basis upon which new reinsurance treaties can be written and existing treaties can be interpreted. [2]

capital.

(1) An amount of money invested in a company by its owners, usually through the purchase of the company's stock. (2) Long-term funds. For insurers, may refer to capital and surplus together. [2]

capital and surplus.

For insurers, the amount remaining after liabilities are subtracted from assets; owners' equity in an insurance company. Also known as *owners' equity*. [2]

capital and surplus account.

An account that represents a company's value and shows the difference between the company's assets and its liabilities. [11]

capital ratio.

A financial ratio that expresses the relationship between an insurer's capital and surplus and its liabilities. [2]

captive reinsurer.

A reinsurer that is formed for the purpose of providing reinsurance by an insurance company or another type of company and that is controlled by that company. [1]

cash value reimbursement.

An amount a reinsurer pays to a direct writer when a life insurance policyowner surrenders a policy reinsured under a coinsurance or modco reinsurance agreement in exchange for the policy's cash value. [11]

cat cover.

See **catastrophe coverage**.

catastrophe coverage.

A type of nonproportional reinsurance designed to partially protect direct writers from (1) a single catastrophic event resulting in multiple claims or (2) an annual total of claims in a catastrophic amount. The coverage usually is a backup for accident or casualty coverages. The coverage usually requires the reinsurer to pay claims on the direct writer's total claims above a stated amount, subject to (1) a minimum number of qualified claims or minimum amount of claim benefits and (2) a maximum total reinsurance payout. Also known as *cat cover*. [3]

ceding commission.

See **allowance**.

ceding company.

See **direct writer**.

cession.

Both the unit of insurance that a direct writer transfers to a reinsurer and the document used to record the transfer of risk from a direct writer to a reinsurer. [1]

claim administration.
The process of evaluating claims and determining the insurer's responsibility for paying those claims. [9]

claim file.
An organized collection of all the information relevant to a claim. [11]

claim fraud.
An action by which a person intentionally uses false information in an unfair or unlawful attempt to collect benefits under an insurance policy. [11]

claim provision.
A reinsurance agreement provision which states the terms and conditions of the reinsurer's liability for claims submitted under reinsured policies. [6]

claim worksheet.
A standard form that a reinsurance analyst uses to document the progress and results of the claim administration process. [11]

claims bordereau.
In some self-administered reinsurance arrangements, a report that includes information about the individual claims received and/or paid by the direct writer on reinsured policies and the reinsurer's obligation under those claims. Also called a *loss bordereau*. [5]

close notice.
See **drop notice**.

coinsurance.
A basic type of proportional reinsurance, suitable for life, annuity, health, disability income, and long-term care coverages, in which a direct writer and a reinsurer proportionately share the obligations of a policy, including paying the death benefit and the nonforfeiture values, and establishing the policy reserve. [3]

coinsurance allowance.
In a coinsurance arrangement, an allowance that the reinsurer provides to the direct writer to acknowledge expenses. The coinsurance allowance can be calculated as a specified proportionate share of the coinsurance gross premium. *See* **allowance**. [3]

coinsurance gross premium.
In a coinsurance arrangement, the reinsurance gross premium including reinsurance allowances. [3]

coinsurance net premium.
In a coinsurance arrangement, the amount the direct writer must pay to the reinsurer after subtracting the coinsurance allowance from the reinsurance gross premium. [3]

combined retention.
See **corporate retention limit**.

commercial automobile insurance.

A type of property insurance that comes in three forms: business automobile coverage, which is similar to personal automobile coverage; garage coverage, which covers businesses that sell, service, park, or store automobiles; and motor carrier coverage, which covers businesses that provide transportation of people, goods, or both, as specified in the policy. [1]

commercial liability insurance.

A type of liability insurance that covers bodily injury and property damage liability, personal and advertising injury liability (such as defamation), and medical payments. [1]

commercial property insurance.

A type of property insurance that covers buildings and personal property owned by a business and personal property of others in the care of the business. [1]

compensatory damages.

In the context of a claim contest, monetary awards paid to a claimant for damage suffered as a result of an insurer's improper denial of a claim. Also known as *actual damages*. [6]

complete bordereau service.

A bordereau service that includes reports on every case covered by the reinsurer. [5]

compliance unit.

The insurance company functional area that performs a wide variety of activities to ensure that company operations adhere to applicable laws and regulations and company policies. [9]

computer virus.

A computer program that attaches itself to other programs and activates itself, often destroying data and programs or disabling computers in the infected system. [9]

condition.

See **schedule**.

conditional premium receipt.

An insurance premium receipt that specifies certain conditions that must be met—for example, the insurer must find the proposed insured to be insurable—before the temporary insurance coverage provided by the receipt becomes effective. [4]

conservatorship.

See **receivership**.

consulting engagement.

See **external audit**.

consumer credit report.

A report prepared by a consumer reporting agency that (1) bears on a consumer's credit worthiness, credit standing, credit capacity, character, general reputation, personal characteristics, or mode of living and (2) is used or collected as a factor in establishing the consumer's eligibility for insurance or credit. [9]

consumer reporting agency.
A person or organization that assembles or evaluates consumer credit reports and furnishes these reports to other people and organizations in exchange for a fee. [9]

contest.
In the context of insurance claim administration, a court action to determine the validity of a claim. [6]

contestable claim.
A claim for life insurance policy proceeds following the death of an insured during the policy's contestable period. [11]

contestable period.
In a life insurance policy, a specified time period following policy issuance or reinstatement—typically two years in the United States—during which the insurer has the right to rescind the policy if the application for insurance contained a material misrepresentation. [11]

continuation.
For an insurance policy, an event that occurs either when (1) the provisions of an in-force policy are significantly modified or (2) a policy replaces an existing policy from the same direct writer. Additionally, a continuation of an insurance policy differs from a new policy in at least one of the following ways: the policy is not subject to the company's new business underwriting requirements; the direct writer does not pay full first-year commissions to the insurance producer; the policy does not introduce a new suicide exclusion period; or the policy does not introduce a new contestable period. [5]

continuation coverage.
The coverage provided to the customers of a failed insurance company under an assumption reinsurance arrangement. [6]

continuations provision.
A reinsurance agreement provision that addresses which reinsurer(s) should provide the reinsurance, the amount of reinsurance, and the effective date of reinsurance for continued policies. [5]

controlling interest.
Ownership of enough voting shares of stock in a company to control company policy. [11]

conversion.
A new policy that is issued on the basis of the policyowner's contractual right to change the policy form, as provided in the original policy. [5]

conversions provision.
A reinsurance agreement provision that typically states (1) that the direct writer must continue the reinsurance on converted policies with the original reinsurer unless the reinsurer releases its right to reinsure the policies and (2) any conditions under which the direct writer or the reinsurer can cancel the reinsurance on conversions. [5]

corporate retention limit.
In reinsurance, the maximum amount of risk that a group of affiliated companies will retain on any one life. Also known as *combined retention*. [8]

corridor.

See **retention limit corridor**.

CRC.

See **Canadian Reinsurance Conference**.

credit.

A specified change made to the monetary value of an account that (1) increases the value of liability accounts, capital and surplus accounts, and revenue accounts and (2) decreases the value of asset accounts and expense accounts. [11]

Credit for Reinsurance Model Law.

A sample law sponsored by the National Association of Insurance Commissioners (NAIC) in the United States to provide requirements for taking reserve credits for the risk transfer in reinsurance. The Model Law is designed to protect the interests of the public and ensure payment of valid reinsurer obligations. [2]

Credit for Reinsurance Model Regulation.

A sample regulation sponsored by the National Association of Insurance Commissioners (NAIC) in the United States to provide guidance for using trusts and escrow accounts, letters of credit, and funds withheld to provide financial backing for reserve credits in reinsurance transactions. Specifies how to implement requirements of the *Credit for Reinsurance Model Law*. Provides language for a certificate, Form AR-1, for an assuming insurer (reinsurer) to provide to the proper insurance commissioner. [2]

crime insurance.

A type of property insurance that covers losses of money, securities, and tangible property resulting from the commission of certain specified crimes, such as burglary, robbery, theft, employee dishonesty, and forgery. [1]

currency of risk.

The currency, specified in a reinsurance agreement, that is to be used in calculating the amount of risk reinsured. Also known as *original currency*. [7]

D&O liability insurance.

See **directors and officers liability insurance**.

data integrity check.

A periodic review of electronic data to determine if the data has been duplicated, deleted, or incorrectly linked in the various databases that a direct writer or reinsurer uses. [12]

date of expiry.

The date on which a reinsurer will cancel a reservation of reinsurance capacity if the reinsurer does not receive a cession or other placement information from the direct writer. [10]

debit.

A specified change made to the monetary value of an account that (1) increases the value of asset accounts and expense accounts and (2) decreases the value of liability accounts, capital and surplus accounts, and revenue accounts. [11]

desk audit.
  In reinsurance, the systematic and ongoing review of a direct writer's quality of administration, performed by the reinsurer's staff at the reinsurer's own offices. [12]

direct premium.
  In reinsurance, the direct writer's premium on the original policy. [7]

direct writer.
  An insurer that sells coverage directly to consumers. Also known as *ceding company*. [1]

directors and officers (D&O) liability insurance.
  A type of liability insurance that covers directors and officers of a corporation for their own liability resulting from failing to exercise the appropriate standard of care when discharging their corporate duties. [1]

disintermediation risk.
  For an insurance product, the risks that interest rates will change and (1) policy loans and surrenders will increase or (2) maturing contracts will renew less frequently than was assumed in the product design. [3]

divisible surplus.
  The amount of an insurance company's surplus that is available for distribution to policyholders who own participating policies. [7]

document management system.
  A technology that stores, organizes, and retrieves documents that have been (1) created electronically and converted to digital images by computer or (2) created on paper and converted to digital images through imaging. [9]

domicile.
  In the United States, the state in which an insurance company is incorporated. Also known as *domiciliary state*. [2]

domiciliary state.
  See **domicile**.

drop notice.
  A written notification from a direct writer to a reinsurer stating that the direct writer no longer needs reinsurance that it previously requested and asking the reinsurer to cancel the reservation. Also known as a *close notice*. [10]

dual control.
  See **segregation of duties**.

due diligence review.
  See **external audit**.

early warning financial ratio tests.
  For insurance companies, a set of standards and financial ratios that regulatory examiners use to analyze an insurer's financial statements and to create a customized examination plan that focuses on the risks identified from the insurer's financial information. [2]

e-commerce.
See **electronic commerce.**

EDI.
See **electronic data interchange.**

electronic commerce (e-commerce).
The use of the Internet and other computer networks to deliver commercial information and to facilitate business transactions and the delivery of products and services. [9]

electronic data interchange (EDI).
The computer-to-computer exchange of data between organizations using a data format agreed upon by the sending and receiving parties. [9]

encryption.
A technology that encodes data and information so that only an authorized person possessing the required computer equipment and/or programming can decode the data. [9]

entire agreement provision.
A reinsurance agreement provision stating that the written agreement and any amendments represent the whole agreement between the parties, which have no further agreement than that stated in the written document. [4]

errors and omissions provision.
A reinsurance agreement provision which states that if either party to the agreement fails to comply with the terms of the agreement through unintentional mistake or clerical error, then both parties will be restored to the position they would have occupied if the mistake or error had not occurred. [6]

escrow account.
An amount of money that one party to a transaction sets aside in a restricted account for the benefit of the other party to the transaction until specified requirements of an agreement have been met. [2]

examiner.
In the United States, a representative of a state insurance department who participates in market conduct and/or financial condition examinations by visiting insurers' home offices or regional offices and reviewing the insurers' business records. [2]

exception report.
An internal management report that selects data on the basis of very specific rules to identify process exceptions. [12]

excess and umbrella liability insurance.
A type of liability insurance that provides additional liability limits for underlying coverages. [1]

excess-of-loss ratio reinsurance.
See **stop-loss reinsurance.**

excess-of-loss reinsurance.

A type of nonproportional reinsurance in which a reinsurer is responsible for paying the entire amount—within a specified range of monetary amounts—of a direct writer's claim benefits paid on a single loss. An excess-of-loss plan specifies both a lower and an upper limit on the reinsurer's monetary obligation for a single loss. The reinsurer covers the entire amount of the loss within the specified coverage range. A type of nonproportional reinsurance which protects direct writers from excessive total claim costs on a single loss. *Contrast with* **stop-loss reinsurance.** [3]

excess of retention.

Generally, in proportional reinsurance, the monetary amount of risk remaining after a direct writer's retention limit is subtracted from the net amount at risk on a case. *See* **net amount at risk**; **retention limit.** [3]

excess-of-retention arrangement.

A method of ceding proportional reinsurance in which the direct writer establishes a dollar-amount retention limit, and the reinsurer agrees to assume amounts over the insurer's retention limit, up to the reinsurer's automatic binding limit. [3]

excess-of-time reinsurance.

See **extended-time reinsurance**.

excess quota share arrangement.

A method of ceding proportional reinsurance in which the direct writer keeps its full retention limit and cedes the remaining risk to two or more reinsurers on a percentage basis. Found mostly in old business. *See also* **retention limit; quota share.** [3]

execution of transactions as authorized.

A control principle that concerns the delegation of authority to perform specified tasks and the communication of that authority. [12]

exhibit.

See **schedule**.

expense account.

An account that shows the uses of a company's funds. [11]

expense allowance.

See **allowance**.

expense risk.

For an insurance product, the risk that an insurance company's first-year or renewal expenses to support the product will exceed the expense level built into the product's design and pricing. [3]

experience refund.

An amount credited by a reinsurer to a ceding company as compensation for the reinsurer's lower than expected mortality experience. [7]

extended-time reinsurance.

A type of nonproportional reinsurance in which the reinsurer takes over paying policy benefits after the direct writer has paid policy benefits for a specified amount of time. The direct writer is not required to repay the reinsurer. Also known as *excess-of-time reinsurance*. [3]

extension request.

A request from a direct writer to a reinsurer to extend the direct writer's reservation of capacity for a specified period so that the direct writer can gather all information needed to move the case from *reserved* to *placed* status. [10]

external audit.

An on-site inspection of a company's procedures, controls, and records conducted by independent third parties who are not employed by the company being audited. Also known as a *consulting engagement*, *risk assessment*, or *due-diligence review*. *Contrast with* **internal audit**. *See also* **audit**. [12]

extra-percentage premium rate table.

A type of substandard extra premium rate table, designed for application to a constant extra risk, that shows premium rates that are a certain percentage greater than the insurer's standard premium rates. [7]

extracontractual damages.

Monetary awards that are given to a party to a lawsuit in addition to compensatory damages. [6]

fac-ob reinsurance.

See **facultative-obligatory reinsurance**.

facultative application.

See **request for coverage**.

facultative certificate.

A short-form reinsurance contract issued by a reinsurance company to cover a specific risk—usually a casualty type of risk—under a specific insurance policy. These certificates typically document a facultative reinsurance arrangement. *See* **facultative reinsurance**. [1]

facultative-obligatory (fac-ob) reinsurance.

A reinsurance cession basis in which (1) the direct writer may choose to submit cases to a reinsurer and (2) the reinsurer is obligated to accept the submitted cases based on the direct writer's underwriting, up to a stated monetary amount, if the reinsurer has available capacity. *Contrast with* **automatic reinsurance**; **facultative reinsurance**. [3]

facultative reinsurance.

A reinsurance cession basis in which a direct writer chooses whether to cede a risk and a reinsurer chooses whether to accept that risk. A reinsurer has no obligation to submit a quote for a case submitted on a facultative basis. *Contrast with* **automatic reinsurance**; **facultative-obligatory reinsurance**. [3]

farm insurance.
A type of property insurance that covers farm property and can also cover the owner's home and personal property. [1]

favorable risk experience.
A better outcome from a reinsured product's operations than the outcome the direct writer and the reinsurer assumed when setting reinsurance premium rates. *Contrast with* **adverse risk experience**. [7]

FDQS arrangement.
See **first-dollar quota share arrangement**.

financial accounting.
A type of accounting that focuses primarily on reporting a company's financial information to meet the needs of the company's external users. [9]

financial capacity.
The total monetary amount of risk an insurance company can accept based on the capital it has available to write new business. *Contrast with* **underwriting capacity**. [1]

financial condition examination.
A type of routine on-site regulatory examination of an insurer for the purpose of identifying and monitoring any threats to the insurer's solvency. *Contrast with* **market conduct examination**. [2]

Financial Regulation Standards and Accreditation Program.
A program sponsored by the National Association of Insurance Commissioners (NAIC) in the United States to provide a method for states to demonstrate that their solvency regulation systems meet specified minimum standards so that other states can be confident those regulatory systems are adequate and effective. [2]

financial reinsurance.
See **finite reinsurance**.

finite reinsurance.
A nontraditional indemnity reinsurance arrangement that allows the direct writer to improve its financial position through the timing and the method of a risk transfer. Also known as *financial reinsurance*. *Contrast with* **traditional indemnity reinsurance**; **assumption reinsurance**. [1]

firewall.
A combination of computer equipment and programming that creates an electronic barrier between the public and private areas of a company's systems. [9]

first-dollar quota share (FDQS) arrangement.
A method of proportional reinsurance in which a direct writer cedes a certain percentage of the entire risk to one or more reinsurers, despite the presence of a retention limit—that is, the direct writer cedes coverage from the first dollar. The arrangement usually states a maximum monetary amount that the reinsurer is willing to accept. [3]

flat extra premium.

A specified flat monetary amount per $1,000 of insurance that a direct writer imposes for insureds in a substandard risk class. [7]

flat extra premium rate table.

A type of substandard extra premium rate table, designed for application to a constant extra risk, that shows a specified extra dollar amount will be added to the standard premium. [7]

fraud.

An act by which one party intentionally deceives another party and induces that other party to part with something of value or give up a legal right. [6]

funds withheld coinsurance.

A variation on basic coinsurance in which the direct writer retains the initial gross premium and the reinsurer retains the initial coinsurance allowance. *See also* **coinsurance; coinsurance allowance**. [3]

gender-specific premium rate table.

A premium rate table that shows different premium rates for males and females of the same age. *Contrast with* **unisex premium rate table**. [7]

good faith.

A party's honesty of intention and avoidance of attempts to deceive or take unfair advantage of another party to an agreement. [6]

gross profit ratio.

A financial ratio that measures the growth in an insurance company's capital. [4]

guaranteed-issue basis.

An underwriting basis under which a direct writer does not conduct individual underwriting and automatically issues a policy to every eligible proposed insured who applies and meets specified conditions. [10]

guaranty association.

An agency that is formed by member insurance companies operating in a given jurisdiction and that is responsible for covering an insolvent insurer's financial obligations to customers and ensuring that these customers are treated equitably when the insurer's assets are distributed. [6]

imaging.

A process of converting printed characters or graphics into digital images by using a device called a scanner, which "reads" the characters and graphics on the document and "translates" them into an electronic file, which is then converted to digital images and stored in an information system. Also known as *scanning*. [9]

incompatible functions.

Job duties in the normal course of employment that, when combined, place an employee in a position where he or she could commit an illegal act or could conceal errors or irregularities. [12]

indemnity reinsurance.
  See **traditional indemnity reinsurance**.

individual cession administration.
  A method of reinsurance record administration under which the reinsurer prepares its own cession records based on detailed information about individual cessions provided by the direct writer. [5]

in-force policy report.
  A reinsurance report that lists all in-force reinsured policies as of a given date and provides detailed information about each policy. [11]

information system.
  An interactive combination of technology, people, and processes that collects, manipulates, and disseminates information. [9]

information technology (IT).
  The insurance company department that develops and maintains the company's information systems and oversees information management throughout the company. [9]

inland marine insurance.
  A type of property insurance that covers property in transit over land and instruments of communication or transportation, such as tunnels and bridges. [1]

insolvency.
  (1) The inability of a business organization to pay its financial obligations as they come due. (2) For an insurer, the inability to maintain capital and surplus above the minimum standard of capital and surplus required by law. [2]

insolvency provision.
  A reinsurance agreement provision that describes the rights and responsibilities of the direct writer and the reinsurer in the event that either party becomes insolvent. [6]

inspection report.
  A type of consumer credit report that is prepared by a consumer reporting agency for use during the insurance underwriting process. [9]

Insurance Companies Act.
  The Canadian legislation that exercises the federal government's constitutional authority to incorporate insurance companies that conduct business outside of a single province and to legislate with regard to insurance companies incorporated in a country other than Canada. [2]

insurance liquidity ratio.
  A financial ratio that measures an insurer's liquidity by comparing the market value of the insurer's liquid assets—which include cash and readily marketable assets—to some measure of the insurer's total reserves. [4]

internal audit.
  A systematic review of a company's operations that is conducted by the company's own employees. *Contrast with* **external audit**. [12]

investment yield ratio.
A financial ratio that shows how efficiently a company has used its investment portfolio to earn a return. [4]

IT.
See **information technology**.

journal.
An accounting document that contains all of the original chronological records of a company's financial transactions. [11]

jumbo limit.
In automatic reinsurance, the maximum allowable monetary amount of total insurance—currently in force plus yet-to-be placed—with all companies on any one life that will qualify for automatic cession. Jumbo limits for automatic cessions control the reinsurer's exposure to risk on any one life. [3]

lapse risk.
For an insurance product, the risk that (1) an insurance policy will terminate prior to the recovery of the insurer's initial expenses for the product or (2) the insured will retain the policy long enough to make a claim. [3]

large face amount (large FA) of life insurance premium rate table.
A premium rate table that shows premium rates for life insurance with face amounts greater than a stated monetary amount. [7]

law department.
The insurance company functional area that handles legal matters, such as contracts and litigation. Also known as the *legal department*. [9]

legal department.
See **law department**.

letter of credit.
A document issued by a bank guaranteeing the payment of a customer's bank drafts up to a stated amount for a specified time period. [2]

level retention basis.
See **per life basis**.

leverage.
A financial effect in which the presence of fixed costs—either operating or financing costs—automatically magnifies risks and potential returns to a company's owners. [4]

leverage ratio.
A financial ratio used for comparing the amount of an insurer's obligations with its resources available for meeting those obligations. A basic form of leverage ratio divides a corporation's liabilities by its owners' equity. *See* **liability; positive leverage effect; negative leverage effect**. [8]

liabilities.
A company's debts and future obligations. An accounting classification that represents a company's monetary value for its current and future obligations. An insurer's liabilities consist primarily of limited debts and vast reserves for future contractual obligations. *Contrast with* **assets**. [2]

liability account.
An account that shows the monetary values of a company's debts. [11]

Life and Health Reinsurance Agreements Model Regulation.
A sample regulation sponsored by the National Association of Insurance Commissioners (NAIC) in the United States to provide guidelines to help determine whether enough risk is transferred in a reinsurance agreement to permit the direct writer to claim reserve credit. Requires that all reinsurance agreements and amendments be in writing and be signed by the insurer and the reinsurer. The Model Regulation does not apply to all forms of reinsurance. [2]

limited death benefit.
The benefit to be paid in the event an insured commits suicide during the suicide exclusion period—typically equal to the amount of the premiums paid for the policy minus any indebtedness owed to the direct writer. [6]

liquid assets.
All cash and readily marketable assets. [4]

liquidation.
In insurer insolvencies, a process in which the receiver works to close down the business after collecting all assets and settling all obligations. [6]

liquidity.
In finance, the ease with which a company can convert its assets into cash for an approximation of their true value. [2]

litigation.
The process or act of resolving a dispute by means of a lawsuit. [6]

loss bordereau.
See **claims bordereau**.

maintenance expense.
For an insurance company, any product-related costs, including renewal commissions and some agency expenses, incurred after an insurance contract is in force and that are necessary to keep a policy in force. Also known as a *renewal expense* or an *administrative expense*. [1]

malfeasance.
See **bad faith**.

management accounting.
The process of identifying, measuring, analyzing, and communicating financial information so that a company's internal managers can decide how best to use the company's resources. [9]

management information system (MIS).
A type of information system that provides information about a company's daily operations and helps employees and managers make decisions and control activities. [9]

market conduct examination.
A type of routine on-site regulatory examination of insurers for the purpose of verifying that, in dealings with customers, the insurer is complying with all applicable statutes and regulations regarding sales, advertising, underwriting, and claims. *Contrast with* **financial condition examination**. [2]

market conduct laws.
State insurance laws that are designed to ensure that insurance companies conduct their businesses fairly and ethically. [2]

marketing.
The processes and activities a company uses to develop, price, promote, and distribute its products and services. [9]

material misrepresentation.
An untrue statement made by one party to a contract which induces the other party to enter a contract that it would not have entered had it known the truth. [6]

medical basis.
An underwriting basis under which a direct writer has a physician perform a medical examination of the proposed insured and record the results of the examination and the proposed insured's answers to health-related questions on a medical report. [10]

merger.
A transaction wherein the assets and liabilities of two companies are combined; one of the companies survives as a legal entity and the other company ceases to exist. Also known as an *amalgamation*. [11]

MIB.
See **MIB Group, Inc**.

MIB Group, Inc. (MIB).
A nonprofit organization established to provide coded information to insurers about impairments that insurance applicants have disclosed or that other insurance companies have detected in connection with previous applications for insurance. [9]

minimum capital and surplus requirements.
Solvency requirements, established by each jurisdiction's regulators, that set specific minimum dollar amounts of capital and surplus for an insurer as a whole and for each of the company's product lines. Also known as *statutory minimum capitalization requirements*. [2]

minimum cession.
For a direct writer, the smallest monetary amount of risk that a direct writer may cede. For a reinsurer, the smallest monetary amount of risk that the reinsurer will accept in an automatic cession. [3]

MIS.
See **management information system (MIS)**.

modco.
See **modified coinsurance**.

modco reserve adjustment.
A periodic adjustment designed to balance the financial impact of the one-sided reserve holdings present in modified coinsurance reinsurance arrangements. The adjustment is payable by the reinsurer if the reserve increases or by the direct writer if the reserve decreases. The amount of the adjustment equals the net of (1) interest on reserves payable by the direct writer plus (2) the change in the reserve. [7]

model act.
See **model law**.

model bill.
See **model law**.

model law.
A sample law that is developed by a national association of state regulators and that the states are encouraged to use as a basis for their laws. In the United States, the National Association of Insurance Commissioners (NAIC) proposes model insurance laws. Also known as *model act* or *model bill*. [2]

model regulation.
A sample regulation designed for use in the United States as a basis for the adoption of regulations by the states' administrative agencies. [2]

modified coinsurance (modco).
A type of proportional reinsurance in which (1) the direct writer maintains the entire reserve for each policy; and (2) the direct writer and reinsurer share proportionately in the reserve obligation, the direct writer's gross premium, and the risks of loss from expenses for death, surrender, other benefits, or lapse. Modco typically is used for cash value life insurance and annuity products; and it is particularly appropriate for interest-sensitive products. [3]

morbidity risk.
For an insurance product, the risk that a health insured will experience sickness, accidents, or impaired condition more frequently or for a longer period than the levels built into the product design. [3]

mortality risk.
For an insurance product, the risk that (1) life insureds will die earlier than the levels built into the product design or (2) a life annuitant or long-term care insured will live longer than the levels built into the product design. [3]

moving average.
An average of the values of a variable over several time periods used to show trends for the latest period. The average for the current period includes the most recent data point and excludes the oldest data point. Also known as *rolling average*. *Contrast with* **weighted average**. [12]

NAAR.

See **net amount at risk**.

NAIC.

See **National Association of Insurance Commissioners**.

National Association of Insurance Commissioners (NAIC).

A private, nonprofit association of insurance commissioners from all 50 states and the District of Columbia that promotes uniformity of state insurance regulation within the United States. The NAIC adopts model bills and regulations which each state can choose to adopt, use as the basis for its own laws and regulations, or ignore altogether. [2]

negative leverage effect.

An effect of earning a lower profit due to the presence of leverage. *Contrast with* **positive leverage effect**. *See* **leverage**. [8]

negative testing.

In an internal audit of a direct writer's reinsurance operations, the process of ensuring that the direct writer ceded all of the policies that met the qualifications specified in the reinsurance agreement and no policies that were not covered by the agreement. [12]

net amount at risk (NAAR).

The difference between the face amount of a life insurance policy—other than a universal life policy—and the policy reserve the direct writer has established at the end of any given policy year. [3]

netting off.

A process by which a direct writer subtracts the claim amount owed to it by a reinsurer from the amount that the direct writer owes the reinsurer for premiums. [11]

network.

A group of interconnected computers and computer devices, including the telecommunications equipment and computer programming that connect them. [9]

new business strain.

See **surplus strain**.

nonadmitted reinsurer.

See **unauthorized reinsurer**.

nonmedical basis.

An underwriting basis under which an insurance producer or an underwriter records the proposed insured's answers to a series of health history questions on a nonmedical supplement form, which then becomes part of the insurance application. [10]

nonproportional reinsurance.

A type of reinsurance arrangement in which neither the reinsurer nor the direct writer knows in advance what share of a risk the reinsurer will ultimately assume. Instead, after a direct writer's losses reach a specified maximum limit, the reinsurer begins to share in expenses for claims. Examples of nonproportional reinsurance plans are **excess-of-loss reinsurance**; **stop-loss reinsurance**; **catastrophic reinsurance coverage**; **spread-loss coverage**; **extended-time reinsurance**. [3]

notice of cancellation.
A written statement by which one party can notify another party of termination for new business under a reinsurance agreement. [4]

notice of expiry.
A document a reinsurer uses to notify a direct writer that an offer to reinsure is due to expire and to request additional information, a cession, a drop notice, or an extension request from the direct writer. [10]

notice of reinsurance.
The document by which information about ceded policies is submitted to a reinsurer to begin reinsurance coverage. Also known as a *reinsurance cession form*. [5]

notification for automatic reinsurance provision.
A reinsurance agreement provision that specifies (1) the details about each policy that a direct writer must send to a reinsurer to begin automatic reinsurance coverage and (2) how frequently the direct writer must notify the reinsurer of new automatic cessions. [5]

notification for fac-ob reinsurance provision.
A reinsurance agreement provision that specifies the (1) information the direct writer must provide to notify the reinsurer of risks ceded and (2) maximum time periods allowed for the reinsurance parties to respond to each other concerning capacity available and capacity accepted. [5]

notification for facultative reinsurance provision.
A reinsurance agreement provision that specifies the (1) information the direct writer must provide to notify the reinsurer of a request for facultative reinsurance coverage, (2) procedures the reinsurer must follow to make an offer of reinsurance to the direct writer, and (3) procedures the direct writer must follow to accept the reinsurer's offer. [5]

novation amendment.
An amendment added to a reinsurance agreement by the reinsurance parties following a merger or an acquisition to describe the new entities involved in the agreement and to specify the date on which the reinsurer becomes liable for any additional risk resulting from the merger or acquisition. [11]

occasional reinsurer.
An insurer that accepts some reinsurance business but is not a professional reinsurer. [1]

occasional retrocessionaire.
A reinsurer whose primary business is not retrocessions but who accepts retrocessions. [1]

Office of the Superintendent of Financial Institutions (OSFI).
In Canada, a federal regulatory agency responsible for supervising all federally chartered, licensed, or registered insurance companies. [2]

original currency.
See **currency of risk**.

OSFI.
See **Office of the Superintendent of Financial Institutions**.

overdue reports check.
> A type of process control in which a company employee investigates periodic administrative reports that are overdue by a specified amount of time. A type of exception report. *See* **exception report**; **process control**. [12]

owners' equity.
> *See* **capital and surplus**.

paramedical basis.
> An underwriting basis under which a direct writer has a paramedical examiner perform specified physical examinations of the proposed insured and record the proposed insured's answers to health-related questions on a paramedical report. [10]

participation limit.
> A reinsurer's maximum monetary limit on coverage currently in force or yet-to-be-placed on any given person. If the total amount of insurance—currently in force plus yet-to-be-placed—with all companies on a given person exceeds a reinsurer's participation limit, the reinsurer will automatically refuse to provide reinsurance on a policy covering that person. [3]

parties to the agreement provision.
> An indemnity reinsurance agreement provision stating that the reinsurance agreement exists solely between the direct writer and the reinsurer. [4]

per life basis.
> A method of administering reductions and terminations of reinsurance that (1) potentially affects the reinsurance on every policy the direct writer has in force on an insured and (2) typically requires the direct writer to maintain its full retention on that life. Also known as a *level retention basis*. [5]

per policy basis.
> A method of administering reductions and terminations of reinsurance under which only the reinsurance on the policy that is being reduced or terminated is affected. [5]

performance standard.
> *See* **standard**.

permanent flat extra premium.
> A flat extra premium that is payable for the duration of a policy. *Contrast with* **temporary flat extra premium**. [7]

physical comparison of recorded amounts.
> An internal control process by which a company regularly counts its assets, revenues, and expenses and compares this independent count to the amounts in its accounting records. The staff must reconcile its internally generated inventory against information provided to it by third parties. [12]

placement.
> A process in which a direct writer and reinsurer activate reinsurance coverage for a new automatic, facultative, or fac-ob cession. [10]

policy audit questionnaire.
A document that allows an audit team to examine the accuracy and timeliness of the data about insureds, compliance with the reinsurance agreement, premium verification, rates and accuracy, and other elements to be examined by comparing the reinsurer's data with the direct writer's data. [12]

policy change report.
A reinsurance report that shows details for all policies that have changed during a reporting period in a way that affects the amount of the reinsurance coverage, the reinsurance premium, or the allowance. Also known as a *transaction report*. [11]

policy dividend.
The amount of an insurer's divisible surplus that is paid to the owner of a participating policy. [7]

policy exhibit.
A reinsurance report that summarizes and reconciles the changes that have occurred in reinsured policies during the reporting period. [11]

policy reserve.
For an insurer, a liability amount that, together with future premiums and investment income, the insurer estimates it will need to pay contractual benefits as they come due under in-force policies. Policy reserves represent the insurer's obligations to customers. [2]

pooling.
See **reinsurance pool**.

portfolio reinsurance.
See **assumption reinsurance**.

positive leverage effect.
An effect of earning a better profit due to the presence of leverage. *Contrast with* **negative leverage effect**. *See* **leverage**. [8]

premium-based reciprocity.
In reinsurance, a type of reciprocal arrangement involving the exchange of blocks of reinsurance business representing approximately the same amount of gross premium on the reinsured risks. *See* **reciprocal arrangement**; *contrast with* **results-based reciprocity**. [1]

premium bordereau.
In some self-administered reinsurance arrangements, a report that provides detailed information about each reinsured policy, including its reinsurance premium. [5]

premium payment mode.
For insurance policies, the frequency—monthly, quarterly, or annually—at which renewal premiums are payable. [7]

premium tax.
Type of tax levied by a government on an insurer's premium income. [7]

preplacement.

The process by which the reinsurer (1) reviews a request for coverage, (2) establishes appropriate records and reserves capacity for the case, and (3) follows up on reservations for capacity that have been inactive for a specified period of time. [10]

principal.

In an agency relationship, the party that authorizes another party, the agent, to act on its behalf. [9]

process control.

A procedure that allows an organization to monitor the accuracy of its processes on a regular, ongoing basis. [12]

professional reinsurer.

An insurance company whose sole or primary line of business is providing reinsurance to direct writers. [1]

professional retrocessionaire.

A reinsurance company whose sole or primary line of business is providing reinsurance to reinsurers. [1]

profitability.

A company's overall degree of success in generating returns for its owners, including its abilities to generate profit and to increase the company's wealth. [4]

proportional reinsurance.

A type of reinsurance coverage for which the direct writer and reinsurer agree to share premiums and claims according to a specified amount or a specified percentage. Examples of proportional reinsurance plans are **coinsurance** and **modified coinsurance**. *Contrast with* **nonproportional reinsurance**. [3]

punitive damages.

Monetary awards that are intended to punish or make an example of an insurance company that has committed fraud or acted in a malicious or oppressive manner toward a claimant. [6]

quality control.

The process of ensuring that an organization accomplishes its objectives and follows its standards. [12]

quality control ratio.

The ratio of the number of files that meet a specific standard to the number of files reviewed for that standard. [12]

quality rating.

An alphabetical grade or rating assigned to an insurance company by an insurance rating agency to indicate the level of the insurance company's financial strength, its ability to pay its obligations to customers, or its ability to pay its obligations to creditors. [4]

quota share.
In reinsurance, each company's fixed percentage share of the total risk being divided between or among companies. In a reinsurance pool, a quota share is the amount or portion each pool member accepts as its liability under a specific reinsurance arrangement. Also known as a *subscription*. [1, 3]

quota share arrangement.
A method of ceding proportional reinsurance in which a reinsurer agrees to accept a specified percentage of each insurance risk, and a direct writer retains the remaining percentage, up to the direct writer's maximum retention limit. *See also* **proportional reinsurance**. [3]

rating agency.
An organization, owned independently of any insurer or government body, that evaluates the financial condition of insurers and provides information to potential customers of and investors in insurance companies. [6]

rating extra.
See **substandard extra premium**.

RBC ratio.
See **risk-based capital ratio**.

recapture.
The process by which a direct writer takes back some or all ceded business from a reinsurer. [4]

receivership.
A trust arrangement in which an individual—known as a *receiver* or *conservator*—is appointed by a court to hold and administer an insolvent insurer's assets and liabilities. Also called *conservatorship*. [6]

reciprocal arrangement.
A two-way reinsurance arrangement wherein two insurance companies cede business to each other and assume risk from each other. Also known as *reciprocity*. [1]

reciprocity.
See **reciprocal arrangement**.

reconciliation by exception.
A common method of reconciliation which involves investigating only the accounting entries that do not match or are out of balance; all other entries are assumed to be correct. [12]

recording of transactions as executed.
In accounting, when a company records all authorized and executed transactions in the correct accounting period, in the correct accounts, in the correct physical units, and in the correct monetary amounts. [12]

records inspection provision.
A reinsurance agreement provision that states the rights of each party to inspect the other party's records and documents relating to the reinsurance provided under the agreement. [5]

reduction of reinsurance.
The process of reducing the amount of reinsurance covering an insurance policy. [5]

rehabilitation.
In insurer insolvencies in the United States, a process in which regulators take over operation of the insolvent company from its management and attempt to restore the company to solvency. [6]

reinstatement.
The process by which an insurer puts back into force an insurance policy that has lapsed due to nonpayment of premiums. [5]

reinstatements provision.
A reinsurance agreement provision that typically specifies that when a reinsured policy lapses for nonpayment of premium, the reinsurance can be reinstated if certain conditions are met. [5]

reinsurance.
A transaction between two insurance companies in which one company—the direct writer (or ceding company)—transfers some of its insurance risk to another company—the reinsurer (or assuming company). Under indemnity reinsurance, the reinsurer agrees to reimburse the direct writer for covered losses claimed under the policies that have been reinsured according to the terms of the reinsurance agreement. [1]

reinsurance account executive.
See **reinsurance marketing officer**.

reinsurance administration.
All of the day-to-day activities conducted by the direct writer and the reinsurer to process and manage each risk that the direct writer cedes automatically or submits for facultative consideration. [10]

reinsurance allowance.
See **allowance**.

reinsurance certificate.
A document that a reinsurer issues to notify a direct writer that reinsurance is officially in force. [10]

reinsurance cession form.
See **notice of reinsurance**.

reinsurance commission.
See **allowance**.

reinsurance company.
See **reinsurer**.

reinsurance effective date.
The date on which the reinsurance coverage for a specific risk takes effect. [4]

reinsurance intermediary.

A party who is not employed by a licensed insurer or reinsurer, but who acts on behalf of a direct writer or reinsurer to place reinsurance. In the United States, laws and regulations recognize two types of intermediaries, the **reinsurance intermediary—broker** and the **reinsurance intermediary—manager**. [2]

reinsurance intermediary—broker.

Any person, firm, or corporation that solicits, negotiates, or places reinsurance cessions or retrocessions on behalf of a direct writer but that is not authorized to enter into a binding reinsurance contract on behalf of the direct writer. [2]

reinsurance intermediary—manager.

Any party that acts as an agent of a reinsurer and either has authority to bind the reinsurer to a reinsurance contract or manages all or part of the reinsurer's assumed business. [2]

Reinsurance Intermediary Model Act.

A sample law sponsored by the National Association of Insurance Commissioners (NAIC) in the United States to provide regulation of the activities of reinsurance intermediaries and of direct writers and reinsurers that use the services of reinsurance intermediaries. The Model Act is designed to (1) ensure that reinsurance intermediaries are qualified to perform their services and (2) enable regulators to account for any funds the intermediary may have handled in the event of the insolvency of a reinsurer. [2]

reinsurance marketing officer.

A reinsurer's employee who sells reinsurance and coordinates the marketing process for the reinsurer. Also known as a *reinsurance account executive*. [9]

reinsurance pool.

In a reinsurance arrangement, a group of two or more reinsurers or individuals who jointly reinsure risks accepted on their behalf by an appointed representative who represents them in a marketplace. Also known as a *reinsurance syndicate*. A reinsurance pool may operate as a subscription market or an open market. *See* **subscription market**. [1]

reinsurance premium.

A periodic payment from a direct writer to a reinsurer as compensation for indemnity reinsurance coverage. [1]

reinsurance recoverables.

Reinsurance benefit amounts due to the direct writer or owed by the reinsurer. [9]

reinsurance slip.

A short-form document issued to a direct writer by a reinsurance salesperson to describe the essential terms of a reinsurance arrangement while the reinsurance treaty is being drafted. Until the reinsurance treaty is formally executed, the slip governs the reinsurance relationship. [1]

reinsurance syndicate.

See **reinsurance pool**.

reinsurance treaty.

A long and detailed document that provides evidence of reinsurance for a book of business covering a variety of insureds in various locations. A treaty specifies with precision the nature of the transferred risk, the responsibilities of the direct writer and the reinsurer, and the reporting requirements of both parties, among other things. Reinsurance treaties typically document a type of reinsurance cession known as **automatic reinsurance**. [1]

reinsurer.

An insurance company that, for an exchange of value, such as a payment, accepts insurance risks transferred from another company—the direct writer—in a reinsurance transaction. Also known as *reinsuring company* or *assuming company*. [1]

reinvestment risk.

For an insurance product, the risk that funds reinvested will earn a lower rate of return than was built into the policy design. [3]

renewal expenses.

See **maintenance expenses**.

request for coverage.

The document that a direct writer uses to request reinsurance coverage on a particular insured or group of insureds. Also known as a *facultative application*. [10]

request for proposal (RFP).

A detailed bidding document that is sent by a direct writer to one or more reinsurers and that states the direct writer's needs and provides the product, pricing, and service details that reinsurers must address in their proposals. [4]

required reserves.

Reserves calculated according to regulatory requirements. Also known as *statutory reserves*. [2]

rescission.

The cancellation of a contract under which the parties are returned to the positions they would have occupied had no contract been created. [6]

rescission provision.

A reinsurance agreement provision that describes the notification and administrative procedures required when the direct writer rescinds a reinsured policy. [6]

reserve credit.

In the United States, an accounting entry used by a direct writer to record the reduction of reserves, due to the use of reinsurance, in its Annual Statement. [2]

reserve listing.

A reinsurance report that shows all policies reinsured and the reserve held for each policy. [11]

reserved capacity.

The portion of a reinsurer's capacity that a reinsurer sets aside to fund its financial obligations under anticipated new business. [10]

reserves.
> *See* **policy reserve**; **required reserves**.

results-based reciprocity.
> In reinsurance, a type of reciprocal arrangement involving the exchange of blocks of reinsurance business representing approximately the same monetary amount of projected claims experience. *See* **reciprocal arrangement**; *contrast with* **premium-based reciprocity**. [1]

retention limit.
> A specified maximum monetary amount of insurance that an insurer is willing to carry at its own risk without transferring some of the risk to a reinsurer. [3, 8]

retention limit corridor.
> In reinsurance, an amount above the ceding company's retention limit that a risk must meet or exceed before any part of the risk is ceded to a reinsurer. The purpose of this corridor is for the ceding company to avoid ceding small amounts of coverage. Also known as *corridor*. [8]

retention schedule.
> A written presentation of all of an insurer's retention limits, organized by applicable categories such as product, product line, issue age, and underwriting classification. Also known as a *table of retention limits*. *See* **retention limit**. [8]

retro pool.
> *See* **retrocession pool**.

retrocession.
> (1) A transaction by which a reinsurer cedes risks to another reinsurer, known as the retrocessionaire. (2) The unit of insurance that a reinsurance company cedes to a retrocessionaire. (3) The document used to record the transfer of risk from a reinsurer to a retrocessionaire. *See also* **reinsurer**; **reinsurance**; **retrocessionaire**. [1]

retrocession claim file.
> A file prepared by a reinsurance analyst that contains all the information relevant to a claim, plus information about the retrocession on the case, to use when the reinsurer notifies its retrocessionaires of the claim. [11]

retrocession pool.
> A group of two or more professional retrocessionaires or reinsurers that jointly reinsure retroceded risks. Also known as a *retro pool*. [10]

retrocessionaire.
> A reinsurer that accepts risks transferred from and provides reinsurance to another reinsurer. *See also* **reinsurer**; **reinsurance**. [1]

return.
> Any reward, profit, or compensation an investor hopes to earn for taking a risk. Compensation to an investor in the forms of interest; dividends; appreciation of principal; cash; or rent. [8]

revenue account.
An account that shows the sources of a company's income. [11]

RFP.
See **request for proposal**.

right of recommendation.
The right of a reinsurer to review a claim and offer its opinion to the direct writer on whether to pay the claim. [11]

risk assessment.
See **external audit**.

risk-based capital (RBC) ratio.
In the United States, a requirement for insurers to use a specified formula to demonstrate to regulators the adequacy of the insurer's capital relative to the riskiness of the insurer's operations. [2]

risk management.
A practice of systematically identifying, assessing, and dealing with risk. [8]

risk-return tradeoff.
The relationship between risk and return that can be expressed in the following manner: as the level of risk increases, the level of return increases; as the level of risk decreases, the level of return decreases. [8]

rolling average.
See **moving average**.

safeguarding of assets.
A principle of internal control designed to protect the organization's assets and information against the risks of theft, destruction, waste, and deterioration. [12]

Sarbanes-Oxley Act of 2002.
A U.S. federal law that requires public companies in the United States to take specific precautions related to corporate governance, effective internal controls, and preventing and detecting fraudulent behavior on the part of management and external auditors. [12]

scanning.
See **imaging**.

schedule.
A part of a reinsurance agreement that covers one or more variable elements of the agreement. Also called an *exhibit* or a *condition*. [4]

security.
The physical, technical, and procedural steps a company takes to prevent the loss, wrongful disclosure (accidental or intentional), or theft of information. [9]

segregation of duties.
A principle of internal quality control under which an employer designs jobs so that incompatible functions are assigned to different individuals. Also known as the principle of *dual control*. [12]

selective bordereau service.
A bordereau service that includes only exceptional cases, such as large amount policies, those with frequent or large-amount claims, new business, and other specific categories. [5]

self administration.
A method of reinsurance record administration in which the direct writer maintains detailed records for each ceded policy and sends the reinsurer periodic reports describing the individual risks ceded and reinsurance premiums due for each policy. [5]

self-insured retention limit.
A stated maximum monetary amount of risk that a self-insured entity will carry at its own risk. [8]

smoker/nonsmoker premium rate table.
A premium rate table that shows different premium rates for otherwise similarly situated smokers and nonsmokers. [7]

solvency.
(1) A company's ability to meet its financial obligations on time. (2) For an insurer, the ability to maintain capital and surplus above the minimum standard of capital and surplus required by law. Also known as *statutory solvency*. [2]

solvency laws.
Insurance laws that are designed to ensure that insurance companies are financially able to meet their debts and pay policy benefits when they come due. [2]

special termination.
A reinsurance agreement provision that allows a direct writer to completely withdraw from a reinsurance agreement if the reinsurer experiences a specified business event—such as the loss of its insurance license or the loss of a significant proportion of its capital and surplus. [4]

spread-loss coverage.
A type of nonproportional reinsurance arrangement—similar to a loan—between a direct writer and a reinsurer. In spread-loss coverage, the reinsurer agrees to pay the direct writer if the direct writer's total claims for a specified block of business in a stated period exceed a specified monetary amount. In return, the direct writer is required to repay the reinsurer's funds over time with interest payable according to specified terms. [3]

standard.
A statement of either (1) minimum acceptable levels of performance or results, (2) outstanding levels of performance or results, or (3) the acceptable range for levels of performance or results. Also known as a *performance standard*. [12]

standard aggregate premium rate table.
A premium rate table that shows one set of premium rates for all standard underwritten policies. [7]

statutory minimum capitalization requirements.
See **minimum capital and surplus requirements**.

statutory reserves.
See **required reserves**.

statutory solvency.
The legal minimum standard of capital and surplus that every insurance company must maintain. *See* **capital and surplus**; **solvency**. [2]

stop-loss ratio reinsurance.
See **stop-loss reinsurance**.

stop-loss reinsurance.
A type of nonproportional reinsurance which protects direct writers from excessive total claim costs in any one operating period. On reinsured policies, stop-loss reinsurance usually requires the reinsurer to pay for a portion of claims between stated lower and upper limits. Also known as *stop-loss ratio reinsurance* or *excess-of-loss ratio reinsurance*. *Contrast with* **excess-of-loss reinsurance**. [3]

subscription.
See **quota share**.

subscription market.
In reinsurance, an exchange market where appointed agents for reinsurance companies accept shares of coverage on given risks; the share accepted varies from company to company. *See* **reinsurance pool**. [1]

substandard extra premium.
An extra premium that continues throughout a policy's premium-paying period. Also known as *rating extra* or *table rating*. [7]

substandard extra premium rate table.
A premium rate table that shows additional premium rates that apply only for substandard risks. [7]

substandard risk.
An insured who represents a significantly greater-than-average likelihood of loss within the context of an insurer's underwriting practices. [7]

surplus.
For an insurer, an amount that represents the money a company has over and above its reserves and other financial obligations. For insurers, may refer to capital and surplus together. [2]

surplus relief.
A decrease in potential surplus strain. [2, 8]

surplus relief ratio.
A direct writer's net cost for or net earnings from ceding and assuming reinsurance divided by the company's surplus. A type of financial leverage ratio. *See* **surplus relief**. [8]

surplus strain.
A decrease in an insurer's surplus, caused by the high initial costs and the reserve requirements associated with new products. Also known as *new business strain*. *Contrast with* **surplus relief**. [2, 8]

suspense account.
In accounting, a temporary account where deposited funds can be held until the billing statement has been processed and the funds have been allocated to the appropriate accounts. [12]

table of retention limits.
See **retention schedule**.

table rating.
See **substandard extra premium**.

telecommunications.
The electronic transmission of communication signals that enables organizations to link computer systems into effective networks. [9]

temporary flat extra premium.
A flat extra premium that is payable only for a specified temporary period after policy issue, such as for 10 years or until the insured reaches age 65. *Contrast with* **permanent flat extra premium**. [7]

temporary insurance agreement (TIA).
See **binding premium receipt**.

termination.
The complete cancellation of a reinsurance agreement for both new business and in-force business. [4]

termination for new business.
A reinsurance agreement cancellation under which the parties to the agreement no longer cede or assume new business, but reinsurance coverage continues on business already in place. [4]

termination of reinsurance.
The process by which a direct writer cancels the reinsurance covering a policy it issued. [5]

TIA.
See **binding premium receipt**.

time-series analysis.
See **trend analysis**.

traditional indemnity reinsurance.
A type of reinsurance used to effect, in most cases, a partial transfer of business and to form a basis for sharing the risks of the insurance business. *Contrast with* **assumption reinsurance**. [1]

transaction report.
See **policy change report**.

trend.
A change that occurs over time. [12]

trend analysis.

A type of financial analysis that involves assessing numerical patterns in order to identify changes over time, usually over several successive years. Also known as *time-series analysis*. [12]

trust.

A legal arrangement whereby one or more persons—called the trustees—hold legal title to property on behalf of another person—called the trust beneficiary—and are responsible for administering the property for the benefit of the trust beneficiary. [2]

unauthorized reinsurer.

In the United States, an insurer that does business in a particular state without becoming licensed to do business in that state in accordance with that state's law. Also known as a *nonadmitted reinsurer.* [2]

underwriting.

The staff function and process of *selecting* and *classifying* the risks that an insurer will accept, where selecting is the process of deciding to accept or decline a risk and, after a risk is accepted, classifying is the process of assigning the appropriate premium rate to charge for the insurance policy. [1]

underwriting basis.

The amount and type of medical information that the direct writer gathers about a proposed insured to assess the risk the person presents. [10]

underwriting capacity.

The highest monetary amount of risk that an insurance company should accept so that unusual claim volatility will not damage the ongoing solvency of the company. *Contrast with* **financial capacity**. [1]

unisex premium rate table.

A premium rate table that shows a single set of premium rates for both males and females. *Contrast with* **gender-specific premium rate table**. [7]

virtual private network (VPN).

A secure computer network that uses computer equipment and/or programming to act as a "tunnel" through the Internet so that only people in possession of the required technology have access to data and information traveling through the network. [9]

VPN.

See **virtual private network**.

waiver of premium (WP) for disability benefit rider premium rate table.

A premium rate table that shows a premium rate for optional waiver of premium for disability coverage. [7]

weighted average.

A type of average in which the members of a set of data points are assigned different weights before the average is calculated. A weighted average assigns greater significance to some data points than to others. *Contrast with* **moving average**. [12]

weighted moving average.
  A statistical average that is both a weighted average and a moving average. A type of moving average in which the data points are weighted differently, with greater weight being assigned to the most recent data points and lower weight being assigned to the oldest data points. *See* **average**; **moving average**; **weighted average.** [12]

withheld funds.
  In reinsurance, amounts of money that the direct writer would otherwise pay to the reinsurer but, by agreement, the direct writer continues to hold as security for the reinsurance transaction. [2]

workers' compensation and employers liability insurance.
  A type of liability insurance that covers liability resulting from employee injury or death on the job. [1]

WP for disability benefit rider premium rate table.
  See **waiver of premium for disability benefit rider premium rate table**.

yearly renewable term (YRT) reinsurance.
  A type of reinsurance that is used to reinsure only the mortality portion of a life insurance risk. For YRT reinsurance, the direct writer pays a one-year term insurance premium to the reinsurer on the anniversary date of each reinsured policy. [3]

YRT reinsurance.
  See **yearly renewable term reinsurance**.

INDEX

Aa

ability to accept risk 151
accepting risk and not controlling it 146
access 231
access to records provision 237
accident insurance 16
accident or casualty coverages 47
accidental death benefit (ADB) rider
    premium rate table 131
accidental death benefits, coverages 42, 130
account(s) 210, 230
account payable 54
account receivable 54
accounting 168–169, 210
    entry 210–211
    errors 233
    period 230
    staff 233
accreditation of state insurance departments 24
accreditation for reinsurers 27
accredited reinsurer 27
accumulated reserves 56
accumulation at interest option 137
acquisition 213, 238
acquisition expenses 12, 149
actual damages 114
actual experience 52
actual values 52
actuarial projections 154
actuary(ies) 154, 164–165, 186
ADB rider premium rate table 131
administration 53
    expense 12
    records 233
administrative processes 237
administrative reports 234
administrative supervision 121
admitted assets 33
admitted reinsurer 27
adverse risk experience 138
affiliated reinsurer 156
age of insured 56
agency 163
agent 163
agent of a reinsurer 28
aggregate premium rate table 131
aggressive business practices 146
agreement effective date 73
allowance(s) 12, 51, 87, 129, 130, 134, 135, 136,
    140, 149, 205, 209–211, 214, 244
alpha file 188
amalgamation 213
amount of surplus relief 148, 150
anniversary date 55, 76
annual basis 134
annual internal control report 231
annual reinsurance meeting 25
annual report 237
Annual Statement 29
annuity(ies) 16, 53, 54, 146
antivirus software 176
application for insurance 137
arbitration 72, 118–120, 121
arbitration provision 118–120
arbitrator(s) 118, 119, 120, 121
arithmetic mean 234
articles 69
    reinsurance coverage articles 79
asset account 210
asset risk 52
assets 29, 137, 210
assigning risk 51
association examination 31
assumed investment earnings rate 11
assuming company 5
assumption certificates 9
assumption reinsurance 3, 9, 26, 123
Assumption Reinsurance Model Act 26
assumptions 52
attachment point 45
attorney 33
attorney-in-fact 27
audit(s) 169, 170, 232, 235–245
    committee 231, 235
    findings 239
    processes 242
    report 243
    statement 237
    team 237, 239, 242
auditing claims 242
auditing functions 235
authority 237
authorization level 230
authorized reinsurer 18, 27, 29
automated reinsurance administration systems 233
automatic binding limit 42, 44, 51, 80, 95, 242, 244
automatic cession basis 41, 44
automatic reinsurance 41–42, 51, 103, 117, 152,
    161, 182, 196

automobile insurers 146
average 234
average premium tax rate 140
avoiding risk 145

B

B2B e-commerce 175
bad faith 115
balance sheet 29
basic accounting equation 29, 30
basic coinsurance 52, 136
billing process 239
billing statement 205, 208, 212, 221, 224, 233
binding premium receipt 76, 94
board of directors 137, 154, 231, 237
boiler and machinery insurance 17
bordereau 91
bordereau service 91
bulk administration 88, 90, 209, 224
bulk-administered reinsurance 165
business income insurance 187
business-to-business (B2B) e-commerce 175

C

Canada 24, 25, 140
Canadian Reinsurance Conference (CRC) 25
Canadian Reinsurance Guidelines 25
capacity 43, 151
capital 29, 137, 148
capital and surplus 29–30, 122, 148, 151, 210
capital and surplus account 210
capital and surplus requirements 28, 30
capital ratio 31
captive reinsurer(s) 7
case file 184, 190–192, 194, 196
cash dividend option 137
cash refund 135
cash value 55, 57, 129, 136
cash (surrender) value reimbursement 205, 212
casualty 16
cat cover. *See* catastrophe coverage.
catastrophe coverage 45, 46, 47
catastrophic amount 47
ceding commission 12
ceding company 5
cession 5, 28, 42, 132, 152, 154, 196, 244
cession amounts 242
cession basis 41, 42, 43, 44, 152

changes to the reinsurance 72, 95
claim(s) 73, 154, 155
    administration 13, 111–115, 171, 214–225, 242
    analyst 171, 214–215, 218, 221–222, 224
    bordereau 91
    contest 112, 113, 116
    denial 112
    file 214, 218, 222
    fraud 222, 223
    investigations 114
    liabilities 48
    procedures 112, 242
    provision 111
    staff 242
    volatility 13
    worksheet 215, 218, 220, 222, 224
claimant's statement 215, 216, 221
classifying 12
clean 34
close notice 193
coinsurance 48, 49, 129, 130, 137, 222
    allowance 53
    gross premium 53
    net premium 53
collateral 146
combined retention 152
commercial automobile insurance 17
commercial liability insurance 17
commercial property insurance 17
commissions 53
commute 10
compensatory damages 114
complete bordereau service 91
compliance unit 166, 167
compliance with the reinsurance agreement 237
computer programs 233
computer virus 176
conclusion of the agreement 76
condition 69
conditional premium receipt 76
consequences for inaccurate billing statements 136
conservative business practices 146
conservator 122
conservatorship 122
consultation 13
consulting engagement 235
consumer credit report 171–172
consumer reporting agency 171–172, 174, 175
contest. *See* claims contest.
contestable claim(s) 222, 242

contestable period 100, 112
continuation(s) 100–102
    coverage 10, 123
    provision 100–102
contractual increases 98
control cycle 229
control systems 237
controlling interest 213
conversion(s) 103, 208, 244
    provision 102
corporate governance 231
corporate retention 186, 188–189
corporate retention limit 152, 154
corridor 152
cost of insurance 133
CRC 25
credit(s) 210–211
Credit for Reinsurance Model Law 26, 32–33
Credit for Reinsurance Model Regulation 26, 32–34, 54
creditors 237
crime insurance 17
critical illness 42
currency 129
    exchange difficulties 141
    exchange values 141
    for reinsurance 140
    of risk 140, 141
custodial tasks 230

D

D&O liability insurance 17
data errors 233
data integrity check 232–233
date of expiry 192–193
death benefit 53, 55
debit(s) 210, 211
deceptive business practices 23
declarations section 15
defaulting entirely on reinsurance premium payment 135
delegation of authority 230
desk audit 232, 243–244
desk audit report 245
destruction 231
deterioration 231
direct premium 130, 134, 135
direct writer 5
directors and officers (D&O) liability insurance 17

disability income 42, 47
    insurance 16, 47, 53
    policy 46
disaster recovery plans 231
disintermediation risk 52
dividend options provision 137
divisible surplus 137
document 5, 14–15
document management system 175
documentation of reinsurance arrangements 14–15
domestic currency 141
domicile 23
domiciliary state 23
drop notice 193
dual control 230
due date 141
due date of reinsurance premiums 132
due diligence (review) 67, 235
duration of the agreement provision 72–73

E

e-commerce 175
early warning financial ratio tests 31
earnings potential 147
EDI 174, 175
EDI network 174
electronic commerce (e-commerce) 174, 175
electronic data 233
electronic data interchange (EDI) 174
employees' medical expenses 146
encryption 176
entire agreement provision 71, 72, 73
errors (and omissions) 73, 116, 230, 238
errors and omissions provision 116–117
escrow account 33
estimate for NAAR 56
estimated values 52
Europe 18
evaluation criteria for reinsurance partners 67–69
evergreen 34
examiner 31
exception report 233
excess and umbrella liability insurance 17
excess-of-loss ratio reinsurance 46
excess-of-loss reinsurance 45, 46, 47
excess of retention 48–49
excess-of-retention arrangement 49, 51, 106
excess-of-retention for coinsurance 49
excess-of-time reinsurance 47
excess quota share 51

excess quota share arrangement 51
excess risk 43
exchange market 8
exclusions from automatic cession 80, 81
execution of transactions as authorized 230
exhibit 69
expected obligations 149
expense account 210, 211
expense allowance 12
expense of reinsurance administration 155
expense risk 52
expense risk associated with early withdrawals 146
experience refund 129, 136, 138, 212, 244
exposure to risk of loss 147
extended-time reinsurance 45, 47
extension request 193
external audit(s) 229, 231–232, 235, 237–239
external replacement 101
extra-percentage premium rate table 132
extra premiums (substandard premiums) 130
extra risk 130
extracontractual damages 113

F

fac-ob arrangement 44
fac-ob reinsurance 43–44, 184, 196
facultative application 183
facultative certificate 14
facultative coverage 117
facultative-obligatory (fac-ob) reinsurance 43
facultative provision 41, 43
facultative reinsurance 14, 43, 75, 90, 91, 92, 103, 117, 152, 161, 166–167, 183–184, 196
   application 183
   certificate 14
   provision 41, 43
   underwriting 190
facultative reinsurance underwriting 190
failure to pay reinsurance premiums on time 135
farm insurance 17
favorable risk experience 138
FDQS arrangement 571
federal tax laws 32
federally incorporated 25
federally licensed financial institutions in Canad 25
financial accounting 168, 203
Financial Analysis and Solvency Tracking (FAST) System 31
financial capacity 12, 13, 44, 156
financial components of a reinsurance arrangement 129

financial condition 27, 28, 31, 123
   examination 28, 31
financial design 52
financial provisions 129
financial ratios 30–31
Financial Regulation Standards and Accreditation Program 24
financial reinsurance 10
financial reporting systems 28
financial report(s), reporting 29, 231
Financial Services Commission 25
financial statements 27
financial strain 47
financial strength 29
financial transaction 230
finite reinsurance 10
firewall 176
first-dollar quota share (FDQS) reinsurance 48, 51, 88, 99, 106
first-year allowance 51
fixed cost 147
flat extra premium 130, 131, 134
flat extra premium rate table 132
flat monetary amount of risk 53
Form AR-1 26
fraud 112, 114, 115
fraudulent behavior 231
funds withheld coinsurance 26, 33, 48, 53, 129, 136, 137
funds withheld modco 48, 54

G

gender-specific premium rate table 130, 131, 133
generally accepted accounting principles (GAAP) reserves 32
geographic dispersion 3
good credit 146
good faith 114, 116
gross profit ratio 67, 68
guaranteed-issue basis 186
guaranty association 10, 123
Guideline on Unregistered Reinsurance and Reinsurance in the Ordinary Course of Business 25

H

health insurance 16, 46, 47, 53
health maintenance organization (HMO) 146
high tolerance for business risk 146
hybrid arrangements 14

I

illegal act 230
imaging 175
impaired insurers 30
incompatible functions 230
increases in benefits with evidence of insurability 133
increases in benefits without evidence of insurability 133
increasing death benefits 98–100
indemnity 16, 18
indemnity reinsurance 3, 10, 14, 149, 155
independent public accounting firm 237
individual cession administration 87, 89, 90, 133
individual cession reinsurance 194
in-force 181–182
    business 10, 11, 155, 203, 244
    policy report 203–204
information system 173–176, 188, 190, 192, 193, 196, 199, 212, 237, 238
information technology (IT) 173–174
initial gross reinsurance premium 54
initial reinsurance allowance 54
initial reinsurance premium 132
inland marine insurance 16, 17
insolvency 10, 23, 73, 121–125
insolvency provision 123–125
inspection report 172
insurance commissioner 24, 27, 33
Insurance Companies Act 25
insurance department 27
insurance liquidity ratio 67, 68
insurance producers 24
insurance regulator(s) 10, 29
insurance risks 5
insured 42
interest adjustment 135
interest earned on the reserves 139
interest earnings on the invested assets backing reserves 129
interest on beginning policy reserves 54
interest payable 47
interest penalty 135
interest-sensitive products 54, 55, 87
internal audit 232, 235, 236
internal audit team 229
internal control principle 231
internal controls 231
internal financial control systems 231

internal replacement 101
international partnership 140
international reinsurance transactions 129
interviews 237
introductory letter 239
investment yield ratio 67, 68
irregularities in reinsurance administration 238
irrevocable letter of credit 33, 34
IT 173
IT unit 174

J

job titles 28
journal 210
jumbo limit 42, 43, 44, 83, 151, 221, 242, 244

K

keying errors 233

L

lapse 54
lapse risk 52
large face amount (FA) of life insurance premium rate table 130
large face amounts of life insurance 130
law department 166
legal action 27
legal department 166
legally binding 14
letter of credit 26, 33, 34
level retention basis 104
leverage 67, 147
    effect 147, 156
    ratio 148
liabilities 29, 137, 210
liability account 210
licensed insurance company 6
licensing of reinsurers 6
    of direct writers 26
    intermediaries 27
    process 27
    requirements 24, 27
    standards 26
Life and Health Reinsurance Agreements Model Regulation 26, 36
life coverages 42
life cycle 66–67

life insurance 16, 42, 45, 47, 48, 49, 53, 54, 55,
    100, 130, 131, 134, 137
life reinsurance premiums 133, 134
limit cash flows 53
limited audit 236
limited death benefit 115
liquid assets 67
liquidation 123–124
liquidity 29, 67
    measures 67
litigation 118, 119
Lloyd's of London 8
loans 146
long-term care insurance 16, 47, 53
long-term care reinsurance 48
loss bordereau 91
low rate of inflation 141
low tolerance for business risk 146

M

maintenance and administrative costs 14
maintenance expense 12
management accounting 168, 169, 203
management information system (MIS) 173
market concentration 3
market conduct examination 31
market conduct laws 23
marketing 163, 164
marketing representatives 27
material misrepresentation 115, 222
maximum total reinsurance payout 47
medical basis 186
medical report 186
merger 9, 14, 213, 237, 238
mergers and acquisitions 9, 238
MIB Group, Inc. (MIB) 173, 174, 190, 222
minimum amount of claim benefits 47
minimum capital and surplus requirements 30
minimum cession 42, 43, 82
minimum dollar amount of capital and surplus 26
minimum number of qualified claims 47
minimum ratio value 31
MIS 173
misstatement of age or sex 115
modco reinsurance 129, 130, 136, 222
    interest rate 54
    reserve adjustment 54, 129, 135, 138
model act 24, 26

model bill 24, 26
Model Hazardous Condition Regulation 122
model law 24, 26
model regulation 24, 26
Model Rehabilitation Act 121
Model Supervision Act 121, 122
moderate business practices 146
moderate tolerance for business risk 146
modified coinsurance (modco) 48, 49, 54
    reserve adjustment 54
modified reserves 32
monetary amount of reinsured claims 45
monetary amounts 230
monitoring costs 14
mortality 165
    cost 56–57
    portion of a life insurance risk 55
    risk 56–57, 131, 137
moving average 234
mutual insurance companies 14

N

NAAR 57, 223, 224
NAIC Accreditation of State Insurance
    Departments 24
National Association of Insurance Commissioners
    (NAIC) 21, 24
negative leverage effect 147
negative modco reserve adjustment value 54
negative testing 237
net amount at risk (NAAR) 49, 55, 57, 82, 87, 214,
    222, 223, 224
net cost for the reinsurance 151
net earnings from reinsurance ceded and assumed
    149, 151
net funds withheld 54
net worth 148
netting off 224
network 174, 176
new business 10, 12, 13, 77, 78, 100, 149, 150, 155,
    244
new business strain 32
new policy issue 133
Newfoundland 25
non-life coverages 45
nonadmitted reinsurer 27
noncontractual increases 100
nonforfeiture values 53

nonguaranteed direct premium rates 136
nonmedical basis 186
nonpayment of reinsurance premiums 78
nonproportional reinsurance 45, 79, 82
North America 16
notice and disclosure requirements 26
notice of cancellation 78
notice of expiry 193
notice of reinsurance 89
notification for reinsurance provisions 92
   notification for automatic reinsurance 88, 89
   notification for fac-ob reinsurance 91
   notification for facultative reinsurance 92
novation amendments 213
number of the reinsured claims 45

O

objectives 229
occasional reinsurer 6, 9
occasional retrocessionaire 6, 9
off-premises storage 231
offset of the amounts 135
Office of the Superintendent of Financial Institutions (OSFI) 25
old business 51
on-site regulatory examinations 31
one-year term insurance option 137
one-year term insurance premium 55
open market 8
original currency 140
OSFI . See Office of the Superintendent of Financial Institutions.
outstanding report 234–235
overdue report checks 232
overdue reports 234
overdue reports check 232, 234
owners' equity 29

P

paid-up additional insurance option 137
paramedical basis 186
paramedical report 186
partially modified coinsurance (partco) 48, 54
participating policies 137
participation limit 42, 43
parties to the agreement provision 71, 72
per life basis 104–106
per policy basis 106
percentage of risk 53

percentages retained and ceded 51, 74
performance standard 229
permanent flat extra premium 131
personnel changes 238
physical comparison of recorded amounts 231
physical units 230
placement 181, 182, 193
plan 42
policies 229
policy audit questionnaire 239
policy cash value 56–57
policy change report 205, 206, 207, 208
policy dividend(s) 55, 129, 136, 137, 138, 205
policy dividend payment reimbursements 212
policy exhibit 205, 206, 209
policy maximum 47
policy reserve 12, 29, 48, 49, 53, 56, 57, 87, 116, 129, 165, 203, 210, 213, 214
policy terminations and lapses 237
policy year 49
policyholders' and shareholders' equity 29
policyowners 237
pooling 8, 80, 190
poor credit 146
portfolio reinsurance 9
positive leverage effect 147
positive modco reserve adjustment value 54
premium-based reciprocity 8
premium billing statement 136
premium bordereau 91
premium income 139
premium payment mode 132
premium rate(s) 41, 130
premium rate tables 130
premium receipts 76
premium reduction option 137
premium refund 205, 214, 221
premium tax refund 212
premium tax 53, 72, 129, 139–140
preplacement 181, 182, 184
principal 163
probability of a claim 57
procedural documentation 236
procedures 229, 232
   manuals 237
   to begin coverage 72
process control 232, 236
process exceptions 233
product design 52
product liabilities 155
product model 52

product pricing 52
product-line retention limits 152
professional reinsurer(s) 6, 9, 27
professional retrocessionaire 6, 9
professional risk managers 145
profitability 67
proof of loss statement 215, 218
proof of payment statement 215, 219
property 16
property/casualty insurance coverages 16, 17
proportional reinsurance 47
provincial Insurance Act 25
provincially incorporated 25
provisions 71
public disclosure 237
public interest 23
punitive damages 114

Q

quality control 136, 229, 232
quality control ratio 229
quality control reviews 229
quality control system 230
quality rating 67
quarterly mode 132
quota share 8, 51, 221, 244, 245

R

rating agency 123
rating extra 131
rating factor 133
ratio analysis 31, 149
recapture 10, 76, 77, 95–98, 124, 125, 238, 244
recapture provision 76
receiver 122, 123
receivership 122
recertification review 24
reciprocal arrangement 3, 7, 8
reciprocity 7
reconciliation by exception 231
recording of transactions as executed 230
recordkeeping 141
recordkeeping and administration 54
records inspection 72
records inspection provision 95
reduction(s) of reinsurance 103–104, 208
registered mail 135
regulation of reinsurance 24–25, 27, 166
regulators 237

regulatory examinations (examiners) 31, 237
regulatory requirements 27
rehabilitation 122–124
reinstatement 101, 103, 205, 208, 222, 244
reinstatements provision 103
reinsurance 5
Reinsurance (Canadian Companies) Regulations 25
Reinsurance (Foreign Companies) Regulations 25
reinsurance account executive 28, 163
reinsurance activities 161, 162
reinsurance administration 13, 83–107, 154, 161–163, 179–199, 201–225, 233, 235, 243
    costs 154
    databases 233
    unit 162, 163
reinsurance agreement 63–141, 184, 221
    establishment 69–70
    negotiation 70
reinsurance agreement provisions 71–73
    arbitration 73
    change to the reinsurance 72
    claims 73
    errors and omissions 73
    insolvency 73
    premium taxes 72
    procedures to begin coverage 72
    records inspection 72
    reinsurance coverages 72
    reinsurance rates and premiums 72
    reporting 72
    rescission 73
    scope of the agreement 72–73
    termination 72, 77
reinsurance agreement schedules 74, 79–82
reinsurance allowance 12
reinsurance analyst 162, 163, 169, 171, 172, 173, 174, 188, 189, 190, 209, 214, 215, 218, 219, 221, 222, 224, 225
reinsurance arrangements 5
reinsurance certificate 194–195
reinsurance cession form 89
reinsurance claim notice 215–216
reinsurance commission 12
reinsurance company 5
reinsurance contract 14
reinsurance costs 154
reinsurance coverage articles 79
reinsurance coverages 72
reinsurance death benefit 133
reinsurance effective date 74, 75

reinsurance gross premium 12
reinsurance intermediary 26–28, 171, 174–175
reinsurance intermediary—broker(s) 28, 171–172
reinsurance intermediary—manager 28
Reinsurance Intermediary Model Act 26, 28
reinsurance intermediary's authority 28
reinsurance liability 57
reinsurance marketing officer 28, 163
reinsurance net premium 12
reinsurance partner 67
reinsurance pool(s) 3, 8, 80, 190
reinsurance premium(s) 11–12, 41, 47, 53, 87, 130, 132, 133, 134, 155, 205, 209–212, 214–215, 218, 221, 224, 244–245
  account 233
  check 233
  payment(s) 129
reinsurance premium rates 136, 237
  charged 237
reinsurance quality control 232
reinsurance rates and payment 72
reinsurance record administration 87–88
reinsurance regulation 23
reinsurance reports 94
reinsurance reservations 229
reinsurance salesperson 15
reinsurance syndicate 8
reinsurance transaction 3
reinsurance treaty 14
reinsurer 5
reinsurer insolvency 124
reinsurer's liability 57
reinvestment risk
renewal expenses 12
renewal premiums 132
renewal reinsurance premiums 132—134
  annual mode 132
  quarterly mode 132
  monthly mode 132, 134
reporting 72, 94
  party 203, 205, 209
  requirements 29
request for coverage 183, 184, 185
request for payment 135
request for proposal 70
required reserves 31, 138, 139
rescission (provision) 72, 78, 115, 116
rescission 72, 78, 115, 116
reserve credit 23, 26, 27, 32–33, 36, 51, 149
reserve listing 205, 208

reserved capacity 181
reserves 149, 156
reserves on the reinsured business 55
results-based reciprocity 8
retained earnings 29
retention 186, 188, 245
retention check form 186, 187, 188
retention limit 42, 46, 51, 82, 95, 112, 145, 151–155, 164, 184, 188, 242
retention limit corridor 152
retention limits schedule (retention schedule) 82, 153, 188
retention management 242
retro pool 190, 191, 196
retrocession(s) 5, 28, 182, 184, 190, 192, 196, 219
  claim file 219, 225
  pool 187, 190
retrocessionaire 5, 8, 154, 187, 190, 191, 192, 196, 209, 219, 225
return 146
revenue account 210–211
riders 130
right of recommendation 221
risk 145
risk assessment 235
risk-based capital (RBC) ratio 30
risk management 143–156
risk-return tradeoff 146, 147, 148, 154
risk protection 147
risk tolerance 154
risk transfer (in reinsurance) 23, 26, 36
rolling average 234
rules of recordkeeping and reporting 28

S

safeguarding of assets 231
sample, sampling, sampling process 229, 236, 239, 242
Sarbanes-Oxley Act of 2002 231
scanning 175
schedule 69, 80–81
  reinsurance coverage schedules 81
  retention limits schedule 83, 153, 188
Schedule of Binding Limits 83
scope of the agreement 71, 72
securities transactions 23
security 176
segregating incompatible functions 230
segregation of duties 230

selecting 12
selective bordereau service 91
self administration 87, 89, 209
self-administered reinsurance 203, 234
self-insured retention limit 146
service of process 27
service standards 236
settlement options provision. *See also* payout
    options provision
shared risk 53
shopping 184
shortfall of funds 149
single catastrophic event 47
small block of business 155
small cession 42, 152
smaller allowances 51
smoker/nonsmoker premium rate table 131
software 155
solvency (laws and regulation) 13, 23–24, 27, 145
    provisions 28
spread-loss coverage 45, 47
standard 229
standard aggregate premium rate table 131
standard risks 133
state insurance department 23, 24, 34
state insurance laws 23
state regulators 30
statistical sample 229
status codes 184–185
statutory minimum capitalization requirements 30
statutory reserves 31
statutory solvency 30
stockholders 237
stop loss 47
stop-loss ratio reinsurance 46
stop-loss reinsurance 46–47
submission stage 181
subscription (market) 8
subsidiary company 7
substandard extra premium 131
substandard extra premium rate table 132
substandard risk(s) (class) 130, 133, 134
suicide exclusion period 115
surplus 29, 137, 148, 149
surplus relief 32, 148, 149, 150
    ratio 149, 151
surplus strain 32, 51, 55, 148, 149, 156
surrender 54, 55
surrender charge 146
suspense account (reconciliation) 232–233
systems conversions 238

T

table of retention limits 153
table rating 131
tax jurisdiction 139
tax reserves 32
taxation laws 23
taxing authority 140
telecommunications 174
temporary flat extra premiums 130
temporary insurance agreement (TIA). *See* binding
    premium receipt
term life insurance 57
term life insurance policy 55
termination(s) (of reinsurance) 72, 77, 78, 162, 182,
    205, 208, 213
    costs 14
    for new business 77
    of reinsurance 104, 214
    of the agreement 77
    provision 72, 78–79
    stage 181
theft 231
third parties 237
TIS. *See* temporary insurance agreement.
time-series analysis 233
trading partners 174
traditional indemnity reinsurance 10
transaction costs 14
transaction report 205
transferring risk 145
trend 233
    analysis 232–233, 235
    analysis report 234
    data 234
trust(s) 27, 33
    and escrow accounts 26
    beneficiary 34
    document 34
    fund 33
trusteed surplus 33

U

U.S. dollars 140
U.S. federal law 231
unauthorized reinsurer(s) 27, 33
unconditional 34
underwriters 130

underwriting 12, 13, 41, 42, 154, 161, 166, 172, 173, 186, 189–191, 196
   administration 242
   basis 185, 186, 194, 221
   capacity 13
   classifications 244
   criteria and policies 142
   evaluation 43, 44
   philosophy and guidelines 43, 238
   practices 130
unexpected obligations 149
unexpected outcome 145
unexpected trends 234
unfair competition 23
unfavorable currency changes 141
Uniform Insurers Liquidation Act 121
unisex premium rate table 130
United States reinsurance regulation 23
universal life policy 49
unscheduled external audit 238

V

virtual private network (VPN) 176
volume of reinsurance 238
VPN 176

W

waiver of premium for disability 130
waiver of premium for disability rider premium rate table 1301
waiver of premium for disability claim 98, 114
waste 231
weighted average 234
weighted moving average 234
withheld funds 34
workers' compensation and employers liability insurance 187
workflows 237
worse-than-expected experience 156
written contract 28
written documentation 229
written policies 231

Y

yearly renewable term (YRT) reinsurance 48, 55, 56, 102, 136, 137, 222
YRT reinsurance 55
YRT reinsurance premium 56–57, 135
YRT reinsurance premium rate 56, 57, 130, 133, 134, 136